The journey of the Lost Boys of Sudan is both heartbreaking and inspiring.
It speaks to the strength of the human spirit to survive and grow under even
the most abject circumstances. Their plight eloquently shows us the terrible
consequences for children of war, and their personal triumphs over adversity
symbolize a great hope for Africa and the global community.
— Former President **JIMMY CARTER**, winner of the 2002 Nobel Peace Prize

A compelling story about four courageous and persistent young men who
overcame enormous adversity before arriving in the United States. I am
especially taken by the Lost Boys' intense desire to gain a college education
and by the personal sacrifices they are willing to make to achieve their goal.
I find *The Lost Boys of Sudan* to be an excellent introduction to a remarkable
group of newcomers to this nation of immigrants and refugees.
— **GEORGE RUPP**, president of the International Rescue Committee

In this moving tale of two years in the life of four so-called Lost Boys resettled
from Sudan in Atlanta, Georgia, Mark Bixler brings the story of the American
dream screeching up to the minute. The four young men are not typical
refugees. They arrive in Atlanta after a childhood separated from their parents
and spent wandering through the charnel house of Sudan's civil war. They
have dodged bullets and been hunted by hyenas. They know nothing of flush
toilets, air-conditioners, or automobiles, but they have a dream — to get an
education. Without sentimentalizing their journey, Bixler has written a book
that is sometimes sad, sometimes funny, but most of all deeply inspiring.
— **DEBORAH SCROGGINS**, author of *Emma's War: An Aid Worker, a Warlord, Radical Islam,
and the Politics of Oil — A True Story of Love and Death in Sudan*

Mark Bixler shows what the refugee experience is like for tribal, traditional, and
traumatized people as they crash into modern America. While there are quite
a few books on the Sudanese in America, this is the one that connects personal
stories to history, foreign policy, and public policy. It's erudite and readable,
a rare combination. — **MARY PIPHER**, author of *The Middle of Everywhere: The World's
Refugees Come to Our Town*

A touching story of survival, faith, tenacity, courage, and optimism both before
and after the Lost Boys resettled in America. A worthy read!
— **RALSTON H. DEFFENBAUGH JR.**, president of Lutheran Immigration and Refugee Service

This is a remarkable book that everyone interested in the Sudan should read. With insight, compassion, and integrity, Mark Bixler weaves together complex threads of extraordinary developments that, for many children, span a decade: the outbreak of a genocidal war that uprooted thousands of children, and the remarkable survival of significant numbers of these children against human foes, wild beasts, and dangerous waters. Although it is an account of tragedy, it is as entertaining as it is educational. The story is well told and well documented.

—**FRANCIS MADING DENG**, professor of international politics, law, and society at the Johns Hopkins University School of Advanced International Studies; former Sudanese Minister of State for Foreign Affairs and Sudanese ambassador to the United States, Canada, and the Scandinavian countries; representative of the UN Secretary-General on Internally Displaced Persons from 1992 to 2004

A compelling account of the extraordinary hardships the Lost Boys underwent in Sudan, Ethiopia, and Kenya and the at times wrenching difficulties they encountered after coming to the United States. In addition to chronicling the experiences of several of those boys, Bixler provides essential background about the civil war that led to the uprooting of millions of southern Sudanese and about U.S. policy toward refugees. *The Lost Boys of Sudan* should appeal not only to readers drawn to the dramatic story that unfolds in its pages, but also to U.S. government officials and private organizations involved in refugee resettlement who want to improve their programs.

—**DONALD PETTERSON**, former U.S. ambassador to Sudan and author of *Inside Sudan: Political Islam, Conflict, and Catastrophe*

Mark Bixler's fascinating narrative follows four young men coming of age as they navigate from a past that saw the slaughter of their families, the destruction of their communities, their flight to years of temporary asylum, their childhood denuded of adult assistance and supervision, in at best a fourth-world environment, to, suddenly, the most complex and competitive society on earth. Bixler also plumbs the strategic limits of American society; the rescue and resettlement of individual refugees such as these is tied to the principled oversoul of America. These young men will succeed here; as they do, we succeed too.

—**ROGER WINTER**, executive director of the U.S. Committee for Refugees from 1981 to 2001 and assistant administrator for democracy, conflict, and humanitarian assistance at the U.S. Agency for International Development

THE LOST BOYS OF SUDAN

MARK BIXLER

THE LOST
BOYS
AN AMERICAN STORY OF
THE REFUGEE EXPERIENCE
OF SUDAN

THE UNIVERSITY OF GEORGIA PRESS   ATHENS AND LONDON

© 2005 by The University of Georgia Press

Athens, Georgia 30602

All rights reserved

Set in Garamond Pro

Printed and bound by Maple-Vail

The paper in this book meets the guidelines for
permanence and durability of the Committee on
Production Guidelines for Book Longevity of the
Council on Library Resources.

Printed in the United States of America

09 08 07 06 05 C 5 4

Library of Congress Cataloging-in-Publication Data

Bixler, Mark, 1970–

The lost boys of Sudan : an American story of the
refugee experience / Mark Bixler.

    p.   cm.

Includes bibliographical references and index.

ISBN 0-8203-2499-X (hardcover : alk. paper)

1. Refugees—Sudan. 2. Refugees—Georgia—Atlanta.
3. Orphans—Sudan. 4. War. I. Title.

HV640.4.S73B59 2005

962.404'3—dc22   2004026942

British Library Cataloging-in-Publication Data available

To Arden Layne Bixler, with hope for the future

Learning is good
We have found it so,
Learning is the best
We have found it so.
I will not leave the school
I am a man
I have liked it;
I will not leave the school.
I am a gentleman of the future.
Those children who run away
They have no hearts
They do not even bid their masters farewell;
Those children who run away
They have no hearts.
Even if we tire
We shall endure.
We shall find its sweetness later on;
Even if we tire
We shall endure
To find its sweetness later on.

"Gentlemen of the Future," a song sung in the
1940s by some of the first children in southern
Sudan to receive a formal education

CONTENTS

PREFACE

In the spring of 2001, airplanes were landing around the United States to deliver new lives to some of roughly thirty-eight hundred refugees known as the Lost Boys of Sudan, men in their late teens and early twenties with stories that captivated Americans. In the late 1980s, when they were children, war in their native southern Sudan forced them from home and away from families. Several thousand boys wandered for months without mothers or fathers toward the promise of safety. Many died of hunger, disease, or animal attacks, but survivors came of age relying on one another, a teeming brotherhood that would later endure more months of wandering before settling in a refugee camp in Kenya. Acting on humanitarian grounds, the United States opened its doors to the young men in late 2000 and 2001. Unlike most refugees, these young men arrived with little understanding of life in the West. Most had never seen tall buildings or microwave ovens. They had no experience with flush toilets, refrigerators, or cell phones. Many had never climbed stairs.

I first met several of these men as a newspaper reporter at the *Atlanta Journal-Constitution*. Their stories intrigued me. Many refugees who come to the United States have relatives in the country to whom they can turn for advice on where to catch the bus and how to establish phone service; the Lost Boys of Sudan would have to rely on each other and the kindness of strangers. Despite the challenges posed by knowing so little about everyday life in the United States, these men, like most refugees, were expected to find jobs and support themselves after a few months of government assistance. After an initial news story about their resettlement in Atlanta prompted more than a hundred readers to donate time or money, my editors and I decided to tell a more complete story by focusing on one group of young men as they adjusted to life in the United States. So I went to the Atlanta airport one afternoon and met four refugees on the cusp of rebirth. They let me drop in on them every few days for the next several months, as they explored a kitchen, rode a train, and looked for a job. The resulting story was the impetus for this book. Mine was one of many newspaper accounts around the United States that documented a resettlement initiative without parallel in U.S. history. Never before had the federal government opened its doors to refugees such as these, young people unaccompanied by parents and unfamiliar with everyday life in the modern world.

To chart the results of the government's experiment beyond the first few months, I followed the four young men I met at the airport for their first two years in the United States. I was there as they saw tall buildings for the first time, and as they interviewed for jobs, learned to drive, and stared at shapely young women who pranced enticingly across their television screens. I spent many hours documenting their struggle to receive what most Lost Boys said they wanted more than anything else in the United States—an education. What emerges, I hope, is a portrait that bears resemblance to the experiences of so many other Lost Boys around the nation and to the larger experience of the more than 2 million refugees resettled in the United States since 1980. I have aimed, as well, to place the story into context by exploring the forces underlying a devastating war in Sudan that has rarely made the evening news. My hope is that the story unfolding in these pages appeals to a wide audience but also that it proves of value to scholars and to those who resettle and serve refugees, particularly as Africans supplant Asians and Europeans in coming years as the leading refugee population resettled in the United States.

There often is a story behind the story, and I have tried to uncover and convey what the journalist Carl Bernstein calls "the best obtainable version of the truth." That is not easy. People who are being written about often have an interest in how their story is told, and the writer must consider a person's motivation for portraying events in a certain light. I encountered numerous descriptions of the war in Sudan, the U.S. refugee resettlement program, and the refugee experience that were simplistic and clichéd. In addition, accounts of what forced children from parents in southern Sudan in the late 1980s, repeated in news stories around the United States, typically failed to acknowledge the hushed reality that various reasons cast these children into a life of danger. Most Lost Boys said they were tending cattle away from home, as is customary for boys of that age and in that culture, when Sudanese soldiers or aligned militias attacked their villages and killed or kidnapped their relatives. They said they survived only by walking into the wilderness. For some, that prepackaged story was true, but for others it covered a deeper truth that some denied even to themselves. It is clear years later that no one account of leaving home applies to every refugee who came to be called one of the Lost Boys of Sudan. Whatever the reason boys were separated from their parents, though, my goal is to make plain that nearly all endured a childhood trauma uncommon to most.

While most Americans who sought to help the young men invested time and energy out of the spotlight, a few courted recognition by anointing themselves guardians on less-than-altruistic impulses. I have sought to dispassionately chronicle the activities of both groups. As for portraying the Lost Boys themselves, I have tried to move beyond the common, simplistic depiction of the refugee as a noble soul who survives suffering to triumphantly surmount obstacles in a new world. The young men in this book clearly have traits of victim and hero, but I have tried to portray them as no more and no less than complex human beings. I believe that their story of being forced from parents, marching into desolation, and coming of age with a desire to learn resonates because the emotions and experiences that run through it, such as grief, resilience, and the yearning to transcend, are common to all people. Another recurring theme, familiar worldwide, is the ability of faith to sustain, even amid brutality, and in that respect, the strong Christian faith of the young men in this book may resonate with people who find solace in religion.

The book also explores a U.S. refugee policy that often is described as an altruistic enterprise helping the neediest of the needy but actually has been guided more by U.S. foreign policy than compassion. Refugee advocates speak of the American tradition of offering shelter to people fleeing persecution, but less frequently discussed is the role that geopolitical concerns play in guiding refugee admissions. Historically, the United States has offered shelter to people fleeing persecution in countries where it has deep interest, such as Vietnam or the former Soviet Union, while accepting relatively few refugees from countries such as Sudan, where war has displaced more than 5 million people since 1983, more than in any other nation.

I have tried to avoid oversimplifying a complex war that has claimed at least 2 million lives since the early 1980s, mostly southern Sudanese civilians who died of war-induced famine or disease or as a result of military attacks that frequently target noncombatants. The war often is described as a conflict between Arab Muslims in northern Sudan and black Africans in the south who practice Christianity or animist religions. This description is not far off the mark but does not capture the complexity of a war that, as the historian Douglas H. Johnson points out, is actually a series of "multiple and recurring civil wars." The war has been described, notably by some conservative Christians in the United States and the champions of militant Islam in northern Sudan, as a clash of Islam and Christianity, even though it has pitted Muslim against Muslim and Christian against Christian. The reality that killer and victim sometimes shared the same faith became obvious after black African Muslims in the western Sudanese region of Darfur rebelled in 2003 against the Sudanese government, which responded by aiding Arab Muslim militias in carrying out a campaign of rape and killing that the U.S. Congress condemned as genocide. The government and aligned Arab militias killed an untold number of black Africans in Darfur and forced more than 1 million others from their homes. Extended analyses of U.S. refugee policy and the war in Sudan are beyond the scope of this book, but I have tried hard to provide a concise yet thorough look at shifting U.S. attitudes toward refugees and the forces behind a war that former president Jimmy Carter has called "the most long-lasting and devastating war in the world."

Following the journalistic approach of documentary narrative, I based this case study on hundreds of scenes witnessed and interviews conducted over more than three years with refugees, volunteers, resettlement-agency workers, authors, historians, and political figures including former president Carter, who has a history of deep involvement in Sudan, and former senator John Danforth, who was President George W. Bush's special envoy to Sudan until he became the U.S. ambassador to the United Nations. Several interviews were conducted in my role as a reporter for the *Atlanta Journal-Constitution*, but most were done solely for this book. I have enclosed in quotation marks only dialogue I heard firsthand except as indicated in the notes. Past events were reconstructed based on separate and, typically, multiple interviews with the participants. These reconstructions are indicated as such in the notes. The four men I met at the Atlanta airport were the focus of most observations and interviews, but I compared their experiences often in conversations with dozens of other southern Sudanese youth, resettlement-agency workers, and volunteers in Atlanta and cities such as Annapolis, Louisville, Nashville, Houston, Phoenix, Pittsburgh, and Sioux Falls. For the sake of accuracy and precision, I have focused as much as possible on events I personally observed, though it has been difficult to know to what degree my presence altered events. I struggled to balance the detachment and objectivity expected of journalists and authors with the need to not simply enter these young men's lives in hopes of obtaining information. As a gesture of gratitude to them, a portion of the proceeds of this book will support two-month refugee-orientation sessions at Jubilee Partners, a Christian community in Comer, Georgia, that has welcomed more than twenty-five hundred refugees of all faiths from nearly thirty countries since 1980. A portion of the proceeds will also go directly to Lost Boys themselves, to help pay for textbooks or tuition or cover medical or other costs as they see fit.

Finally, I hope the reader takes note of the subtitle—"An American Story of the Refugee Experience." The story of these young men from southern Sudan is in many ways emblematic of the experience of so many other refugees resettled in the United States. It is an American story in the most literal sense because most of the book is set in the

United States, following newly arrived refugees for their first two years in this country. The narrative also reminds us that the United States is and has been a nation of immigrants, where most people can trace their ancestry to another part of the world. In addition, it is an American story in its embodiment of themes that run through so much of American culture, history, and literature. These include the emphasis on individual freedom and the idea—too often dismissed as myth—that despite its disparities and imperfections, the United States offers even its most vulnerable newcomers the opportunity to achieve through sacrifice and hard work.

LANDING

The city of Atlanta appeared through the airplane window like a distant island in a sea of green, a cluster of buildings surrounded by trees. A road unfurled like a whip in the world below, teeming with squat moving specks of indeterminate color, sunlight gleaming off metal, cars and trucks and vans going who knew where in the middle of the day. In the center of the city rose a stand of office towers that seemed to climb higher as United Airlines flight 1905 descended, its landing gear down, seats returned to upright positions. Passengers peering through thick, rounded glass windows could distinguish parking lots and green interstate signs on a brilliant summer afternoon. Among those looking out the windows in coach were four young men seated in a row near the wing. They were tall and slender and dark as night. Each wore white canvas tennis shoes with thin red stripes and an oversized gray sweatshirt that said "USRP" across the chest, gifts from people in Nairobi hired by the United States Refugee Program to outfit the young men for a trip into modern America. They sat still in their seats at the end of a three-day journey, on the brink of a new life somewhere in the landscape unfolding before them.

They took turns leaning forward or sitting back so that one or another could try to divine something of the new world rushing up toward them, their eyes darting right and then left, intent, focused on a landscape that yielded few secrets from the air.

Those four young men called each other "colleague" or "brother" but were not colleagues or brothers in the strictest sense of the words. They had been separated from parents in the swirling chaos of civil war in Sudan nearly fourteen years earlier and had marched through the violent desolation of East Africa with thousands of boys in similar straits. They had come of age in the wilderness and in refugee camps and had grown accustomed to eating one meal a day of corn or sorghum or some other donated grain. They would tell you about month-long spans on a diet of unripe mangoes or cassavas and whatever water might have collected in a hollow on the ground. At times they had eaten soft mud and drunk their own urine to survive, but others had succumbed to hunger. The men flying into the United States on that brilliant afternoon in July, a day so full of possibilities, could not banish the memory of friends who had starved to death, the image of skin pulling taut over ribs, the sound of rattling wisps of breath. And so they had not known quite how to react in the last three days when smiling European and American men and women in tidy slacks and skirts strolled down airplane aisles wheeling stainless-steel carts to deliver more food than any of them could fairly have expected to see in months not so long ago. Trays arrived bearing exotic green leaves and unfamiliar meat. There was bread, which they recognized, beside small foil-wrapped squares of a cold, hard, yellow substance, which they did not recognize. And there were three-pronged plastic instruments everyone else used to eat. So much was strange to them. Even the lemon juice, they would say. The lemon juice tasted different than the lemon juice they'd been given in the refugee camp in Kenya, their home for the last nine years.

As a voice crackled throughout the airplane to announce a final approach to Atlanta, one of the four, Jacob Ngor Magot, clutched a white plastic bag and a small black knapsack that held all that he owned—immigration documents, a book outlining what refugees could expect in the United States, and a change of clothes. He and the three men sitting nearby would live together in Atlanta, to be joined in a few weeks by two others from the refugee camp. Nearest to Jacob sat Peter Ayuen Anyang, the oldest and darkest and tallest of the four, a man in his early twenties with a high, sloping forehead and an overbite that defined his grin. He had planned to bring a book of Christian songs in his native Dinka language, but someone told him that U.S. authorities did not allow new arrivals to bring books, so he left the hymnal and arrived instead with letters from others in the refugee camp to friends who were sprinkled around the United States, in Boston, Dallas, San Diego, Seattle, and Sioux Falls. In the refugee camp, Peter had lived near Daniel Khon Khoch and Marko Aguer Ayii, two other young Sudanese men who were on flight 1905 that day and who also would be his roommates in the United States. Daniel and Marko had been together most days for the last fourteen years. They had eaten together, played soccer and gone to church together, watched boys succumb to dehydration and disease and attacks from lions and hyenas. Daniel was like the protective older brother to his shy younger friend. He wore a purple plastic rosary around his neck as he had every day for the last nine years, since an Italian priest named Father Joseph had given it to him in 1994. Daniel had sung in church choirs in the refugee camp and dreamed of becoming a priest. Marko, who could not speak English as well, talked about maybe becoming a pilot or soldier or doctor.

Jacob, Peter, Daniel, and Marko knew as the airplane delivered them to Atlanta that somewhere down there, beneath the trees, in one of the many buildings, awaited a home to replace the one they left in Africa. An apartment, probably, though people in the United States were rumored also to live in houses of wood or stone or other materials not often found in southern Sudan or the sprawling refugee camps of Ethiopia and Kenya. Somewhere, too, they knew, awaited the first jobs they would hold, jobs they had to find within four months, before their government assistance ended. The prospect excited them, the idea that they could earn money and spend it as they wished and as their budget allowed. They would be in a position to feed hungry relatives or send sick friends to the hospital, to pay for a cousin to go to boarding school in Nairobi or Kampala. They were coming to the United States as responsible people, adults, with fresh power and a sense of duty to remember the majority who had to stay behind. They had been told that America was a land of opportunity and already had committed to memory terms such as *entry-level job*, *self-reliance*, and *self-sufficiency*.

They knew, too, that some of the buildings revealing themselves from beneath the clouds were schools, where they might learn more about commerce and mathematics and literature and science. This was a country of learned people, they knew, where two brothers invented a flying machine a hundred years ago and others went on to give the world automobiles and computers. If they were to one day rebuild the desolation of their native southern Sudan, Jacob, Peter, Daniel, and Marko would need to continue their education. They were told in the refugee camp that those who were under eighteen would go to high school in America. Those who had finished high school would be eligible for college, though it was not clear how much that cost or who would pay. The majority of the refugees were over eighteen, according to the best estimates of the United Nations, but had not finished high school. Once they arrived in the United States and found a job, they were told, they would have a chance to study for a test that would result in a General Education Development (GED) diploma, the equivalent of a traditional high-school diploma, which would open the door to college. The distinctions were important; Jacob and his fellow refugees believed that unless they got an education, their kinsmen in southern Sudan risked continued confinement to the violence of a preindustrial age, where the assault rifle is among few tangible signs of a modern world beyond the horizon. They would tell you that the one thing they wanted more than anything else in the United States was to go to school.

And what better place for education than the United States, where children could go to school for free, where the law actually *required* their attendance? It was right there on page fifty-three of *Welcome to the United States: A Guidebook for Refugees*, a spiral-bound volume that Jacob, Peter, Daniel, and Marko had tucked in white plastic bags alongside their immigration documents.

"In the United States," the guidebook says, "education is accessible to everyone, regardless of a person's age, race, religion or social class.

Public education is free and required by law for all children ages 6 to 16, and may also be available for children older or younger, depending on local school district regulations." And then, this: "Most Americans view education as a way to qualify for more satisfying jobs and improve their standard of living. After deciding to continue their education, adults usually continue working full-time and attend courses in the evening or on the weekend."

The obstacles seemed daunting. One of Jacob's friends, bound for Atlanta the following week, referred to residents of the United States and Europe as Special People from the Gods, for he could not conceive of human beings with the capacity to design, for example, a jet airplane. Who could say what combination of metal and glass and plastic and steel would lift it from the ground? What person could list the thousands of parts to be fitted together to make this flying machine, and in what shape and of what material the parts should be fashioned and in what order they need be assembled and connected to each other to carry aloft people otherwise chained to the earth?

Yet clearly someone had known, for the young men on flight 1905 could not claim to be dreaming. They had climbed inside an airplane for the first time in their lives three days earlier, on a dusty red airstrip in a refugee camp in northern Kenya, and had flown to Nairobi, where relief workers outfitted them in USRP sweatshirts. Then they had flown to Brussels and walked through the airport toward another gate. It was here that they first saw a moving staircase. They were in a group of about forty young men like them. The one who happened to be in the lead approached the staircase and stepped on in hopes of going to the second level, but some invisible force pushed the stairs down, not up, and the leader fell back into a crush of bodies with refugee sweatshirts like his. His fellow travelers laughed at him and he laughed at himself. They stepped cautiously onto another escalator—going up—and soon boarded an airplane that landed several hours later in New York. They spent the night in a hotel and the next day they flew to cities around the United States.

The flights were part of a remarkable migration coordinated and financed by the United States government for thirty-eight hundred teenagers and young men who had been separated in the late 1980s from parents in the chaos of war in the vast, flat expanse of southern Sudan, the largest African country in size and one with fifty-six ethnic groups split into more than 570 tribes that speak at least one hundred languages. Aid workers and journalists called them the Lost Boys of Sudan after the *Peter Pan* orphans who were cast as children into the world of adults. They arrived in cities such as Atlanta, Boston, Chicago, Cleveland, Dallas, Denver, Houston, Kansas City, Las Vegas, Philadelphia, Phoenix, Pittsburgh, Salt Lake City, San Diego, Seattle, Tampa, St. Petersburg, and Washington. They could not have fathomed as boys that they would one day be reborn in a world as alien and strange as the bottom of the ocean, in places with names like San Jose, California; New Haven, Connecticut; Jacksonville, Florida; Des Moines, Iowa; Louisville, Kentucky; Omaha and Lincoln, Nebraska; Rochester and Utica, New York; Charlotte, North Carolina; Fargo, North Dakota; Sioux Falls, South Dakota; Memphis and Nashville, Tennessee; Richmond, Virginia; Burlington, Vermont; and Tacoma, Washington. They attracted a great deal of attention after airplanes delivered them to new homes around the United States, most noticeably from mothering American women who tended to be white, middle-aged and middle- to upper-class. Yet there had been a time when the outside world knew little of their plight.

In 1987 and 1988, relief workers and diplomats were reporting that roughly seventeen thousand "dying young boys" and "walking skeletons" had arrived in refugee camps in Ethiopia after walking hundreds of miles from their homes in neighboring southern Sudan. A cable sent to the U.S. State Department from an American diplomat in Ethiopia on April 4, 1988, painted a grim picture: "[A]ll had the dull concentration camp stare of the starving" and "compared poorly with pictures of Nazi concentration camp victims and were as bad or worse as anything seen in Ethiopia during the 1984–86 famine." Some estimated that three in five boys who embarked on the trek died along the way of hunger, disease, or animal attacks. Tens of thousands of adults from southern Sudan also were filtering into the camps, many in the same perilous physical condition, but the presence of so many boys without parents was unusual. The question of how they came to be separated from their families would become one of the many controversies of a brutal war. Most offered accounts that were similar in many respects to the one that Jacob Magot gave not long after United Airlines flight 1905 touched down in Atlanta.

Jacob said he was five or six when he last saw his parents. He has no birth certificate and so does not know his precise age, but he remembers those last days in Mathiang, a village of grass huts spread out over several miles. He was like any other boy that age, just beginning to learn to care for cattle, the primary responsibility of any boy in Dinka culture, which reveres cattle for meeting almost all their worldly needs. The day it happened, Jacob said, he was at home with his mother. His father was in the field, working, when Jacob heard strange sharp noises. Like thunder almost, but without the lingering rumbles. More like a whip cracking. Then screams, people running in every direction. Jacob ventured outside and saw men with rifles. Arabs, he remembers, from northern Sudan. He watched them shoot neighbors. He did not know what to do, but instinct told him to do something, so he ran from that grass hut, away from his mother and father, and he did not stop until the sound of shooting and screaming went away. He has worked it out in his mind; he cannot figure what else he could have done. He closes his eyes and sees himself in a stand of trees outside his village, waiting, a boy cast into a world of grinding violence, alone, just like that. Jacob would later say, matter-of-factly, that he had taken his own direction that day and that his parents had taken their own direction. His brother and two sisters? Gone. It would be ten years before he learned whether any of them were alive.

For the first three nights, he said, he slept in the bush. Occasionally he heard shots and saw smoke rise from the grass huts on the flat plains around Mathiang. What else could he do? On the third day, survivors from his village wandered past. Most were boys, like him, but there were some girls and a few men in their twenties. The adults played the role of decision makers, which is otherwise reserved for elders in Jacob's Dinka tribe, the most numerous ethnic group in Sudan. Most Dinka are tall and thin, known for exceptionally dark skin and a reverence for cattle. The adults in the band of refugees that stumbled on Jacob on his third day in the wild told him they were walking east, toward Ethiopia, and that he should come. He did. No one told him the camps were roughly

250 miles away, about the distance from New York to Washington, D.C. (Daniel, Peter, and Marko were from another part of southern Sudan. They walked roughly 450 miles to the camps in Ethiopia, about the distance from New York to Cleveland.) Jacob said his group moved at night, guided by moonlight and stars, and rested during the day. He ate fruit and wild leaves he had never seen before, dry skin from dead animals when it came to that.

Danger lurked everywhere. One night as they were walking, Jacob said, a lion emerged from tall grass and lunged at a boy in front of him, swatted his face as if he were a doll. The boy's eye tumbled from its socket; there was terrible screaming and blood. Jacob would speak of it years later with less emotion or flourish than one might in recounting a trip to the dentist. "An eye from that boy was removed," he said. "Somebody came running—an elder person who was having a spear. He speared the lion. Then it turned away." The maimed boy lived, but others died of dehydration, disease, or hunger.

Survivors in Jacob's group walked for weeks before reaching a refugee camp in Panyido, Ethiopia, just across the border from Sudan. Having crossed an international border, Jacob registered as a refugee with the United Nations High Commissioner for Refugees. The UNHCR fed the boys despite concerns that SPLA officers in the camp were providing military training after aid workers left, one of many decisions that raised questions about the unintentional role of international aid organizations in helping one side or the other in Sudan's war. Jacob and about ten thousand other unaccompanied minors, as they were known to international relief workers, were kept away from the much larger refugee population at Panyido. An instructor in the camp befriended him and invited Jacob to live with him. Jacob accepted and helped the man maintain a paltry collection of books. Other instructors taught him to speak a lilting, British English. They schooled him in Christianity and encouraged him to choose a Christian name. He chose *Jacob* and began a dual existence. His fellow Dinka continued to call him Ngor Magot or by one of several nicknames, but the white, Western aid workers and missionaries would call him Jacob Magot. (The name Magot was his father's first name. It became his second or "last" name in accordance with Dinka naming traditions.)

Peter Anyang, Marko Ayii, and Daniel Khoch were born in remote villages not far from Aweil, in the Bahr El-Ghazal province of southern Sudan. Jacob Magot was born a few hundred miles away, near Bor, in the Upper Nile province of southern Sudan. In the late 1980s, they and thousands of other "Lost Boys" walked hundreds of miles to refugee camps at Itang, Panyido, and Dimma in Ethiopia. After rebels overthrew Ethiopia's government, several thousand of the boys wandered for about a year before settling in a refugee camp at Kakuma, Kenya.

Jacob lived in the camp for about four years, until May 1991, when he and nearly 250,000 other southern Sudanese refugees at Panyido and other Ethiopian camps fled in a panicked evacuation, most with nothing but the clothes they wore. The Ethiopian dictator, Mengistu Haile Mariam, was on the verge of being overthrown, and rebels ousting him were hostile to southern Sudanese refugees in Ethiopia. Jacob was about nine. He and a crush of humanity moved en masse toward Sudan. Anti-Mengistu rebels fired on the column a few miles outside the refugee camp, killing several. Others trudged on and came in a day or so to the banks of the swift-moving Gilo River dividing Ethiopia and Sudan, a place that remains etched in Jacob's memory as a reminder of all that was chaotic and violent and senseless then. The unaccompanied minors had crossed the river several years earlier as they had entered Ethiopia, but its waters had been low and calm then. This time, hundreds of boys lined up along the banks of a river swollen by heavy rain. Crocodiles lurked in the water. Yet Ethiopian fighters with automatic rifles were closing in, firing at SPLA soldiers among the refugees and those they viewed as the SPLA's child recruits. Jacob watched hundreds of boys leap into the river. Some were sucked under by the current, never to surface alive. Others were eaten by crocodiles, the carnage turning the water into a churning red cauldron of parts of bodies and scraps of clothing. One of Jacob's teachers threw an inflatable tire into the river and leaped in. Jacob followed. "I made myself to be courageous," he would recall years later. "God made it for me to cross the river."

After they walked back into Sudan, fighting pushed the Lost Boys from one makeshift camp to another. A raid on one camp, at a place called Pochalla, triggered an SPLA order to move thousands of boys further south in Sudan. Workers with the International Committee of the Red Cross provided safe drinking water and transportation for some of the sick and disabled, but most trudged through an unforgiving landscape, from one tanker truck of potable water to the next. Though bandits shot and killed several boys along the way, most arrived at their destination, the city of Narus, about one hundred miles north of the Sudanese border with Kenya. They built a camp and dug foxholes, but just as they were settling in came news of an advance by the Sudanese military. A major rebel stronghold, the city of Kapoeta, fell, and the Lost Boys joined tens of thousands of desperate refugees streaming into Kenya, some among them bombed by the Sudanese air force on their way to safety.

The story of several thousand Sudanese children wandering through wilderness without parents, falling prey to bullets and wild animals and disease, would receive widespread news coverage ten years later, after the United States opened its doors to some of the survivors. These Lost Boys of Sudan eventually would receive more attention in the United States than the 2 million Sudanese who have died since 1983 and the roughly 4.5 million who have been forced to leave home and settle elsewhere in the country, known in the parlance of relief workers as "internally displaced persons." In the early 1990s, though, few people in the United States kept up with events in far-off Sudan. Americans were preoccupied with news of the 1991 Gulf War and the 1992 election between President George Bush, Governor Bill Clinton of Arkansas, and Ross Perot, the eccentric billionaire from Texas. Stories of devastation from East Africa had a hard time penetrating the American consciousness, though several reporters and photographers told the story, including journalists for the *Atlanta Journal-Constitution*, the *Baltimore Sun*, the *New York Times*, and the *Toronto Star*. The June 1992 issue of *Life* magazine carried a nine-page story under the headline "Lost Boys of the Sudan." It appeared alongside accounts of the Los Angeles riots that followed the acquittal of white police officers accused of beating a black motorist named Rodney King and advertisements for Life Savers candy that asked, "Isn't life delicious?"

"Hunted by lions and hyenas, living on leaves and bark, swarms of boys wander the wilderness in a nation ravaged by a long and bloody civil war," the story begins. "Abandoned by adults, they are fighting a heroic battle for survival in their Republic of Children—but nobody seems to care."

One of thirteen color photographs accompanying the article shows a boy with a blanket of red, yellow, and green draped over his shoulders. He holds two rats by the tail in his left hand. "Lack of adequate protein can be fatal to these young children, whose diet consists mostly of grain," the article reads. "To survive, the boys must kill and eat small animals—even rats." Another picture shows a boy of about seven or eight sitting down to face a boy who looks like he might be three or four. The caption says, "Older boys often 'adopt' younger boys who cannot fend for themselves. As surrogate parents, they offer advice, protection and sometimes consolation."

Years later, when news of the Sudanese resettlement made headlines, some Americans would remember the *Life* article and feel compelled to act, as if circumstance had finally provided an outlet, they would say, to funnel lingering empathy into something concrete, as if, by some miracle, the opportunity arrived to nurture young men who so seemed to need nurturing. They would remember the photo of a boy in a long-sleeved white shirt, notebook in his left hand, tracing multiplication tables in sand with the fingers of his right hand. There also is a shot of boys huddled on a classroom floor, a rail-thin adult instructor in front of a blackboard with the words "English" and "7 days in a week" and "Sunday" scrawled in white chalk.

"If hunger is the permanent condition of life in the camps, getting an education is the constant dream," the story reads. "The boys devise crude writing implements and scavenge for school supplies as they do for food. During the hardest times, groups of children often select one member to go to class while the others hunt for food. After supper they sit around a dying fire and listen avidly as their surrogate recounts the day's lesson."

Psychologists who interviewed the Lost Boys of Sudan reported findings that rank them among the most war-traumatized children in a world with no shortage of wars that injure, maim, and kill. They said 74 percent of the boys were survivors of close shelling or aerial bombardment and 85 percent had seen someone starve to death. Ninety-two percent said someone had shot at them and 97 percent had witnessed a killing. Whether ruthless attack or the promise of education pushed these boys from their homes, and whether or not some of them later received military training, what is certain is that nearly all lost a childhood and endured hardships that many people in the United States would find difficult to fathom.

By the spring of 1992, Sudan's civil war had chased Jacob and roughly ten thousand other young Sudanese refugees out of their native country and into Kenya. They wound up at the Kakuma refugee camp, a collection of thousands of tents and mud huts perched on a broiling tabletop plain of northern Kenya. Aid workers showed the boys how to build huts of dried mud and concrete, and soon several thousand small huts peppered the landscape. Jacob lived near other boys from the same part of Sudan. Peter, Daniel, and Marko moved into their own huts, with floors of dirt and roofs of plastic sheets and leaves. Like Jacob, they typically ate one meal a day, usually corn or sorghum or maize. They went to school from 7 a.m. to 2 p.m., attended church on Sundays, and moved into adolescence with a routine of class work and soccer and grinding grain for dinner. Each day merged into the next. Weeks blurred into months, rolling forward, unceasing, repeating the pattern of everyday life.

As the boys grew into young men, several thousand of the original ten thousand "unaccompanied minors," as they were called, left Kakuma. Some returned to southern Sudan to search for relatives or join the fight against the government. Others left to try to make their way in Kenya working as illegal immigrants in the underground economy, but most faced an uncertain future. The United Nations body that feeds, clothes, and shelters refugees prefers to return them to their native countries if stability allows, but war still raged in southern Sudan. Repatriating the Lost Boys was impractical. The agency's second priority is to integrate refugees into a country near their own, but the Kenyan government would not let them work, so the Lost Boys were stuck in a camp that unfolds over a few miles and houses eighty thousand refugees, including about sixty thousand Sudanese, fifteen thousand Somalis, and smaller numbers from Ethiopia, Uganda, and other countries. A small group in the U.S. State Department and a few refugee advocates started to argue in 1998 that the United States should open its doors to some Lost Boys.

Each year, the United States offers shelter to a limited number of refugees, often chosen with foreign-policy priorities in mind. More than three of four refugees admitted since 1980 came from the Soviet Union, Indochina, or Bosnia, but the government lets in a very small number strictly for humanitarian reasons, and word began swirling through Kakuma in 1999 that some unaccompanied minors might fly across the ocean to a new lives in the United States. The rumors were confirmed when Americans arrived to begin questioning the first of several thousand young Sudanese men at Kakuma.

They were officers of the U.S. Immigration and Naturalization Service, dispatched to Kenya to determine who among the Sudanese might qualify for refugee status in the United States. The INS officers interviewed one young man after another, looking for evidence in their life stories of persecution based on race, religion, national origin, political opinion, or membership in a social group, the five legal grounds upon which a foreign national can legally enter the United States as a refugee.

The federal government had never before welcomed so many young refugees without parents or close relatives. Rarely had so many refugees arrived with such a profound lack of knowledge about life in the modern Western world. These were people who knew nothing of microwave ovens or refrigerators, who had never seen tall buildings, who could not imagine fast-food restaurants with drive-through windows and supermarkets where fresh bread and meat and vegetables and eggs appeared every day. They never had held jobs or written checks or received bank loans with principal-and-interest payments. Like many refugees from less-developed nations, they viewed time as an abstract concept, placing less insistence on punctuality than Americans accustomed to fighting traffic to get to work or soccer practice on time.

Yet Jacob, Peter, Daniel, Marko, and the other Sudanese youth would arrive under the same terms as each of the other 2.2 million refugees the United States has resettled since 1980. The federal government would pay their rent and power bill for up to four months as they adjusted to life in the United States. A nonprofit resettlement agency would help them find a job and a place to live. Then they would be on their own. It would be up to them whether to heed or ignore the advice outlined in *Welcome to the United States*, the spiral-bound guidebook they carried as United Airlines flight 1905 touched down at Hartsfield International Airport just south of Atlanta at 3:51 p.m. on July 18, 2001.

"One lesson that you will learn quickly is that most Americans value self-reliance and individual responsibility," the guidebook says. "You will be expected to go to work as soon as you can find a job and begin to support yourself and your family. . . . As a refugee, you may have lost everything, but in the United States you are offered a chance to start over and rebuild your life. Starting over may not be easy, but it can be done."

The manual offers tips: Understand American culture without criticizing it. Speak English. Get a job as soon as possible. Focus on how far you have come, not how far you have to go.

When the airplane had rolled to a stop, everyone crowded into the aisles. Jacob, Peter, Daniel, and Marko joined the slow procession toward the front of the plane and stepped off at gate T-15 to meet the first Sudanese man they had seen in three days who was not wearing a USRP sweatshirt. He wore a short-sleeved shirt and khaki pants instead, and an easy smile. His name was Mathew Kon, and he worked for the International Rescue Committee, one of ten resettlement agencies the federal government pays to guide refugees into life in the United States. The IRC was one of five agencies in Atlanta that would resettle 156 Lost Boys. Mathew was the caseworker assigned to shepherd Jacob, Peter, Daniel, and Marko through the rhythms of everyday life. He was the one they would call when they could not figure how to work the gas oven or adjust the thermostat. He would help them apply for Social Security cards and send them on their way to finding a job. Mathew would walk with them to a station of the Metropolitan Atlanta Rapid Transit Authority (MARTA) and teach them to read bus and train schedules.

In the airport, however, he had more immediate concerns. He was leading his wards down the concourse when he realized they were no longer behind him. Marko had encountered a revolving door and frozen, uncertain how to proceed. Mathew backtracked and showed him how to just step in and push the metal bar. The four young men filtered through in silence. They were all the way to a bank of glass doors leading to the parking decks outside, sunlight streaming in, before one of them finally spoke up.

"Tell me," Jacob said, "what is Atlanta like?"

BREAD IN THE DISHWASHER

Outside, in the airport parking deck, they climbed into the backseat of Mathew's Chevy Blazer and sat still as rocks as he started the engine. They stared through windows as he navigated out of the airport, merged onto Interstate 85, and picked up speed. What they noticed right off was the number of cars, trucks, buses, and motorcycles. There were thousands, moving at breathtaking speed, and the Blazer zoomed right along with them, so fast that each broken white line on the pavement blurred into one. Messages bombarded them from the side of the road. First came a blue sign with white letters that said "We're Glad Georgia's on Your Mind" and "Atlanta—Site of the 1996 Olympic Games." Words gracing the tops of buildings seemed written in a language they did not understand: "Holiday Inn" and "Econo Lodge." A dull gray concrete bridge came and went. The interstate flowed up and gently to the left and all of a sudden there it was in the distance, like a mirage, that cluster of buildings surrounded by trees, towers the colors of gunmetal and dry earth. One building came to a point like a sharpened stick. Another jutted up in a solid rectangular hulk, like a fencepost. A few seconds passed, and then the interstate dipped down and the skyline receded beneath the trees as suddenly as it had arrived. The road shrank from three lanes to two and widened again and then veered left on the arc of some invisible circle, dumping Mathew's Blazer into an even more crowded river of traffic—seven lanes pulsing with cars and trucks and vans and buses of every size and shape.

The four young men in USRP sweatshirts sat in silence, hands on their laps, looking out the window to absorb and record. They passed under more concrete bridges of dull gray; a sign on the far right shoulder said "North 75/85." Three or four minutes more and they crested a hill to see tall buildings once again, the ones they had seen from the air, arrayed before them in magnificent panorama. Through the lower right portion of the windshield they saw a building with a dome of gold topped by the statue of a woman with her arm raised toward the heavens. Much taller towers rose like fingers. They saw a cylindrical glass building with "WES-TIN" on top and a darker rectangular one that said "EQUITABLE" on the highest floor. Meanwhile, the Blazer kept speeding past signs on the side of the road. There was a pale neon-yellow billboard dominated by the oval shape of a black man's face, eyes covered by dark sunglasses beneath an enormous Afro of jet-black hair. The word "Atlanta" was written above his face and, below it, in bright orange letters, "Home of So So Def Recordings." To the right, just beyond the Bullpen Bar and Grill, rose an assemblage of dark green and black metal several stories high. Lights on top seemed poised to illuminate an open space inside. On the outside of the building were the images of human forms in baseball hats, frozen in the act of swinging a stick or throwing a ball. Outside, between the structure and the interstate, a sign said "Turner Field," the words separated by a white ball with red arcs inside, at the top and bottom, curving toward each other.

Twenty minutes later, Mathew stopped the Blazer in the parking lot of the Decatur Inn, a two-story motel of brick and glass. He had planned to deliver them to their apartment, but there was a last-minute problem with the key, so he rented two rooms at the motel instead. He climbed stairs to the second floor and they followed, watching as he unlocked the door. Mathew took a step inside and pointed to a switch on the wall, then flicked it up with his finger; on came the lights. He moved the switch up and down, up and down, and the light flickered on and off, on and off. Jacob, Peter, Daniel, and Marko had seen electric lights in the buildings the United Nations employees occupied in the Kakuma Refugee Camp in Kenya, their home of the last nine years, but they knew about electricity in the abstract, the way you know the air is thin atop Mount Everest without having ever been there.

"Let me show you something," Mathew said. "This is the air conditioner."

Mathew would leave them with survival skills for one night; the real lessons would begin the next day, when he would take them to their apartment and explain thermostats, alarm clocks, and stovetop burners in what would be their home for at least a year. Mathew wanted to be certain they knew a few things, though, so he led them into the bathroom and knelt beside the tub. "There is always hot water on the left side," he said. "Put your hand here and feel it."

The four young men knelt down in turn and put their hands into the stream of water coming out of the faucet. They shook their heads and grinned when they felt heat. Mathew pointed to the commode, then showed them how to flush by pressing the stainless-steel handle. They took turns pressing the handle just as they had during weeklong cultural-orientation sessions in Kakuma. American instructors had explained the flush toilet as part of a crash course in what to expect in the modern world. Daniel and each other refugee in his orientation session had been made to sit on the toilet and flush. Teachers had passed around U.S. currency and ice. They had explained that people in the United States could dial 911 on their telephone—most apartments and houses had telephones—to summon police, paramedics, or firefighters. They had talked about jobs, schools, and apartments, but no one had expected refugees with so little familiarity with the modern world to retain it all. So people like Mathew Kon waited in cities around the United States, caseworkers who were responsible for dozens of refugees at a time.

Mathew showed them the peephole in the door and told them to look through it if someone knocked. "Don't open unless it's me," he said.

He pointed out the telephone, scrawled his number, and told them to call if they needed to. He strode to the television set and pressed a button that conjured images and sound.

"Senator," a woman on television was suddenly saying, "if you believe that life begins at conception, how can you then favor [the use of] embryonic stem cells?"

Daniel leaned down until his face was two inches from the screen. He peered into the eyes of Judy Woodruff, an anchor for CNN who was talking with Senator Bill Frist of Tennessee.

"Well, senator," she was saying, "I know you're aware that those who disagree with you say if there's any chance those embryos could survive, they potentially are human beings, and to treat them as anything other than that is just immoral."

Daniel focused on buttons near the one that Mathew had pressed. "How is it possible to adjust the volume?" he asked.

A few feet away, Marko stepped through the open hotel-room door, out onto the covered walkway. Peter closed the door and held his left eye to the small glass circle in the middle of the door. "There is Marko," he announced. "I see him."

Jacob took his turn looking through the peephole and shook his head and looked at Peter to confirm that, yes, he, too, saw Marko. Mathew lingered for a few minutes longer and then suggested he leave to buy some chicken, bread, and Coca-Cola. He would eat with them and maybe watch TV, then they would go to sleep after he left. He was on his way toward the door when Jacob picked up a black plastic rectangle with numbers and buttons. "What's this?" he asked.

"A remote control," Mathew said. "You can use it to see different channels."

The next morning, Mathew herded them back into his Blazer and eased into traffic. Soon they were on a leafy two-lane road that followed railroad tracks past gas stations and old wooden houses. Peter cocked his head and looked through the rear window at the treetops. He was accustomed to a flat landscape that let him see for miles, but here trees and buildings rose everywhere to obscure the horizon. He wondered how he would figure out where the sun rises and where the sun sets.

Jacob noticed all the traffic—even on this small road. "Most of us will be having no vehicles," he said. "It will be difficult if you get a job far from your living area." What if they had to walk? "If you walk randomly, maybe a vehicle will knock you."

The Blazer turned left onto North Indian Creek Drive, passed under a railroad trestle, and followed the road as it arced to the right. A curtain of trees parted to reveal a sign on the left heralding the Clarkston Village shopping center. Signs in the strip mall advertised *halal* meat, prepared in accordance with Islamic guidelines. The Pho Truc restaurant trumpeted its Vietnamese beef noodle soup. They saw a yellow sign with red Arabic letters and the Global Pharmacy and Thriftown grocery store. Next to the strip mall, on the same side of the road, they saw a building with dull gray siding spiced up by a colorful sign that read "Inserection Adult Fantasy Store."

Mathew steered the Blazer down a hill and turned left just past a sign that said "Olde Plantation Apartments." He drove into the complex over bumpy, potholed pavement, and turned right and then left through a maze of two-story buildings, this one made all of brick, that one of brick with black shingles that covered the exterior wall of the upper level. They passed a beat-up burgundy Nissan Maxima with the word *asshole* scratched into the passenger side and a minivan with stickers displaying the flags of the United States and Kurdistan. A Somali woman strolled toward them in a colorful *hijab*, the head scarf many Muslim women wear. Five young African American men sat in chairs on a porch stoop, passing around a forty-ounce bottle of beer in a paper bag. The Blazer groaned to a stop in front of building 40.

The four young men stepped out and heard the whoosh of traffic on a nearby interstate filtering through trees like a stream in the woods. Mathew led them toward a black door off its hinges and stepped into a stairwell covered in paper-thin green carpet. He climbed six stairs to a landing with a bare lightbulb mounted halfway up the wall and turned to walk up six more stairs that led to a freshly painted black door with the letter "G" nailed just above the peephole. He turned a key in the lock and they followed him into an empty room with beige carpets and plain white walls. The only furniture in the living room was a wooden butcher-block table with three wooden chairs and three folding chairs. A corridor led to three bedrooms, each with two twin beds, a bathroom, and a walk-in closet. Mathew opened one closet door. "It is not a room," he said. "You must put your things in here."

They followed him into a room with no carpet and recognized the appliances from photographs in a book. Jacob opened the freezer and inspected a package of frozen beef, turning it over in his hands. "I have tried milk and orange juice, but I have not tasted cow meat," he said.

Peter picked up a sponge. "What is this?" he asked. Not waiting for an answer, he read aloud the words on a small plastic bottle full of blue liquid: "Dish detergent."

Jacob grasped a bottle of deodorant someone had left on the counter. "Is it detergent, too?" he asked.

Jacob and Peter moved to the stove. Peter read the words printed there: "Front. Rear. Oven Settings. General Electric." He stared through a grimy plastic panel at a clock showing the wrong time.

"Is it broken?" Jacob asked.

Peter leaned in closer. "It is written here, 'Push to Set Clock,'" Peter said.

Mathew stood in front of the stove, Jacob, Peter, Daniel, and Marko around him, and twisted one of the knobs. He held his hand above one of four black coils on the stovetop, kept it there until he felt something, and smiled. Next Jacob reached his hand to the place where Mathew's had been. Heat raced up and he jerked his hand away. He laughed. Peter and Daniel and Marko did that, too, looking at each other with wide grins. Then Mathew showed them how to open, close, and lock two windows in the living room, how to lock and unlock the front door, how to plug in a lamp. "If you have a radio or TV or you want to play a cassette, you can get the power from here," he said, pointing to a receptacle in the wall.

Mathew busied himself installing blinds in two living-room windows while the four young men, still in USRP sweatshirts, khaki pants, and thin white canvas shoes with red stripes, filed down the hallway and into a bedroom. Peter climbed on the bed first and then Jacob and Daniel and Marko until they all sat there in a row, feet dangling over the edge.

"We have never lived in such a house," Jacob said. "I have my clothes in the drawer over here. You know, I have everything. I get water in my house. I can prepare food without difficulty, but when I was in Africa, these things were very difficult." He tried to wrap his mind around the future. "We were told that America is a place of freedom. Also, they told us that America is a place of self-reliance and self-sufficiency," he said. "According to what we were told, there is something called entry-level jobs, like the cleaning, carrying things in a factory. You are the one to determine your need. If you fail, you will not blame anyone."

He had questions about the United States: Is it true that bandits knock on your door at night and if you open it they will terrorize you? Is it true that sometimes bandits with guns will stop your car and take it from you? What is the minimum and maximum cost of a college education? What is a bank loan? How much does a used car cost? They say in America there is freedom. You can go to any church you want. Is this true? What about women? We were told that, here, if you want to make friends with a girl, she might have had a boyfriend and that boyfriend might go and kill you. If a girl asks to make a friendship and you say no, will she kill you?

Similar questions were arising around the United States. In Boston, a Sudanese man riding in the backseat of an American family's minivan glanced at the shrubs in a suburban neighborhood and asked whether lions lurked in the bush. In a grocery store in Fargo, North Dakota, a refugee who had spent the previous nine years eating mushed-up grain strolled down an aisle with a writer who was there to cover the resettlement. The newcomer plucked a can from the shelves and asked the writer, "Can you tell me what this is?"

"Um," the writer said, "that's food for our dogs."

The young man paused. Many such cans lined the shelves. "Tell me," he said. "What is the work of dogs in this country?"

In Georgia, a mile or so from the apartment where Jacob, Peter, Daniel, and Marko were settling in, a young man named Lueth Mou Mou got a lesson in cooking an egg one Tuesday afternoon from a new American friend named Dee Clement, a former exercise physiologist who also had helped Vietnamese and Bosnian refugees adjust to life in Atlanta. She is a whirlwind of a woman who flitted from one apartment to the next in 2001, delivering donated underwear, shirts, towels, and secondhand telephones and radios to newly arrived Sudanese. She opened a cabinet in Mou Mou's kitchen at the beginning of her lesson to discover half-empty jars of Knott's Berry Farm strawberry preserves and Prego Mini-Meatball pasta sauce. She raised them into the air as if they were exhibits in a trial. "You see that?" she said. "That's mold. If you eat that, it will make you sick." She threw away the jars before Mou Mou could react.

He opened the dishwasher. "We were shown that if you want to wash, you put the soap in there and then you turn the handle," he said. He could not open the plastic lid for detergent and looked to Dee for help. She reached over to help but stopped when she saw what was inside.

"What's this?" she demanded. "Why is there bread in the dish-washer?"

The first few days were dull inside apartment 40-G at Olde Planta-tion. Mathew was a phone call away, but others of the dozens of Lost Boys already in Atlanta had questions for him, too, and there was a never-ending procession of paperwork at his office. Jacob, Peter, Daniel, and Marko knew he was busy. They spent most of their first few days talking with one another, test-driving the thermostat and oven, trying to figure what to do with a bag of sugar. They ventured out in search of friends from Kakuma in other units at Olde Plantation, one of five or six rundown complexes where resettlement agencies were placing the latest of fifty thousand refugees that the federal government had sent to Georgia since 1980.

The agencies had been steering refugees for more than ten years to the town of Clarkston, a place where tall trees sway in the wind above old white wooden houses. The city was founded in 1882 and named for Colonel W. W. Clark, a lawyer and director of the Georgia Railroad and Banking Company (the fact that he owned slaves forestalled plans in 2000 to name a middle school near Clarkston in his honor). It thrived for de-cades as a mill town sustained by the railroad tracks that still pass through the center of town. Despite its proximity to downtown Atlanta—it's an eleven-mile drive down Ponce de Leon Avenue—Clarkston retained the air of an insulated, small southern town for most of the twentieth century, a mostly white city with its own supermarket, post office, and police station. In the early 1980s, apartment buildings offering cheap rents went up, altering Clarkston's demographics. White families began packing up after larger numbers of blacks discovered the city. Whites accounted for 90 percent of Clarkston's population in 1980 but only 37 percent in 1990. The black population went from 7 percent to 57 percent.

Meanwhile, a subtler shift was underway. Nonprofit refugee resettlement agencies, with offices two or three miles down the road, saw opportunity in Clarkston's falling rents and access to public transportation. They began renting apartments there in the 1980s for refugees from around the world. The agencies placed refugees in many cities, but no place in Georgia changed as a dramatically as Clarkston because of an influx of refugees. It was a convenient first home from the refugees' standpoint because the town was close to resettlement offices that offered English classes, help finding jobs, and advice on dealing with the much-feared Immigration and Naturalization Service. In 1980, only 3 percent of Clarkston residents were born outside the United States, but the number soared to 33 percent in 2000, when head counters with the U.S. Census Bureau said that 2,301 of 6,826 Clarkston residents were born abroad.

Thousands of towns in the United States, primarily southeastern and midwestern communities that had little recent history of foreign-born settlement, underwent similar transformations in the 1990s, but the forces diversifying Clarkston were unique. Most communities in Georgia and similar states changed as a result of an unparalleled migration of Latino immigrants, mainly from Mexico but with smaller numbers from Guatemala, El Salvador, Honduras, and Colombia. Many such newcomers bypassed traditional immigrant destinations, such as Chicago, Los Angeles, Miami, and New York, in favor of emerging immigrant communities in states such as Georgia, Iowa, and North Carolina. Tens of thousands of Asians did the same thing, and many were drawn to Atlanta by a white-hot economy that created job openings in the mid- to late 1990s faster than employers could fill them. Several hundred thousand immigrants poured into Georgia, and soon they were working side-by-side with whites and blacks born in the United States.

Immigrants filled jobs in an array of industries, but large concentrations gravitated to specific fields. Indian computer programmers and software engineers became a major force in Atlanta's booming high-tech industry. Others from the subcontinent followed each other into the hospitality business with such vigor that Indians owned more than half of all roadside motels in Georgia by the end of the 1990s. Not all computer programmers or motel owners were Indian, of course, and not all Indians programmed computers or owned motels, but many followed relatives into established businesses. Many immigrants from India gobbled up restaurant franchises and ran hundreds of Dairy Queen, Dunkin Donuts, and Blimpie's restaurants. At the same time, Korean families were investing twelve-hour days in dry-cleaning businesses and liquor and grocery stores. Thousands of Vietnamese refugees went to work in nail salons. The United States had resettled large numbers of Vietnamese refugees after the fall of Saigon in 1975, about the same time that chemicals used to bond teeth in the dental industry were modified to make artificial nails. That change had happened amid a dramatic rise in popularity of the hand-held hair dryer, making trips to the beauty salon less time consuming and more affordable. Manicures, once the realm of socialites and starlets, soared in popularity. In the late 1970s and '80s, just as tens of thousands of Vietnamese refugees were looking for a new livelihood in the United States, entrepreneurs opened more and more nail salons. It took little time for some Vietnamese manicurists in California to spread word of their success. They followed each other into the industry with such abandon that by 2000 nearly four in five nail-salon operators in Georgia were Vietnamese. It seemed every new strip mall that opened in metro Atlanta—there were hundreds—had a salon where Vietnamese women chatted in their native language while hunched over the fingers and toes of white and black women born in the United States.

The concentration of immigrants in particular industries perhaps was most obvious in Georgia's burgeoning Latino community. Immigrants from Mexico, mainly men, followed brothers and cousins to jobs that paid more than they could make in Los Angeles or Chicago and ten times what they could earn in their native country. Soon they dominated the workforce in carpet mills and poultry plants. Most of the people cutting lumber and hammering nails in Atlanta subdivisions spoke Spanish. So did many of the men who raked leaves and trimmed bushes and the women who made beds and vacuumed carpets in hotel rooms. In the fields of south Georgia, where farmers raise a Vidalia onion crop worth $70 million a year, nine of every ten people picking onions at harvest time were born in Latin America.

Yet the forces altering Clarkston were different from those changing other Georgia cities. The foreign-born residents of Clarkston were refugees escaping persecution, not immigrants chasing jobs. Some had endured torture or imprisonment for political or religious beliefs. Many carried with them the memory of relatives who had been kidnapped, beaten, raped, or killed. They came from Afghanistan, Bosnia, Cambodia, Iran, Iraq, Kosovo, Laos, Somalia, the former Soviet Union, and Vietnam. Resettlement agencies put so many of them in apartments in Clarkston that in 2000, the city had the highest concentration of Africans and Europeans of any town or city in Georgia, and the second highest concentration of Asians. It became a place where the library offers audiocassettes in Arabic, Cambodian, Serbo-Croatian, Somali, and Urdu, where the magazine rack displays copies of *Ebony* and *Better Homes and Gardens* alongside *Azizah—For the Contemporary Muslim Woman.* At the police department, in a two-story brick building, the police chief has a photograph of Barney Fife on his wall with a caption that reads, as if he needs reminding, "Hell No This Ain't Mayberry."

This world outside apartment 40-G awaited Jacob, Peter, Daniel, and Marko. On their fourth day in the United States, they had just reunited with some friends from Kakuma who now lived in apartment 35-E, so they sat and traded stories about the journey and their new home. Dee Clement dropped by to introduce herself and deliver donated clothes. Jacob got a long-sleeved blue shirt with an intricate pattern of white diamonds and rectangles, blue jeans a few sizes too big, and black shoes. Peter got khakis and a belt that looped around his waist one and a half times. Marko wore stonewashed blue jeans and a T-shirt that said "Goodwill Games." The green nylon workout pants with white stripes and white sun visor that said "BellSouth Cellular Corporation" went to Daniel. Dee left them her telephone number and told them to call if they needed her. They asked her about going to school and getting a job.

They had asked Mathew about that, too, and he drove them to his office at the International Rescue Committee one morning to talk about it. They followed him into the office, which he shared with a Bosnian caseworker, and watched in silence as he opened a file drawer and took out a stack of forms. They stood and waited as Mathew filled out one form after another and then, when Mathew got up, they turned to follow him like ducks through the corridors, past one office and then another, into a room stacked with books and boxes of clothes. A smiling woman greeted them as if they were long-lost relatives. She handed each of them a plastic bag with toothpaste, shampoo, deodorant, and soap. She also gave them a soccer ball and told them to take their pick of shirts. Peter chose red and white Timberland T-shirts and a beige button-down from Joseph A. Banks Clothiers. Jacob picked three oxford shirts—navy, light blue, and cream-colored.

The woman took from a shelf two books wrapped in a silver ribbon with a bow on top: a dictionary and a study guide for the GED. "Thank you," Jacob said. "Something good." They turned to leave but she stopped them. She had forgotten to give them an aqua-colored plastic pail and a bottle of Pine Sol. Jacob took the bucket and held up the bottle for inspection. "How do you apply this?" he asked.

"What you do is, put a little bit of this in the bucket and then add water," she said. "Mathew will show you."

They followed Mathew through the office, back outside, and down a flight of concrete stairs to put the clothes, books, and cleaning supplies into his car. Mathew wanted to make sure they knew how to use buses and trains because they would take public transportation to whatever job awaited, so he walked them a quarter-mile or so to the Kensington MARTA station, where signs with arrows and strange phrases awaited: "Kiss Ride . . . Avondale Estates . . . Five Points . . . Hamilton E. Holmes."

A train pulled into the station at 11:55 a.m. Its doors whooshed open and they followed Mathew inside. "This is my first time riding a train," Peter said. "It is very, very, very, very long and fast."

Mathew shepherded them off the train at the next stop and walked them to a place where buses idled in the midday sun. He told them to look for bus 125 because it was the one that would pick them up at a stop just outside their apartment and take them here, to the train station. Catching the 125 and riding it to the train station would become an important ritual. To practice, they climbed aboard bus 125 and rode for forty-five minutes, past fourteen stops. Then they boarded a bus going the opposite direction, got off at the train station, and rode back to the station where they began. Jacob peered out the train windows and spied a sign as it slowed. "Kensington," he told the others. "We are supposed to alight here."

More flights from Kakuma were landing in Atlanta and cities around the country, and within days a fifth roommate arrived at apartment 40-G. He went by the name John, and he was from the same village as Jacob, in the Upper Nile province of southern Sudan. John was the one who had talked of people in Europe and the United States as Special People from the Gods, as if they had been born with a scientific prowess that let them harness nature for their own purposes. His view had been reinforced when he had heard news in 1998, while still in the refugee camp in Kenya, that a U.S. missile fired from some great distance had flown without a pilot over Sudan to destroy a pharmaceutical factory in Khartoum, in retaliation, it was said, for the destruction by terrorists of the U.S. embassies in Kenya and Tanzania. Who else but the Americans could conceive of a missile that could slice through the air for hundreds of miles, no human eye to guide it, to destroy a target in unfamiliar territory?

The sixth roommate in apartment 40-G, William, came two weeks later. Unlike most Lost Boys, who were Dinka, William belonged to the Bari ethnic group, found in southernmost Sudan, near the borders with Ethiopia and Kenya. He spoke Bari, Arabic, Kiswahli, and a limited English peppered with grunts when he did not understand. The five Dinka roommates usually spoke their native language with each other, but they spoke with William in Arabic, a language they all understood.

And so, on William's first morning in Atlanta, when he bounded into the living room in a panic, they knew what he was saying when out poured Arabic in a tone of urgency and fright. William had just realized that his five roommates were walking out the door and that he would be left in the apartment by himself. The five were bound for a daylong lesson in cooking and computers from a new American friend and mentor. William could not go because he had an appointment at his resettlement agency to fill out new-arrival paperwork. He stood there wearing boxer shorts and a white T-shirt and a look of fear. Jacob listened and patted William's arm, showed him how to lock the door. Peter told him to look through the peephole if anyone knocked and to keep the door closed unless he recognized the visitor. Then Peter and the others left. In the stairwell, they laughed sympathetically. William did not want to be left alone, they would say later, because he worried that bandits would attack.

Outside in the parking lot was a woman named Cheryl Grover. She was in her late thirties, with a perpetual smile. They strode to her with arms outstretched and shook her hand, one by one. She was an Air Force brat from central California who worked part-time as a real-estate consultant for a cell-phone company. She negotiated deals when the company wanted to buy land, but she had been telling herself lately that she should find some volunteer work that would let her work one-on-one with someone. She had volunteered before, mainly on committees of local governments and chambers of commerce, but once as a mentor with a Boys and Girls club. When she read a newspaper story about the Lost Boys of Sudan she saw another opportunity to connect with someone and possibly be of some service. Cheryl let the idea of volunteering stew for a few weeks. Then she reread the story and called the International Rescue Committee, the agency that was steering Jacob, Peter, Daniel, and Marko into their new lives. Something about the Sudanese refugees beckoned her, she would say, something about their—what was it exactly? Their vulnerability? Their lack of parents? The way they were young men chronologically but seemed to be boys psychologically? Cheryl and her boyfriend of more than fifteen years had decided years earlier to forgo having children, and suddenly here was a chance to fulfill a simmering desire to care for younger people, to nurture and guide without long-term commitment. And if volunteering with Sudanese refugees met some need to connect for her, it also gave the men of apartment 40-G a desperately needed guide who could explain such mysteries as tax returns and cordless telephones.

They piled into Cheryl's car that morning for a rare excursion out of

Clarkston. They were going to Cheryl's house about twenty miles north, in a place called Duluth, on the outer edges of the suburbs. They rode on Interstate 285, the perimeter that loops around the city in up to thirteen lanes, and came in about ten minutes to the junction of that road and I-85. The two interstates meet in a web of eight interlacing beige concrete bridges that rise high into the air, a humming crossroads famously known to the 4.2 million people of metro Atlanta as Spaghetti Junction. Told this, Jacob took out a pocket-size blue day planner and made a note to himself: "Spageti Juncho."

"This one is really very, very technical," he said. "Some cars are moving up and others are moving down."

Twenty minutes later, they pulled into the driveway of Cheryl's house, a split-level place with a boat parked in the driveway that they mistook for some strange car. She gave them a tour, and Jacob made notes in his day planner. He pointed to a Sunbeam 640 gas grill on the back deck. "What is this?" he asked.

"A barbecue grill," Cheryl said.

"How do you spell it?"

"B-A-R-B-E-C-U-E," she said.

He wrote the letters in his blue book. "You can cook with this?"

"Yes."

They went into the house and Cheryl showed them around. They saw a box in the kitchen that she said would cook food with invisible microwaves and another box in the living room that would make movies flicker on a TV screen. "This machine is called a DVD player," Cheryl said. "Hmm. How do you describe a DVD?"

Jacob uncapped his pen. "DBD," he wrote.

"It's like a VCR," Cheryl said.

"BCR," Jacob wrote.

They were on the sofa, talking, when one of Cheryl's dogs barked from somewhere in the house. Daniel sprang up and bolted toward the sliding glass door by the porch. His roommates laughed, and he smiled sheepishly after Cheryl assured them that there was no reason to worry, that Max and Baby wouldn't bite. Besides, she said, the dogs were in a bedroom with the door closed.

"The dogs have their own bedroom?" Jacob asked.

"No, no," Cheryl said. "They're in my bedroom."

She ushered Daniel, Marko, and John into her basement, where they practiced typing on a computer. Cheryl took Jacob and Peter upstairs to the kitchen, where she had pots and pans and packages of all manner of foodstuffs on the counter.

Jacob picked up one of the packages. "How do you call it?" he asked.

"That one is called oatmeal," Cheryl said. "It's very nutritious. It has vitamins." She showed them how to boil water and pour in the oatmeal. Meanwhile, Jacob examined a packet of Top Ramen chicken noodle soup.

"Oatmeal is usually eaten in the morning as a breakfast food," Cheryl explained. "Noodles would be like lunch or dinner." She poured hot water into the soup mix. "In college, we eat this very much because it is very cheap and nutritious."

Jacob tasted the oatmeal. "It's sweet."

Peter sampled the soup and narrowed his eyes in thought. "I think this one is from wheat," he said.

"This one is good for us," Jacob said, "for someone who is not stable financially to go and buy it."

The lessons continued for two hours.

"What is this?" Peter asked.

"Broccoli. It's a vegetable grown in the ground."

He repeated the word, let it sink in.

Jacob picked up a white clump. "What is this? How do you call it?"

"Cauliflower," Cheryl said. All of this stuff is in your cookbook. See here?" She opened to page 162 of *Betty Crocker's Cooking Basics: Learning to Cook with Confidence* and pointed to a picture of cauliflower. "It tells you what to look for when you shop for it and how to prepare it."

They stirred refried beans, grated cheese, and practiced opening a twenty-eight-ounce can of tomatoes. Jacob picked up a flimsy brown tube and learned it was a hot dog. He wrote the words "seasoning" and "Ramen noodle" in his blue book. Then he turned to a page where he kept names and phone numbers. He found Mathew's number and moved toward a phone Cheryl kept on a kitchen counter. "I want to tell Mathew what we are doing," he said.

The receiver sat on a base that had the numbered buttons on it. To use it, Cheryl would pick up the receiver and then dial a number, but Jacob had little experience with telephones; without lifting the receiver, he dialed Mathew's number. Once he had pressed all the buttons, he picked up the receiver and waited to hear Mathew's voice. Nothing. He replaced it and then just stood there, staring. He pressed another button on the base and suddenly the telephone was talking in a stilted mechanical voice: "Sunday. 11 a.m."

He turned to look at Peter and announced, "It did not go through." Then he shuffled to the counter and picked up a plastic packet. "How do you call this one?" he said.

"Herb and garlic," Cheryl answered. "Most of the herbs in this sauce are from basil." She anticipated the next question. "B-A-S-I-L."

Jacob and his roommates and the resettled Lost Boys of Sudan around Clarkston were relying on lessons from people like Cheryl to unravel the mysteries of everyday life. The resettlement agencies tried to assign an American volunteer to each apartment—the International Rescue Committee matched Cheryl with the men in apartment 40-G—and there were a handful of other women, unaffiliated with any agency, who bounced from one apartment to the next to offer rides to the grocery store and advice on laundry detergent. They would nurse those with back pain or headaches and deliver socks and sports jackets collected from neighbors.

Dee Clement was one of these freelance volunteers who moved from one apartment to another and one minicrisis to another. Her second visit to apartment 40-G was a welcome diversion from the hours Peter spent thumbing through dog-eared copies of *Around the World in 80 Days* and *Body Language in the Workplace*, which told him to be punctual for job interviews and to make eye contact and shake hands with the interviewer. She knocked on their door one Friday afternoon, accompanied by her dog, Polka Dot, and a slender maroon machine with the words "Panasonic Jet Flow" on its side. "This machine is a very, very special machine," she said. "It's called a vacuum cleaner."

Dee picked hair from Polka Dot and dropped it on the floor. She told Jacob to open a box of rice and spill it on the carpet. He asked her twice to make sure he understood. Then out came the rice. They stood and stared at the dog hair and rice as Dee flicked on the vacuum cleaner and moved it back and forth. The rice and hair vanished. Jacob and his roommates laughed.

"What this machine should not do is ever get near water because water and electricity do not go together," Dee said.

She stepped back from the handle and asked the young men of apartment 40-G to take turns pushing the machine. Jacob grasped the handle as his roommates watched. He did just as Dee had and the machine moved forward over beige carpet. His roommates took their turns and each of them also laughed at something so alien and amusing. Who among them could have imagined, having spent their lives walking on a ground of dust and dirt, that they would one day live in a building where the floors were covered with fabric and that they would sweep an electric machine over that fabric to make dog hair and rice disappear?

After the last of them had finished, Dee stormed into the kitchen to teach them to cook scrambled eggs. She turned on a stovetop burner and flung open the refrigerator door but saw only four loaves of Nature's Own Honey Wheat bread. Look in the freezer, someone said. She opened that door and saw cans of Chef Boyardee Cannelloni and Healthy Choice Chicken and Rice soup. There also was a carton of eggs in the freezer, but the temperature had cracked them open. Dee sighed but recovered quickly. She always had a backup plan. "Americans love this thing called a peanut butter and jelly sandwich," she said.

"What is jelly?" Jacob asked.

"It's made from a fruit. It's very sweet." Dee found a jar of strawberry jam and used a knife to spread it and peanut butter on bread. Peter put a pinch in his mouth and chewed slowly. He did not say whether he liked it and Dee did not wait for a verdict. She had found a can of Van Camp's Pork and Beans and launched into a tutorial on the can opener. "This is the sharp point right here," she said. "When it goes in, just turn."

Someone from the resettlement agency had left a glass container of orange powder in their kitchen before they moved in. Peter showed it to Dee. "It is written here 'Tang,'" he said, "but we do not know if it is healthy."

Dee explained and then surveyed the kitchen, looking right and then left. She deciding on a cleaning lesson. Her pupils may have been overwhelmed, but they liked Dee and enjoyed her lessons. They were as eager to learn as she was to teach, so they followed and nodded their heads as she told them how to clean a window. They kept nodding as she sprayed glass with liquid from a twelve-ounce bottle of Mountain Berry Windex (Streak-Free Shine!).

The roommates were most excited that day by Dee's gift of an electric typewriter. She showed them how to plug it in and they put it up on a chair and sat on the floor to hunt and peck. Peter crouched down to hit the keys as the others stood behind him like backup singers. He tried to type his name, and his roommates watched with wide eyes as if the typewriter might at any minute spring to life. The typewriter held magical appeal. Here was an instrument of the written word, a machine for the educated. It thrilled Peter to imagine his Dinka friends in Kakuma knowing he had a typewriter. Peter remembered what an elder said the day before he left Africa, when the man addressed the latest group of Dinka bound for the new world. "When you are an educated person, you can put some things in documents. Some words from past can be found in documents for the educated people," the man had said. "But when you are uneducated, there is nothing. When something happens and you have not recorded it, so it may go. And when it is needed for the reference, it cannot be found anymore. But if you are an educated person, you can put your things in documents and when they are needed to be reviewed again, they can be found in documents."

Now they were in Atlanta, in the United States, the modern world, with a machine that would let them put some things in documents. Daniel supplanted Peter at the machine and started to type as Marko looked over his shoulder. "We all of us speak English Arabic Kiswahli and mother tongueeee," he typed. "America is the land of freedom. America is multicultural land." He paused a moment, then typed, "Arabic soldiers came and shot our people."

The only other time any of the roommates had had a chance to type something, on the computer that day in the basement of Cheryl's house, thoughts also had drifted across an ocean, to a country riven by intractable war, a land they saw now only in their dreams.

"I am John from the land of Cush [Sudan] eager to learn a lot of things," John had written. "I have left my mum and dad in Africa due to the emerge war in my territory. This war caused great separation of relatives in Sudan and many destruction."

THE SPOILING OF THE WORLD

Southern Sudan is one of the most isolated spots on earth, a place that had little sustained contact with the outside world until the nineteenth century. The rhythms of everyday life unfolded much as they had since the time of Christ in the rich savannas where Jacob, Peter, Daniel, and Marko were born. Various ethnic groups have lived and died in that region for thousands of years, and the largest of these is the Dinka, a collection of roughly twenty-five tribal groups with a common culture and language and similar physical characteristics. The Dinka have herded cattle, cultivated grains, and fished in bountiful rivers along with smaller ethnic groups for countless generations. They lived without the structure of the modern state, grouped into lineages and clans, which formed parts of tribes. No single chief, king, or authority held sway over the disparate groups sprinkled across southern Sudan. Members of one lineage or another, and larger groups of one clan or another, allied together at various times to confront grievances that arose with opposing lineages or clans, a traditional East African hierarchy of loyalties described in this Somali proverb:

Me and my clan against the world;
Me and my family against my clan;
Me and my brother against my family;
Me against my brother.

The Dinka historically have viewed themselves as blessed by a variety of crops and domesticated animals such as goat and sheep, but it is the cow that dominates Dinka culture and defines their sense of self-identity. The cow has met most of the material needs of the Dinka for hundreds of years. They use the animal's dung as fuel and fertilizer and its urine as a disinfectant. The Dinka fashion trumpets and spoons from the horns of cattle. Young children supplement a diet of mother's milk with cow milk, and boys are given the crucial task of herding cattle in vast fields around their homes. It is said that Dinka boys are able to distinguish cows from one another among a herd of hundreds of cattle that appear remarkably similar to outsiders. Historian Francis Mading Deng, a Dinka from a prominent family in Sudan, writes that Dinka traditionally have sacrificed cows to protect themselves from "the evil forces of illness and death." Children grow up to compose songs about their favorite cattle and boys often perform elaborate dances in which they leap high into the air, arms raised above them in the shape of the horns of this bull or that. Boys occasionally lead cows far from home, to cattle camps, where the cows get good grazing and the boys escape the scrutiny of adults. Spending time at the cattle camp is "a source of dignity and pride," Deng writes, an experience that "is highlighted by the institution of toc (literally 'lying down'), according to which young men excuse themselves from cultivation, retreat to summer camps, gorge themselves with milk supplemented with meat, and as the word for the custom suggests, lie down, fatten themselves and move as little as possible. They compose songs about matters of special interest to them," mostly about the desire to marry, the attributes of a particular girl, or feelings of despondency at having made a failed proposal. They return from this retreat and "are thought to be attractive as a result of their being fatter and heavier: For since the Dinka are generally very slender and tall, gaining weight usually improves their figures. They attract a great deal of attention as they move around in a group, presenting their songs with a dance and feast for the occasion." Marriage "is the dream of every Dinka," Deng reports, and is accomplished after courtship by the payment of a dowry of cattle by the groom's family to the bride's. The desirability of a bride can be gauged by the number of cows her family receives as a dowry—in more prosperous times, the most attractive young women could fetch up to two hundred cows: "So important for the welfare of the Dinka and so honored by them are their cattle that the Dinka speak of the cow or the bull as the 'creator.'"

The Dinka call themselves *Monyjang*, which means "The Man of Men" or "The People," a title that reflects a traditional perception among the Dinka that their way of life is the best, an ethnocentric view they share with many cultures. The region known informally as Dinkaland covers roughly one hundred thousand square miles in Sudan. Generations have come and gone tending to cattle and raising sorghum, corn, peanuts, and a range of other crops. "Traditionally most southern peoples live in spread-out settlements," Deng writes. "A family . . . usually lives in a settlement comprising several huts and a cow barn, with a distance of about a mile from the next family. A village identified by one name will usually spread over a number of miles with the same pattern repeated." It is a harsh environment where "the blazing sun of the dry season kills the grass and deceives the traveler with moving mirages of rivers and lakes," a place where "the soil dries up, forming wide and deep cracks into which humans and animals fall." Thorns lurk on the ground and in trees, and the wet season can bring days of heavy rains and floods, and lightning that can burn huts and fell trees. Throughout Dinkaland roam lions, leopards, hyenas, wild dogs, rhinoceroses, crocodiles, snakes, and scorpions, but "to a Dinka, his country, with all its deprivations and troubles, is the best in the world. Until very recently, going to a foreign land was not only a rarity but a shame. For a Dinka to threaten his relatives with leaving Dinkaland was seen as little short of suicide."

The Sudan was known in biblical times as Cush and, later, Nubia, a place near the end of the Earth from which the Nile originated. The Greeks and Egyptians dispatched explorers to try to find the source of the Nile, but a foreboding landscape stymied expeditions. A Roman commander who ventured south of Egypt around 23 BC turned back after concluding that the territory ahead of him was "too poor to warrant its conquest." Even in those times, two worlds merged in the land of modern-day Sudan. The northern peoples looked to the Middle East for their sense of identity, an inclination bolstered by hundreds of years of trade, while people in the south pursued a more insular existence that revolved around traditional African notions of culture and religion. A vast swamp, known as the Sudd, created a natural boundary between north and south. It marked the edge of the known world for ancient geographers. The swamp, stifling heat, and fierce resistance from southern inhabitants thwarted incursions from the north for hundreds of years.

Divisions deepened after the advent of Islam in the seventh century and its subsequent spread through Egypt and into the northern regions of Sudan. Arab Muslims with superior weapons defeated the Nubians in 652 and the Beja in 831, two groups who had held sway in what is now northern Sudan. There were several Christian kingdoms in northern Sudan, but they collapsed in 1505, when Islamic armies seized control of a swath of land extending from Alexandria, a Mediterranean port city at the mouth of the Nile, far south to the area on which Khartoum, the capital of modern Sudan, was founded. The north developed increasingly along Arab and Islamic lines, while southerners followed traditional pagan and animist religions. The name Sudan, in fact, is a shortened version of the Arabic *Bilad al-Sudan*, a pejorative reference that means "Land of the Blacks." It was applied at first to a vast territory south of Egypt. During the colonial period, when European powers carved Africa into modern nation-states under their control, French possessions in West Africa, hundreds of miles from modern-day Sudan, were known for a time as French Sudan. Hundreds of years earlier, Greeks and Romans looking beyond the known realms of North Africa referred to the region further south as the "Land of the Burnt-Faced Ones." The names hinted at a mysterious territory, and in fact the south that would produce Jacob, Peter, Daniel, and Marko remained virtually unknown to the wider world until 1820.

It was in that year that Muhammad Ali, the *khedive* or viceroy of Egypt, invaded and seized much of northern Sudan. Ali was a representative of the Ottoman Empire in Constantinople, but had cultivated a formidable military force that needed more recruits to grow stronger. His predecessors in Cairo had relied on Sudan for slaves, and Ali made no secret of similar ambitions in a message to his commander in Sudan in 1825. "You are aware that the end of all our effort and this expense is to procure Negroes," he wrote. "Please show zeal in carrying out our wishes in this capital matter." In 1840, his forces became the first outsiders known to have penetrated the vast swamp dividing north and south, that natural barrier that had thwarted so many previous expeditions. The Arab Muslims of Egypt went south in *Dar al Harb*, the "House of War," to enslave black southerners in the name of *Dar al Islam*, the "House of Islam." The Muslims arrived on horseback, well armed with rifles, and with an appetite for much larger numbers of slaves than historically had been taken by rival groups in the south. Classical Islamic teaching outlawed the enslavement of Muslims but permitted the bondage of nonbelievers. Like some Christians in the American South who rationalized slavery as a divinely ordained method of civilizing barbarians from Africa, many Muslims in Sudan viewed slavery as an opportunity to introduce infidels to Islam. They would lose freedom but win exposure, the theory went, to enlightened Muslim faith and culture. Over the next several decades, the Turks and Egyptians were joined in their journeys south by slave raiders from northern Sudan, Greece, and other parts of Europe. Merchants in the business of flesh built fortified stations along riverbanks in southern Sudan to feed a bustling slave market in Khartoum.

The slave-raiding incursions so disrupted the Dinka pattern of everyday life and so terrified and devastated them that they refer to this era as "the spoiling of the world," a time when history and tradition were turned upside down by forces beyond their control. That the Dinka's world was spoiled at the particular time it was would set into motion a sequence of events that would propel modern Sudan into excruciating civil war more than one hundred years later, in the second half of the twentieth century, again for reasons hopelessly beyond the control of the ordinary Sudanese. It set into motion the historic forces that eventually would force more than 4 million Sudanese from their homes, including several thousand boys who would come to be known as the Lost Boys of

Sudan, for the booming slave trade in southern Sudan unfolded at the very time that antislavery sentiment was sweeping across much of the Western world. Abolitionists scored a major victory in Britain in 1807, when that country forbade its citizens from engaging in the slave trade, and again in 1831, when Britain freed slaves across its far-flung empire. The British navy seized more than fifteen hundred slave ships en route to the Western Hemisphere from 1820 to 1870, freeing nearly 150,000 Africans destined for slavery in the Americas. In the United States, slavery was the major issue in the civil war that began in 1861. President Abraham Lincoln outlawed it two years later. The American attitude toward slavery counted little in Sudan in the second half of the 1800s because the United States had sent no significant military forces to Africa since its infant navy battled pirates off the coast of Libya in 1804 and 1805, but the importance of antislavery opinion in Great Britain was a very different matter.

Dozens of years after Ali's Turko-Egyptian forces invaded Sudan, his grandson Khedive Ismail took control with grand designs to modernize Egypt, a goal that would require an infusion of cash from powers such as Britain and France. He opened Cairo's first opera and built the Suez Canal with backing from European countries, and he responded to their abolitionist pressures. Ismail closed Khartoum's slave market and banned the importation of Sudanese slaves into Egypt, but these measures did little to stop the slave trade. It remained legal to own slaves in Egypt and Sudan, and Ismail himself is said to have owned hundreds of people. The prevalence of slavery troubled British power brokers even though many of their fathers and grandfathers had themselves profited from the buying and selling of Africans. To placate the British and ensure a steady stream of cash for development, Ismail commissioned famous British explorer Sir Samuel Baker and supplied him with a band of Egyptian and Sudanese soldiers for the purpose of suppressing the slave trade. Off went Baker and his men, into the Upper Nile territory of southern Sudan, on a mission that would seem ridiculously naive years later. The idea that "one man in command of a small flotilla could single-handedly extinguish a trade that had been millennia in the making absurdly underestimated its tenacity," writes the journalist and author Deborah Scroggins. "In fact, as the khedive must have known, the plan was so unrealistic as to reassure any Sudanese slavers who had feared he actually intended to put them out of business. But in terms of appeasing British antislavery sentiment, it worked like a charm."

Baker spent two years "battling the slave-traders and their local allies and raising the Ottoman flag over rivers filled with splashing and grunting hippopotamuses" in an effort that was "ineffectual at best" in "actually ridding the Upper Nile of slavery." Baker was succeeded by Colonel Charles George Gordon, an eccentric commander who had earned the nickname "Chinese Gordon" in the British press for his leadership during a successful campaign in 1860 to recapture towns of the Manchu dynasty that had fallen to Taiping rebels. Gordon arrived in Sudan in 1874 confident that he would extinguish the slave trade mainly by sheer will and power of persuasion. He liberated hundreds of slaves and executed a major trader but soon came to realize that the trade in humans was far more entrenched than he had thought, and that the Egyptian and Sudanese soldiers assigned to him saw nothing wrong with it. The slaves he liberated, furthermore, often viewed the prospect of walking home with the dread certainty that they would die of hunger or thirst or fall prey again to slave traders or rival ethnic groups. The goal of eradicating slavery proved extraordinarily difficult to realize and did not enjoy much support from an Egyptian power structure that profited greatly from the slave trade. Disillusioned, Gordon resigned in 1879, but he would return soon enough.

By the time he left, the Dinka and their neighbors in southern Sudan were thoroughly devastated. Arabs and Muslims from the north had invaded their land and spoiled their world. The Egyptians and Turkish forces had been joined by northern Sudanese and others from the Ottoman realm, including Syria, who came to conduct slave raids and trade in ivory. These violent incursions from the north fused in the collective southern outlook an abiding distrust and contempt for outsiders and, particularly, for northern Arabs and Muslims, a hatred that each successive generation would nurse until the country dissolved into civil war in 1955.

That fate was not a foregone conclusion in 1881, however, when southerners allowed themselves a great measure of optimism at the prospect of casting out foreign powers. Hope came in the form of a revolt born in northern Sudan. Its leader was a Muslim holy man named Mohammed Ahmed. He called himself the "Mahdi," or "Expected One," and purported to be someone who would defeat the enemies of Islam. Despite his Islamic message, non-Muslims in southern Sudan were attracted to the Mahdi by his promise to expel the Turko-Egyptian forces, those foreign invaders who had so thoroughly upset the routine patterns of life. The Mahdi led a military campaign that achieved success in 1882 and 1883. Alarmed by his advances, the British government, which had sent troops to Egypt in 1882 to suppress a nationalist rebellion, decided to evacuate several Egyptian garrisons in northern Sudan and Egyptians and British in the capital. It would be an immense undertaking. At least one British commander and several European nuns and priests already had been captured and imprisoned by the Mahdi's force. It was unclear how a British force could extricate several thousand Egyptians without meeting the same fate. Then the idea emerged of dispatching Colonel Gordon, that old hero from China who had marched into Sudan with so much confidence just a few years ago. He accepted the challenge and returned to Sudan in 1884 without a military force of consequence, banking once again on the force of personality. He arrived in Khartoum with clear marching orders: He was to evacuate the Egyptians and British from Khartoum. Yet Gordon, seeing himself as the valiant champion of enlightened Christianity, declined to simply evacuate people and leave the city to be taken by the Mahdi. The Muslim leader laid siege to Khartoum. He offered Gordon safe passage out of the city, if only he would leave, but the British hero refused. Tribal allies betrayed him. Food supplies dwindled. The Mahdi's forces severed a telegraph line that connected him to the outside world. The British government sent a relief expedition, but it arrived two days too late. The Mahdi's forces overran Khartoum and killed Gordon on January 26, 1885.

The Mahdi's victory ushered in an era that the Dinka hoped would free them from the grip of slave traders. In fact, conditions worsened. The region descended into the chaos of famine and tribal warfare. Deng cites estimates that the Sudanese population fell from 7 million before the revolt to 2 to 3 million about twenty years later. He quotes a graphic account of those days given by Rudolph Slatin, an official of the Turko-Egyptian administration who was captured by the Mahdists and converted to Islam to survive. He later escaped and returned to parts of Sudan he had known before the Mahdi's victory. Slatin's description of what he saw, Deng writes, makes the crises in Somalia and Bosnia in the 1990s look "mild" by comparison. Slatin writes,

> Those were terrible months at the close of 1889; the people had become so thin that they scarcely resembled human beings—they were veritably but skin and bone. These poor wretches would eat anything, no matter how disgusting—skins of animals which had long since dried and become decayed were roasted and eaten. . . . Those who had any strength left went out and robbed; like hawks they pounced down on the bakers and butchers, and cared nothing for the blows of the kurbash which invariably fell on their attenuated backs. . . .
>
> Several sold their own children, both boys and girls, pretending they were their slaves; this they did not to obtain money, but simply to save their lives; and when this year of misery was over some parents bought them back again at even higher prices. The dead lay in the street in hundreds, and none could be found to bury them. . . . Every day the waters of the Blue and White Niles swept past Omdurman, carrying along hundreds of bodies of the wretched peasantry who had died along the banks—a terrible proof of the awful condition of the country.

When slave traders increased their raids into southern territories, the Dinka felt betrayed by the Arabs of northern Sudan who had once urged unity to throw off the yoke of foreign domination. An elderly Dinka chief named Makuei Bilkuei recalled in an interview with Deng that the Arabs "would come with camels and donkeys and mules and guns. . . . [They] took the people and sold them. . . . They said, 'La Illah, ila Allah, Muhammad Rasul Allah' (There is no God but the One God and Muhammad is God's Messenger). That was the way they chanted while they slaughtered and slaughtered and slaughtered." Another chief, Albino Akot, was quoted describing Dinka efforts to combat the slave traders: "The Dinka would beat the drums of war. . . . The scouts would go ahead to look for where the Arabs were. . . . The Arabs would stop and sleep, thinking they had left the Dinka behind, but the Dinka . . . would come and attack them. . . . Some people among them would be captured and the people who had been captured by the Arabs would be released." Another chief said the Arab "would go . . . and would kill any people he found. . . . Then the Dinka would go and search for him and attack him at night and kill his people also."

The effects were obvious to Baker when he returned to a land he had earlier tried to clear of slavery. "It is impossible to describe the change that has taken place since I last visited this country," he was quoted as saying. "It was then a perfect garden, thickly populated and producing all that man would desire. The villages were numerous, groves of plant-ens fringed the steep cliff on the river bank, and the natives were neatly dressed in the bark cloth of the country. The scene has changed: All is wilderness. The population has fled. Not a village is to be seen. This is the certain result of the settlement of Khartoum traders. They kidnap the women and children for slaves and plunder and destroy wherever they set their foot."

Slavery and its history in Sudan is critical in understanding the forces that led to civil war and, ultimately, to the refugee crisis that separated so many boys from their parents in southern Sudan in 1987 and '88. Deng notes that "slavery has indeed remained the most glaring reminder of the bitter history of North-South, Arab-African hostilities and animosities." In the dozen years after the Mahdi's victory, as slave raids intensified in southern Sudan and Dinka resentment smoldered, stories of slavery and death filtered out of Africa to audiences in the United States and Europe. In 1896, eleven years after the Mahdi's forces killed Gordon, the British government decided to try to reconquer Sudan. Some Dinka chiefs would later praise the British for delivering them from bondage. They would remember a force bent on eradicating their world of the evil of slavery. A few Dinka chiefs would go so far as to claim credit for persuading the British to intervene. Yet altruism rarely dictates foreign policy or mili-tary adventures. The real impetus was not an honorable desire to avenge General Gordon, as the British public was led to believe, but Britain's growing wariness of a traditional adversary, France. French incursions south of Sudan in the 1890s raised the specter of Britain's old enemy gaining control of the Nile River before it flowed north into Egypt. The British were determined to prevent that. In 1898, military men led by the cry "Remember Gordon!" charged into battle in Sudan. Their machine guns destroyed wave after wave of Sudanese fighters in white gowns on camels and horseback. Soon the British controlled Sudan. The threat of the French meddling with the Nile passed. The British victory ended a fourteen-year reign of destruction and ushered in a colonial era that led to some measure of peace.

Despite radical differences in language, ethnicity, religion, and culture, the peoples of southern and northern Sudan were lumped together into a modern nation state from 1899 to 1955 in an arrangement known as the Anglo-Egyptian Condominium. Technically the country was to be administered jointly by the British and Egyptians, but the British held the real power. One of Britain's most important decisions, one with far-reaching consequence, was a policy of administering Sudan as two entities, north and south. The colonial authorities prevented people in one region from traveling to the other and allowed the two sides to follow separate patterns of development. Northern Sudan, home to about two-thirds of Sudan's land and population, continued firmly along its path as an Arab and Islamic center with more in common with the countries and cultures of North Africa and the Middle East than with the rest of Africa. The south remained largely, as Deng puts it, "a museum of nature," relatively undisturbed by outside influences after so many decades of turmoil. British rule "brought the longest period of peace and security, at least from invasion and the use of crude force, that the south has experienced throughout its recorded history." It also gave people in the West their most comprehensive view yet of the Dinka, a view that even so tended toward the exotic. Deng recounts the report of a British explorer who described the Dinka in 1931 as "a race of long-legged, well built people so tall that a seven-foot man is no uncommon sight, so slim that a white man cannot fit his hand into their shield grips or his body into their canoes," a group of "people clad in nothing but beads and an expansive, cheery grin."

The Dinka were predisposed to oppose colonial rule on philosophical grounds, but they came to trust the British and developed a curiosity about their innovations. This opened the door for a modernizing force in southern Sudan that came in the form of Christian missionaries from the West. The British allowed missionaries from the Anglican, Presbyterian, and Roman Catholic churches to preach and set up schools, giving thousands of people their first experience with a formal, Western education. The native peoples were skeptical at first. Authors Lilian and Neville Sanderson note that the "idea of progress was quite foreign" to most people in southern Sudan in the 1930s and '40s: "There was little evidence that life had ever been different from what it was today, nor, until the coming of the Europeans, that it was ever going to change." The Sandersons captured the opinion of many Dinka about the missionary schools: "Of what practical use was education . . . ? There was no indigenous role that it could improve his capacity to fill; on the contrary, by restricting his opportunities to learn . . . the skills of a . . . pastoralist and of a warrior, it diseducated him for the fundamental roles of an adult male."

Yet the few southerners who attended the schools, mostly boys, learned to read and write and gradually realized how backward they were in comparison to other cultures. They saw that lack of education put them at a political disadvantage compared with northerners. Some came to appreciate the value of modern medicine over traditional remedies. Godfrey Lienhardt, who conducted extensive studies of the Dinka in the 1930s and '40s, says the Dinka came to value missionary education: "The Dinka became increasingly aware that much though they might have preferred to live without external interference in their traditional mode of life, that interference had already begun to endanger their independence. They saw that they needed enough of their own people capable of thinking in foreign ways, of meeting foreigners on their own ground while remaining Dinka in their loyalties, to understand and circumvent encroachments to their own autonomy."

The Dinka criticized Deng's father, a prominent Dinka chief, for sending his sons to a school that opened in 1943, but neighbors were later impressed by skills Deng and his brothers acquired. "The most popular game in our house, where there was always a crowd of tribesmen, was to ask some of us to write on the ground or on paper while others were escorted away and watched to make sure that they did not see what was written," he writes. "To come back and read it accurately elicited loud laughter of astonishment. Whenever we read letters coming to our father from other chiefs about intertribal cases, it was common for the bearers to listen with utmost interest, then remark, 'Exactly, that was what the Chief told his clerk to write,' and an impressed audience would burst into admiring laughter."

Teachers in the missionary schools taught children songs that celebrated the importance of learning. The idea was that the Dinka students would sing these songs after class, so that others their age could hear. It was a way, the teachers thought, to reinforce the importance of education to those who were already enrolled and instill a reverence for Western learning among those who were not yet attending class. One of many songs from that era echoes through time. In it, boys boast about having come to appreciate education as a key to the future success of the Dinka. They equate attending school with a rite of passage. They also mock boys who spent time at school only to run away to return to traditional life. The song's message of education as salvation would resonate decades later, in the 1980s and '90s, when thousands of boys from southern Sudan would be separated from parents to come of age in refugee camps and then, for a few, in modern America, where they yearned for transcendence through the classroom:

> Learning is good
> We have found it so,
> Learning is the best
> We have found it so.
> I will not leave the school
> I am a man
> I have liked it;
> I will not leave the school
> I am a gentleman of the future.
> Those children who run away
> They have no hearts

They do not even bid their masters farewell;
Those children who run away
They have no hearts.
Even if we tire
We shall endure.
We shall find its sweetness later on;
Even if we tire
We shall endure
To find its sweetness later on.

The increasing popularity of mission schools in the south later would sow suspicion in the north, particularly among Muslims committed to the spread of Islam through all of Sudan. Many of them came to view the British and Christian missionaries as conspirators dividing the country and blocking what they saw as Islam's natural progression southward. They blamed the missionaries for the division of the country and for the British administration of Sudan as separate entities, north and south, a policy that the British suddenly reversed as colonialism fell from favor. In 1947, the year the practice of separate development ended, Britain was eager to extricate itself from Sudan. It was a country drained by World War II, a nation that had yielded military supremacy to new superpowers, the United States and the Soviet Union. In preparation for the eventual independence of Sudan, Britain suddenly regarded both regions of Sudan as one integrated whole, but there was no ignoring northern supremacy in education, development, and, most ominously for the south, political power. Northerners dominated conferences to determine the form of government in an independent Sudan. Talk of unification was poisoned by northern suspicions that southerners wanted to create their own nation and by southern fears of northern domination. It was a turbulent process that took a turn toward violence when the government announced that 792 of 800 positions held by the colonial authorities would be filled in the new nation by northern Sudanese.

The northern dominance in shaping an independent Sudan deepened long-standing fears of the north among southerners, who had little experience with modern politics. Fears that northern army officers would hold the real power in the military, and that southern troops would be transferred to the north, led to a mutiny among soldiers from Equatoria, a southern province bordering Kenya, on August 18, 1955. Dozens of southern soldiers broke into an armory and stole weapons and ammunition. They slaughtered northern soldiers and killed Arab prison inmates. They also went house-to-house killing northern soldiers, merchants, and families. The mutiny forever altered the course of independent Sudan. It is of such pivotal importance that northerners and southerners frequently disagree about its causes and effects. Northerners tend to believe that more northerners were killed while southerners maintain that their kinsmen paid a steeper price (there were reports of northern troops killing civilians in retaliation, and several mutineers were later executed). A low-level guerrilla war continued after Sudan became independent on January 1, 1956. The Dinka did not immediately join the fight in large numbers, but the government, dominated by northerners, pursued a policy of Arabization and Islamization for the next several years that would encourage more southerners to take up arms. When the National Assembly appointed a committee to draft a national constitution in September 1956, forty-three of the forty-six members were from the north. Government troops began to burn villages in the late 1950s in an effort to eliminate opposition by targeting educated southerners. The government took control of mission schools and began to teach students Arabic and encourage their conversion to Islam. It declared Friday, the Muslim prayer day, the official day of rest in southern Sudan and outlawed religious gatherings outside churches. In 1964, the government expelled Christian missionaries.

The Dinka soon joined other southern rebels in fighting that evolved into full-fledged civil war in the 1960s and forced hundreds of thousands of Dinka refugees into the nearby countries of Congo, Uganda, Kenya, Ethiopia, and the Central African Republic. According to Deng, refugee status traumatized the Dinka: "For a people who had grown up thinking of themselves and their country as second to none, the indignities of refugee life brought lamentation and a feeling of isolation." A young Dinka in exile sang of the reversal of fortunes that required men to grind grain—a woman's job in Dinkaland—and to beg. The exiled Dinka nursed old grievances. Deng quotes another song in which warriors tout their willingness to fight with a southern rebel army, called the Anyanya after a poisonous insect of the south, in a region of southern Sudan called Bahr El-Ghazal:

The feud of the Southerners with the Northerners;
Our feud will never end.
The army of Deng Nhial and Morwell
Are called the Anyanya.
In Bahr El-Ghazal, we shall shoot
With the northerners—the Arabs;
We shall cut through Bahr El-Ghazal;
We shall revenge the evils of the past;
And if we succeed in our vengeance
We shall be praised by God;
Bless us
We are the Dinka.
O, feud, O, feud.

War became a tragic reality for the newly independent African state, a back-and-forth series of bombings and shootings that ensnared civilians as often as military men. It would rage, with brief respite, for the rest of the twentieth century and into the twenty-first. In the 1990s, a growing number of combatants and outside observers cited the differences in religion between north and south as a major reason for the fighting, particularly after a virulent strain of political Islam took hold in northern Sudan and Christians in the West identified more closely with persecuted southern Sudanese Christians. There is unquestionably a religious dimension to the war, but divisions of race, ethnicity, language, and culture, as well as the discovery of oil and an abundance of fertile ground in the south, also factor into a complex war that defies simplistic descriptions. Deng offers as concise a summary as any when he labels the war "a clash of identities in competition over power and resources." Southerners rebelled in 1955 against what they perceived as northern dominance in forging the first government of an independent Sudan and against attempts to forcibly spread Islam and Arabic culture. Even though many northerners can claim Arab and black African ancestry, Deng says, they "deny the strongly African elements in their skin color and physical features. They associate these features with the negroid race and see it as the mother race of slaves, inferior and demeaned. . . . Until recently, calling the southern Sudanese 'slaves,' abeed, to their faces was a common practice. . . . The term abid (singular for abeed) is the exact equivalent of 'nigger' in American popular usage."

In July 1965, in the southern town of Juba, government forces "intent on liquidating the Christianized-Westernized educated classes" torched three thousand grass-thatched huts and killed at least one thousand inhabitants. A newspaper editor in southern Sudan said at the time that "it became the policy of the government of Sudan to treat every educated southerner, whether or not he was a soldier, as a rebel." This policy of attacking the educated, of targeting education itself, led even to the establishment of torture centers where schoolteachers were among the victims. Teachers were subjected to particularly cruel treatment in one center, as described by Mansour Khalid, former foreign minister of Sudan: "Chiles were put into their eyes and genitals, and each was given two hours' whipping every day tied up to a tree with their heads down. The first to die in these tortures was the headmaster of Dolieb Hill center for girls, and several other casualties ensued."

The first real glint of hope for peace, in the view of the southerners, came after Jaafar Muhammad Nimeiri toppled the government and seized power on May 25, 1969. The new ruler announced socialism for Sudan and pledged autonomy for the south. Negotiations between the government and rebels led to the landmark Addis Ababa Agreement of 1972, which conferred autonomy on southern Sudan.

For the first time since independence in 1956, Sudan was at peace. Thousands of refugees returned to a life of farming in Dinkaland, a life dominated by songs about cattle as it was years ago, way back, before the world was spoiled. A new sense of national unity gripped southerners. Talk of separation faded. For the first time, the concept of Sudan as a nation-state, north and south together, took root in much of the south. The West regarded Nimeiri as peacemaker, as a man who had proven himself willing and somehow able to resolve a seemingly intractable conflict.

Sudan's ties with the United States grew. It was the first Arab country to restore diplomatic relations with the United States, severed after Sudan and other Arab nations declared war on Israel during the Six Day War of 1967. In 1978, Sudan was one of very few Arab nations to support the Camp David Accords, the peace between Egypt and Israel brokered by President Jimmy Carter. The United States began to see Nimeiri as a friend in a hostile neighborhood. It appreciated his opposition to the Marxist government in Ethiopia of Mengistu Haile Mariam to the east and the anti-West Libyan leader Muammar al-Qaddafi to the north. Sudan became the third largest recipient of U.S. foreign aid, after Egypt and Israel. After a failed rightist coup in 1976, however, Nimeiri changed course amid growing pressure from conservative Islamic political forces in northern Sudan.

Political Islam was spreading throughout the Arab world, and conservative Muslims were gaining strength in northern Sudan. Nimeiri appointed leading figures of a conservative Islamic party to key government positions. Deng, who served as Nimeiri's minister of state for foreign affairs and ambassador to the United States, notes the change: "Instead of the liberal president in a safari suit who had won the hearts of the common folk in the peripheral regions and particularly in the South, Nimeiri began to dress in Arab garb, with all the outward symbols of an Islamic sheikh or imam." He threatened a fragile peace with the south by intensifying a program of Islamization, requiring senior government officials, for example, to abstain from gambling and drinking alcohol. With the increasing move to an Islamic state came a growing sense in the south that the tentative peace would not hold, that the old cycle of violence and bloodshed was on its way back.

In 1983, Nimeiri sought to weaken the south by splitting it into three regions—Bahr El-Ghazal, Equatoria, and Upper Nile. His decision that year to impose *shari'a*, Islamic law, throughout Sudan also would be a major force in returning the nation to civil war. The laws dictated public flogging and amputations for criminals. They also disenfranchised non-Muslims by requiring that top government positions be filled only by Muslims. Southerners perceived the changes as an abdication by Nimeiri of the peace agreement of 1972. Civil war resumed after southern rebels took to the bush. Many southerners came to advocate secession from the north, but rebel leaders said they were fighting for a unified, secular Sudan. Perhaps not coincidentally, Deng notes, leaders in the Sudan People's Liberation Army realized that "fighting for justice or equality (was) more likely to win sympathy and support" from other countries "than calling for secession."

Thousands of families around southern Sudan, accustomed to eleven years of peace, soon would be reminded of the brutal chaos of war. Wives would lose husbands, husbands, wives. Whole families would leave homes and battle hunger and indignity as refugees, risking their lives to walk hundreds of miles to the squalor of squatter camps in Khartoum. Others would walk through forest and desert to chase the promise of someplace, anyplace, safe. Thousands of parents would lose track of their children.

Such a fate awaited Magot Garang and his wife, Guet. They lived in a grass hut in a village called Mathiang, in Upper Nile province of southern Sudan. They had two daughters and a son who was about five or six. His name was Ngor. He was about to be separated from his parents and march with thousands of other boys into a vast and unforgiving wilderness where hunger, disease, and wild animals lurked. Years later, Ngor would take a Christian name and be called Jacob Magot.

Hundreds of miles away, in a similar grass hut on a flat landscape peppered with cattle, lived Anyang Deng and his wife, Awud Mamer, with three sons and two daughters. One son, Mel Deng, also would also be separated from his family and grow up not knowing whether his parents or siblings were alive. He would come of age as Peter Anyang. When war resumed in 1983, his parents were raising him in a village called Modhol, in the region of Bahr El-Ghazal. Nearby, Athok Arol, and her husband, Ayii Aguer, lived in a hut with two sons and a daughter. In another hut, Manyoun Mon Achol, and her husband, Dut Akech Khoch, were raising three sons and five daughters. The two groups of siblings had not yet met each other. Separately, one son from each family would join so many other boys on the perilous journey into a place where survival required children to eat soft mud and drink their own urine. They would emerge, at last, on the other side, in a sprawling Ethiopian refugee camp. The two boys would meet and become inseparable, children who could not yet fathom they would grow into their teens and early twenties knowing each other as Marko and Daniel. Many years later, from the comfortable perspective that new beginnings provide, they would recall the days they first met each other, that time in the wild with more deaths to come, and marvel, when they stopped to think about it, that they were alive at all.

A BITTER WIND

It was no secret, to those who cared to look, that civilians were brutalized in southern Sudan after war resumed in 1983. Human-rights organizations uncovered ample evidence that government forces repeatedly bombed civilian targets and burned and looted dozens of villages, often killing or capturing noncombatants. They cited the Sudanese government for stealing cattle and grain from civilians and arming tribal militias who held longstanding grudges against rebels from ethnic groups that included the Dinka and Nuer. The government also shared responsibility for the starvation deaths of hundreds of thousands because it placed severe restrictions on the movement of international relief organizations and United Nations agencies. Yet the rebel Sudan People's Liberation Army was not without transgression. It also was cited for gross violations of human rights. International monitors said the SPLA stole cattle and grain to support its troops and forcibly recruited soldiers. The war had battles in the traditional sense of the word, with clearly defined military forces confronting one another on a battlefield, but just as often the violence engulfed civilians. One example from the lengthy catalog of savagery unfolded on March 27, 1987, in the railroad station at place called Ed Da'ein. Hundreds of Dinka refugees boarded a train there in hopes of leaving town, but members of the Arab Rizeigat tribe, whose ancestors had enslaved the Dinka in the 1800s and who recently had been given machine guns and hand grenades by the government of Sudan, attacked the train in retaliation for an SPLA assault that had killed about 150 Rizeigat three months earlier. Several hundred Dinka inside the train cars suffocated or burned to death. A Rizeigat mob, joined by police, tore through the town in a spree of killing and mutilating Dinka. No one was arrested. The government denied for several months that the massacre had even taken place.

Against this backdrop of bloodshed, this maelstrom of killing and rape, thousands of starving young boys began streaming from southern Sudan into refugee camps in Ethiopia. An aid worker who visited one of the camps in 1987 recalled "only naked bodies, very thin, of boys, as far as the eye could see." A United Nations worker in Ethiopia reported in 1988, "When they come in the camps, they're not even able to stand." Diplomats in Addis Ababa, the Ethiopian capital, estimated that about eight thousand boys had died on the months-long journey from Sudan. Many of the survivors reported having fled remote villages after escaping militia attacks that they said had killed some of their relatives. Daniel would give a similar account years later, after he passed through adolescence and was resettled in Atlanta by the United States government.

Daniel lived with his parents, two brothers, and three sisters in the western part of southern Sudan. One Sunday, he said, he walked with his mother and a brother, Yel, to mass at a Catholic church. He was six or seven years old. After the service, Daniel was outside playing soccer with some other boys when he heard the sound of a "plane they use to bomb the people." Everyone scattered. Daniel ran and did not stop until he thought he was safe. Then he realized he was by himself, his mother and brother having run in different directions. He waited awhile and then decided to walk home, expecting that his mother and brother would have followed different routes back to the house. At home were his father and a sister, Akuol, but his mother and brother never showed up. Nearly fifteen years would pass before Daniel would learn what had happened to them. The next day, Monday, Daniel took cattle to graze in the fields near home. He said he was returning when he heard screaming and gunfire and saw men in green uniforms on horseback. They had rifles—he called them "complicated poisonous weapons"—and they were shooting people. He described the scene in an autobiography he wrote while perfecting his English and teaching himself to type:

> It took me at about 4 o'clock p.m. Sudanese local time when I drove cattle home after I brought them from grazing field. . . . It came a strange sound and screaming of people of which I didn't heard it one day in my live. Within zero minutes, the sound and screaming of people getting louder and louder, immediately, I saw many people running dizzinessly in different directions without control at all. As soon as I saw them, I leave cattle on the spot and looked at them seriously because I was really get confused what to do since I don't know what was going wrong that people were running anyhowly without any sense of control. As sooner as they pass by near me, one of the people who were been running, called out to me with unwanted voice saying, "Please, please, come on. Let us go together. Here are Arabs soldiers. They will killed you if you don't run."

The attackers burned huts and set fire to stores of grain that held supplies of millet, rice, peas, okra, and sorghum. Daniel said he saw the men steal his father's cows and goats. He said he saw them abduct some people from his village (militias aligned with the government were widely accused of taking captives, especially girls, to work as servants). Daniel joined a crowd running from his village. "I thought that my life has come to an end because too many people were dead. Many others were wounded, and I lose my hope as well," he wrote.

Daniel scanned the river of refugees for his mother and father, but he did not see them. His brother, Yel, was nowhere to be found. His sisters also were missing. "If they are dead," he prayed, "just take their souls and put them to your right hand."

Daniel said he found himself in a group of several boys from his village, but there were no elderly men or women, few adults of middle age, and hardly any girls. He explained the predominance of boys by saying that many, like him, were away from home with cattle when attackers struck. Their parents and sisters were at home, in the village, he said, when men on horseback swept in and started shooting. They were therefore more likely to have been abducted or killed. The "senior people" in his group decided it was too risky to return to the ruined village. Instead, they would lead the group toward camps in Ethiopia, where boys could find safety and obtain an education. The SPLA ran camps on Ethiopian soil with the backing of the Marxist Ethiopian leader, Mengistu Haile Mariam. It spread word of the camps in parts of southern Sudan, and many people believed children could get an education there. They did not know, though, how far one would have to travel to arrive at the camps. And so Daniel's group set off for Ethiopia sometime in 1987. They walked for weeks, stumbling into villages to beg for food. Along the way they ate grass and leaves and drank water from holes in the ground. Many starved to death. "In those days, I, Daniel, saw many dead people for the first time in my life," he wrote years later. "I also witness too many people died because of the famine and drought. In more details, some wild animals which were friends to us before and ever, such as hyena, leopard, cat, fox, rat and etc. became the good eaters of flesh."

They walked through forests and marshes before entering a desert that would take nearly four days to cross. "Many remain dead there because of water and food," Daniel wrote. "There was no water and foods for people to drink and eat for three and a half days. As a result, again, we drank our own urine so that to sustain our life. If we were not drunk our own urine and eat soft mud and strange foods, therefore, automatically, we would have died like the rest of colleagues who were been dying. . . . The foods we ate during desert were included dry skin from cows, sheep, goats, some dry bones of animals no matter the animals is. We don't care in this. Other desert foods include termites, soft mud, and the others I don't know their names." The survivors left the desert and entered a town near the Ethiopian border. They feasted on unripe mangoes plucked from tree branches, and then crossed a river onto Ethiopian soil and staggered into a camp at Dimma, where Daniel registered with the United Nations High Commissioner for Refugees.

About seventeen thousand so-called unaccompanied minors registered as refugees in the Ethiopian camps at Dimma, Itang, and Panyido in 1987 and 1988. They told relief workers stories, like Daniel's, of Arabs forcing them from home and away from their families. Most said they were six, seven, eight, or nine and were tending cattle away from home, as is the custom for boys that age in the Dinka and Nuer ethnic groups of southern Sudan, when government soldiers or militias aligned with the government attacked their villages. They said assailants killed and kidnapped relatives, stole cattle, and burned huts and grain before vanishing toward the horizon from which they had come. Sometimes the attackers were turbaned Arab horsemen. In other places, they carried AK-47 assault rifles. Most of the boys said they saw the attack from a distance or learned of it as they walked home. Some saw smoke. Others heard shooting. As young men many would recall walking toward home only to encounter panicked neighbors racing from a village under attack. The boys ran with the crowd until they could no longer hear gunfire. They waited, uncertain. Inevitably, they said, an adult in the group of survivors asserted himself and led them on a treacherous, barefoot, weeks-long march east, toward the promise of safety in refugee camps across the border in Ethiopia.

And so relief workers in southern Sudan reported seeing ragged columns of wasted youth in 1987 and '88, apparitions of boys once alive with youthful hope and mischief, lurching relentlessly across a harsh landscape where lions and serpents kill as efficiently as malaria, hunger and fatigue. A few men usually accompanied the boys, but there were few girls and fewer women. Militias armed by the Sudanese government attacked scores of villages around southern Sudan in 1987 and '88, particularly in the Bahr El-Ghazal region, where Daniel was born, but there actually were a number of reasons children were separated from parents in southern Sudan in the late 1980s. Aid workers and diplomats said some were encouraged to walk toward Ethiopia by the rebel army in southern Sudan, the Sudan People's Liberation Army (SPLA). Few opportunities existed for formal schooling in southern Sudan, and the SPLA said children could get an education in the camps. A friendly Ethiopian government let the SPLA operate in the camps and use its territory to launch attacks against government forces inside Sudan. Human-rights organizations would later accuse the SPLA of luring boys to the camps not only for education, but for military training, as well, in the hopes of building a reservoir of future soldiers in an interminable and complex civil war most commonly described as pitting a government of Arabs and Muslims in northern Sudan against black rebels in the south who followed Christianity and traditional African religions. Some of the Lost Boys of Sudan who were resettled in the United States would acknowledge receiving military training, and a few would talk about fighting for the SPLA, but Jacob, Peter, Daniel, and Marko insisted that instructors in Ethiopia spoke only of subjects such as English and math.

Many boys in the camps talked of having come to Ethiopia to attend school. A report of Human Rights Watch/Africa said "boys interviewed by social and relief workers routinely volunteered 'education' as their reason for going to Ethiopia. . . . Often the boys left Sudan upon hearing from SPLA commanders of the educational opportunities available in the refugee camps in Ethiopia." Most of the few schools in southern Sudan had closed by the mid-1980s. A growing sense among some Dinka of the importance of formal education, first instilled after missionaries set up schools in the 1940s and exacerbated by deepening suspicion of the more-educated north, pulled many boys toward Ethiopia. Others went for "safety reasons" and "some were orphaned by war," but investigators came to believe that many were lured to the camps by a rebel army in search of a manpower reservoir for the future. The Human Rights Watch/Africa report was blunt: "The SPLA has engaged in recruitment of underage soldiers. It has maintained large camps of boys separate from their families and tribes, given them some education and military training and from these camps has drawn fresh recruits." The SPLA's involvement in steering children to the camps would help explain why so few girls trekked to Ethiopia; the rebel army did not use many female fighters. Perhaps more importantly, few families in southern Sudan would have willingly sent girls away from home. Girls are too valuable. They grow into young women who fetch dowries of valuable cattle when they marry.

The United Nations fed and clothed the boys, something it might have been reluctant to do if the world saw the camps as military training grounds. Citing security concerns, the SPLA required nearly all foreign relief workers to leave the camps by late afternoon. Many journalists and aid workers who were in Ethiopia suspected that the military training began after prying international eyes left. The SPLA "instructed the minors in the camps in what to tell expatriate relief workers and other outsiders about their relations with the SPLA," Human Rights Watch/Africa said. "Interviewers over the years remarked on the singular uniformity to answers to questions such as why the minors went to Ethiopia ('Education')." The organization concluded that "the SPLA recruited the boys for both educational and military purposes but attempted to conceal the military purpose." Rebels denied that military training took place in the camps, but journalists and human-rights investigators who looked into the question found evidence to the contrary. One chief in a village in southern Sudan told a journalist in 1991 that the SPLA had taken twenty-nine twelve-year-old boys by force and that their parents had no word of their whereabouts.

The practice, offensive to the West, played on two traditions in southern Sudan involving boys and warfare. Several countries in East Africa had a tradition of "boy soldiers" that dated to at least 1870. These were children who were enslaved by military forces when they were from seven and ten years old, to work as gun bearers for individual soldiers. The boys learned military ways and often were funneled into the fighting forces when they became of age. These boy soldiers served armies in Uganda and Sudan, including the British military forces in Sudan for the first half of the twentieth century. In August 1955, when 1,146 Sudanese soldiers mutinied at a place called Torit, sparking the civil war, their numbers included 380 boy soldiers. In addition, generations of preadolescent Dinka boys have grown up singing about how they would like to prove their strength and valor in fighting, to join the men. The songs lament the elders and their ridiculous rules that say boys cannot fight until they have undergone the ritual scarification that traditionally marked a boy's passage to manhood, usually sometime around seventeen. Several rebel commanders seem to have exploited this tradition in the late 1980s and early '90s by giving some boys the chance to speed the hands of time and become, at last, warriors.

Daniel, Marko, and Peter were among roughly two thousand unaccompanied Sudanese minors in the camp at Dimma, Ethiopia. They lived and studied apart from eighteen thousand other refugees, many of whom were also from Sudan. Dimma and the other two camps in western Ethiopia, Itang and Panyido, were desperate places. Children and adults streamed in nearly every day in the late 1980s. Flies buzzed around the faces of listless boys and girls with the protruding bellies of the starving and arms that were little more than skin stretched tight over bone. Boys spent hours pounding grain with poles because the camps lacked any better way to grind grain. Children sat on dirt floors under thatched roofs to learn English and the multiplication tables from teachers of varying quality. Men and women in Western-style T-shirts, shorts, and skirts crafted a sign in 1990 to show a delegation visiting from the U.S. Committee for Refugees. "American Humanists," it said, "We are naked and uneducated unaccompanied minors."

Marko would say many years later that he was too young when he left southern Sudan to remember much about those days. All he knows, he said, is that an older man named Keiir carried him from his village to Dimma, where the man later died of cholera. Daniel and Marko got to know Peter at Dimma. He, too, said Arabs had driven him from home. He said he was coming home with cattle one afternoon and was on his way to tie up calves when he saw Arab Baggara enter his village and start shooting. The Baggara are an Arab people who have warred with their Dinka neighbors off and on for a hundred years or more. Deng says they "are among the most chauvinistic about their Arabism and racially bigoted against their more African neighbors to the south." Peter remembers people running from his village and telling him to run, too. He said he did run, like Daniel, and eventually joined a band of boys and young men moving east. His future roommate in Atlanta, Jacob Magot, was from a different part of Sudan. He followed a slightly different path to Ethiopia than Daniel, Marko, and Peter. It led to a camp called Panyido, a few miles from Dimma. About ten thousand southern Sudanese boys lived there, the most of any of the Ethiopian camps. Jacob and the other boys at Panyido built their own huts and schools and were kept apart from roughly sixty-six thousand other refugees. A third camp, Itang, had about fifty-three hundred Sudanese boys, mainly members of the Nuer ethnic group, among a total population of about 150,000. Despite widespread desire for education, Human Rights Watch/Africa said the "schooling the boys received in Ethiopia was minimal, no doubt due to the difficult conditions under which they lived and the fact that they had to perform the whole range of feeding and housekeeping chores normally split up among family members according to age and sex." One 1989 survey of the unaccompanied minors found that 90 percent were illiterate or in first grade.

Armed boys were seen in southern Sudan working as bodyguards for SPLA soldiers or defending towns the rebel army had captured. One former SPLA officer told investigators the rebels organized battalions of teenagers it called the Red Army. "In the first few years, the Red Army fought and was always massacred," he said. "Then they were taken off the front line. They were not good soldiers because they were too young."

A few southern Sudanese refugees who were resettled in the United States acknowledged receiving military training in Ethiopia, and a few even said they joined the SPLA, but many insisted they passed several years in the camps without anyone even suggesting they received training as soldiers. Nevertheless, in May 1991, the perception that the camps were affiliated with the SPLA once again endangered boys like Jacob, Peter, Daniel, and Marko.

By then they had spent about four years at the camps, with no word of whether their parents were alive. They ranged in age from about seven to about twelve, though none carried a birth certificate and would ever be certain of his age. They had lived in Ethiopia with the blessing of that country's leader, an ally of the SPLA, but Ethiopia was in the throes of its own civil war, its government on the verge of being overthrown by Eritrean and Tigrean rebels. Rebel attacks in northwestern Ethiopia in late February 1991 achieved success and opened the door for the rebels to march on Addis Ababa. The departure of the Ethiopian president on May 21, 1991, and the approach of rebel armies about to take over the country sparked panic among the unaccompanied minors and roughly 250,000 southern Sudanese refugees at Dimma, Itang, and Panyido. Almost overnight, nearly all of them left the camps to go back to Sudan, a hurried exodus that would plant the seeds of nightmares for years to come.

Daniel remembers leaving with a cup of maize, a blanket, and a bag with one change of clothes. Wearing long pants and a tattered long-sleeved shirt, he joined a stream of so many people that he couldn't see far enough ahead to know where it began or far enough behind him to know where it might end. Barefoot, he followed the person in front of him on a forced march back into a country where men on horseback rode with rifles into villages to shoot and maim and kill, to a land of famine and disease and separated families, to that place of seemingly interminable violence that had robbed him of a childhood just as it was dawning. That line of several thousand souls lurched inexorably toward Sudan, back into the furnace, past a bleak landscape of shrubs and trees. On the first day, after several hours, Daniel heard screams and wailing flow like a bitter wind through the pack of humanity around him. Only later, after parts of the column paused to rest, did he learn what it was about. A lion, they said, had leaped from the bush, mauled one among the many, and dragged off the limp body as survivors watched, helpless. The attack would turn out to be a prelude of things to come.

After two days of walking, Daniel, Peter, Marko, and other unaccompanied minors from Dimma, along with thousands of other Sudanese refugees, came to the banks of the Gilo River, which divides Ethiopia and Sudan, swollen after days of heavy rain. Daniel remembers hundreds of boys about his age on the banks of an overflowing river, crying: "They needed help, but there was nobody to help." He talks about wading into the river, arms flailing, trying to swim, aware even in the chaos of crossing that the current was sucking under one of his friends. He remembers two other friends who were "cut into pieces" by a crocodile that pulled their bodies below water that was "full of blood," but Daniel somehow made it across the river, to the other side, back to Sudan.

The mind retains images of its own accord and replays them later to haunt or restore, regardless of our waking desires, and for Daniel, one scene among many lingers from that time. He sees a boy sitting by a ditch. An SPLA soldier climbs behind the wheel of a tractor and the machine groans to life. Suddenly a blade attached to the front of the tractor lurches toward the boy and smashes into his head, the sound of metal striking bone, life evaporating. It takes two or three seconds. Daniel does not know if it was an accident. He does not know why he remembers it. It's just there, like a record that keeps skipping.

The SPLA directed Daniel and thousands of minors with him to stop at a place called Pakok. They dug foxholes, built small huts, and settled in for five months. Human-rights organizations accused the SPLA of using the unaccompanied minors as bait to secure donated food—some portion went to the boys, the rest to the rebel army.

Jacob and ten thousand other minors from Panyido (also spelled Fugnido and, less commonly, Pugnido) left Ethiopia and eventually created a camp at a small village just inside Sudan. They built small grass huts, called *tukuls*, with foxholes near the door. A journalist who visited them, Scott Peterson, recalls "the acrid camp smell of constantly burning cooking fires, of legumes of some type on the boil, and of wafts of excrement and other human mess." He wrote that their "capacity for affection and other human traits had often been left behind, somewhere on the road. They had nothing, fled with nothing and knew nothing of love nor hope." After another camp for the minors sprung up in the Sudanese town of Nasir, the International Committee of the Red Cross moved in to provide food and protection. By the end of 1991, the ICRC counted ten thousand boys at Pochalla, two thousand in Pakok, and two thousand in Nasir.

Three months after the panicked evacuation from Ethiopia, in August 1991, three SPLA commanders—Riek Machar, Gordon Kong Kuol, and Lam Akol—split with the rebel movement and called for the overthrow of its leader, John Garang, a former Sudanese military officer who had received a Ph.D. in agricultural economics from Iowa State University. Their stated goal was an independent southern Sudan, in contrast to Garang's call for a united, secular Sudan that protected the rights of southerners. They also rebelled in response to the humanitarian crisis created by the evacuation from Ethiopia, a growing concern that one man held too much power, and reports that the SPLA was recruiting children as a manpower reservoir for the future, a suspicion that gathered strength after United Nations relief workers happened upon four thousand ten- and eleven-year-old boys living in an abandoned Italian Catholic mission at a place called Palataka in southern Sudan in March

1990. The boys wore rags, were infested with lice, and lived in old brick buildings popular with rats. When relief workers asked whether they received military training, the boys stayed quiet. The workers concluded that Palataka was a secret SPLA recruitment and training center and that the rebels opposed U.N. plans to open schools nearby for fear they would siphon boys from "schools" run by the rebel army.

The split within the SPLA largely followed tribal lines. Riek Machar, who led the breakaway rebels, is Nuer; Garang is Dinka. It took little time for the fissure to explode into a war within a war, a conflict in which Dinka and Nuer shot, stabbed, raped, and burned each other. The Sudanese government exploited the rift. It reached an agreement to arm Riek Machar's forces and launched a major offensive against Garang's forces, pushing them from one town to the next. The fighting spilled ever closer to the minors' camp. In early 1992, about ten thousand unaccompanied boys evacuated Pochalla in advance of an attack by the Sudanese government. Human Rights Watch/Africa notes that "some relief workers suspected that part of the government motivation for the Pochalla attack was to kill or capture large groups of the minors, whom the Sudanese government viewed as combatants or at least a military reserve force."

Jacob and the other refugees left Pochalla on foot, walking through marshes and desert on the way to the southern Sudanese city of Kapoeta. Workers with the Red Cross had heard accounts of boys starving to death and dying of thirst and disease on their walks to Ethiopia, four or five years earlier. They were determined to avoid a repeat of those deadly marches. The Red Cross set up water tanks and medical stations along the route and ferried the sickest and frailest to Kapoeta in ambulances. In response, the government expelled the ICRC in March 1992, but not before it also helped shepherd unaccompanied minors from other camps toward Kapoeta. Daniel Khoch and the other boys from Dimma, for example, left their ragged camp at Pakok and flowed south. The march took several days. On the second or third night, Daniel and the other boys put empty sacks and leaves on the ground and laid down to rest. A few hours later, the sound of gunfire jolted them awake, and then came screams and the sound of people running. Daniel leaped up and joined a crush of boys running in the darkness in panic and confusion.

He followed other boys for no particular reason, one direction as good as any other. Suddenly he became aware of a sharp pain in his right foot. He reached down, felt the sticky pool of blood around his ankle, and realized he had been shot. In the morning, an SPLA commander "came with many SPLA soldiers so that he can investigate" Daniel wrote later, but "very unfortunately, he didn't find those who are responsible for the cowardly attack."

Daniel said they loaded him and fourteen other wounded boys into a truck that rumbled south toward a city in Kenya, just across the border with Sudan. Only five made it to the hospital alive. Doctors told Daniel they could not remove the bullet because it had lodged between two bones. The only solution, they said, was to amputate, but Daniel would not give them permission. They nursed his wound for the next four months in a hospital crowded with people injured in the war. Eventually, Daniel would walk without so much as a limp. No one would know of his wound unless he told them.

Daniel left the hospital and rode by ambulance back to Sudan, to the city of Narus, the same place where Jacob Magot and so many other unaccompanied minors from Pochalla had ended up. On April 22, 1992, aid workers counted 12,241 unaccompanied minors and sixty-six hundred "teachers and dependents" in Narus, but the refugees would not stay there long. On May 28, 1992, the Sudanese military unexpectedly captured nearby Kapoeta. Tens of thousands of refugees were forced to move again. Nearly all the unaccompanied minors in Narus surged into Kenya. In a final indignity, the Sudanese air force bombed the column of refugees as it streamed south.

Crossing an international border had some advantages. In the eyes of the United Nations, it made them refugees, as opposed to "internally displaced people." As such, they were entitled to protection from the United Nations High Commissioner for Refugees, the primary organization that cares for refugees around the globe. By June 1993, UNHCR had directed twenty-eight thousand Sudanese refugees to a camp at Kakuma, on the broiling tabletop plain of northwestern Kenya. It was a sprawling camp with a population in 1993 that included 10,500 unaccompanied minors who would later be known as Lost Boys. Kakuma would be their home for the next nine years, a final destination after nearly a thousand miles of wandering, from homes across southern Sudan, through forest and marshes and desert, into Ethiopia and back again, across a river to a wasteland of chronic violence and, finally, to this bleak Kenyan camp prone to sandstorms and flash floods and year-round temperatures near one hundred degrees Fahrenheit.

Dinka boys such as Jacob, Peter, Daniel, and Marko built mud brick and straw huts with dirt floors and roofs made of plastic sheets and leaves. They often sketched scenes that reminded them of home. A reporter who visited Kakuma in 1994 described a drawing in pastel colors that showed "a fat cow, a radio, a pot of flowers and a smiling woman with outstretched arms labeled 'Mrs.'" A thirteen-year-old friend of the artist explained the work: "That's his mother," he said. "She is not here." When asked about the future, many children prefaced their answers to an interviewer by saying "If I am not dead" or "If I am alive in the year 2000."

Many lived in sections of Kakuma with others from the same part of Sudan. Daniel and Marko lived next door to each other. They each had three roommates who were, like them, from Bahr El-Ghazal. Peter, from that same region of Sudan, lived nearby. Most often the minors ate once a day, a meal of maize, beans, sorghum, or corn that they crushed and sometimes mixed with water and cooked over heated stones or wood. Despite the spartan meals, here, finally, was a place without constant threat of attack, sanctuary from a war that ground up life like a tornado skipping from place to place. Even so, violence flared occasionally in Kakuma between the Dinka majority and their Nuer neighbors, violence that mirrored the split within the rebel forces of southern Sudan. A clash in June 1996 killed six boys and injured one hundred others, but the boys were safer in Kakuma than in southern Sudan. Some of the unaccompanied minors eventually left the camp to try to make their way in the world or, sometimes, to slip back into Sudan and join the SPLA. Yet most viewed the camp as a safe harbor. Years later, one of the thousands of young southern Sudanese who had been in Kakuma invoked the experience of past decades to explain a vision that gave the minors hope. He believed, as many around him did, that they would one day play a critical role in rebuilding their homeland: "We were uneducated, so it was the people in the north who were running the government, the business, the universities." In Kakuma, they believed, they could equip themselves with an education that they would one day need to reconstruct their shattered country. Children in Kakuma attended school in three kindergartens, twenty primary schools, and one high school. Merchants sold sugar, shoes, clothes, batteries, and flashlights. Repairmen fixed watches and radios while the few refugees who could afford to do so occasionally paid a few Kenyan shillings to watch CNN or movies such as *Basic Instinct* and *Die Hard*.

Yet life remained rough for the boys from southern Sudan. A psychologist who specialized in treating children for the effects of war described the unaccompanied minors as "one of the most traumatized groups of children I have ever met." She said many were "haunted by flashbacks from the long trail of terror, physical suffering, and loss. The most common manifestation was sound: piercing aural memories that sprang back without warning." She said the boys "could vividly hear" the sound of "screaming from suffering, frightened adults or friends."

One twelve-year-old boy in Kakuma told an interviewer about the effects of trauma: "People were shot, and I saw it. Some of these things are often in my mind. Some of them always. Some people were killed and put in a car. . . . When I am happy, the memory goes away. I am laughing sometimes. Then it goes away, for a while."

The image of skeletons lingered inside the mind of a thirteen-year-old boy. "I saw their bones," he said. "I see these pictures sometimes still, maybe two times a month. They come suddenly. They bother me very much. The picture of a pregnant mother who was killed also."

A twelve-year-old had trouble sleeping. "It all comes back as a film," he said. "There was heavy fighting. People were killed during that fight. I saw them, I saw a lot of people being killed. I had relatives among those who died. I did not carry the dead bodies, but I saw them. In the fight 51 people were killed. . . . Sometimes, especially at night, these pictures come to my mind. When I am asleep I can hear sounds of shooting so I suddenly awake. I really have some sleeping problems."

Years later, after he came to Atlanta, Peter Anyang would recall trying to fend off memories of terror. Occasionally, he said, he would stand alone after school in Kakuma, smoking, trying to stop his mind from grappling with questions about his family. Were his parents alive? Would he see them again? Sometimes, he said, a cigarette helped take his mind off of it.

Daniel found himself increasingly drawn to church. Several denominations conducted services in Kakuma. Daniel gravitated to the Catholic church. After he had arrived at Kakuma, an Italian priest named Father Joseph had given him a purple, plastic rosary that Daniel would wear around his neck every day for the next nine years, until he could afford to replace it with a gold-plated crucifix. He sang in the choir and helped set up chairs before services at Holy Cross Parish. It was a noble thing, he decided, to dedicate one's life to the work of peace and service and spreading the word of Jesus Christ. Daniel said he envisioned himself hearing confession, standing behind an altar, preaching. He often doubted he would wear a collar outside of his imagination, but this vision of the future sustained him no matter how impossible it seemed. He told himself it was God's will. He had faith. One day he would be a priest. Maybe by then the war would be over. Maybe he could return home to teach boys to care for cattle as his father had taught him. His father. It had been nearly ten years since Daniel had seen his father, mother, three brothers, and four sisters. Occasionally he let himself wonder why God allowed the agony of uncertainty, but other times he held out hope. Maybe it was only a matter of time before he would know, before he would see his family again. He knew that other people were finding answers.

Jacob Magot lived in a part of Kakuma favored by other Dinka from the Upper Nile province. New arrivals flowed into the camp all the time, so many that the camp's population increased from about twenty-eight thousand in 1993 to sixty-six thousand in 1999. One day in the winter of 1998 a man came to Kakuma from Labone, a refugee camp in southern Sudan. He was from Upper Nile and settled near Jacob and others from that province. He and Jacob got to talking and discovered they both were from the village of Mathiang. People from southern Sudan have a remarkable grapevine network despite being scattered in squatter neighborhoods inside Sudan and refugee camps outside the country, so

Jacob knew there was a chance this man would have news of his family. He asked whether anyone else from Mathiang lived in the Labone camp. The man mentioned someone named Ayoum, whose wife, Apajok, was from Mathiang. Jacob's pulse quickened; his sister was named Apajok, and he had not seen her for more than ten years. Jacob asked whether this Apajok had any brothers or sisters. Yes, the man said, a sister named Awuoi and a brother named Abraham Agau. Jacob said he knew then, for the first time since he had left home at the age of five or six, that his brother and two sisters were alive. He wrote a letter reintroducing himself to his long-lost relatives, sent it through the Red Cross, and received a reply. His siblings told him they were in danger in their refugee camp, near the border with Uganda. A rebel group in that country, the Lord's Resistance Army, occasionally attacked civilians in refugee camps, apparently with arms and urging supplied by the Sudanese government. Jacob's relatives asked whether Kakuma was safer. Jacob hurried off another letter encouraging them to join him, and they eventually made plans to meet at a point on the border between Kenya and Sudan. Jacob and his siblings were reunited early in 1998, and they came to live with him in Kakuma.

Around this time, just as the first rumors spread that the United States might eventually open its doors to some of the unaccompanied minors, other unaccompanied minors in Kakuma were finding answers about their relatives. One was Abraham Yel Nhial, a man with a soft voice and serious eyes that conveyed gravity. Like many people in southern Sudan, Abraham was born into a family that practiced traditional African religion. His parents sacrificed cows and goats to ward off illness or ask forgiveness for sins. When Abraham was about nine, his younger brother fell sick and died. Abraham remembers wondering: Where is my brother now? What happens to a person after death? He turned it over in his mind after war tore him from his parents. At Dimma, the camp where Daniel, Marko, and Peter lived, Abraham attended services one Sunday at a Christian church. He remembers people in the congregation who welcomed him with hugs even though they did not know him. More importantly, Abraham was intrigued by the pastor's sermon about Jesus Christ and the promise of eternal life. He told the pastor he wanted to join the church. A few weeks later, after sessions with a Sunday School teacher, someone in the church gave Abraham a compact, dark-blue, Dinka-language Bible, printed in 1959 by the Bible Society of Sudan, with red letters on the front cover that said "Lek Jot de Yecu Kritho"—"The Good News of Jesus Christ." Abraham carried it with him after being forced to leave Dimma. He had it with him when he crossed the river and on the deadly months-long march to Kakuma. Christianity so appealed to Abraham that he decided to become a priest. A natural leader, he was ordained as a deacon in the Episcopal Church of Sudan and led services in the camp for hundreds of people. That position gave him the rare opportunity to leave Kakuma and return to his home in southern Sudan in 1999. He accompanied an Episcopal bishop on a flight from Lokichokio, Kenya, to the Aweil district of southern Sudan. There, at a church the bishop visited, Abraham recognized some people in the congregation—his mother's relatives. They did not recognize him at first, but after talking with him they realized straightaway that Abraham was one of the boys who had left so many years ago. They had sobering news—though his father, two of his sisters, and a brother were alive, Abraham's mother, two other sisters, a stepbrother, and grandmother had died, mainly due to disease. "I could not even cry," Abraham recalled. "I made myself to be strong."

His mother's relatives sent for one of Abraham's uncles. Two days later, he arrived with plans to take Abraham home, so he could see his father and siblings again. They rode on bicycles for ten hours to the remote village where Abraham was reunited with his surviving family members. Later, after an emotional visit, Abraham left again, this time with one of his sisters. She was sick, and Abraham hoped she might receive treatment in the hospital at Kakuma.

Meanwhile, news of relatives arrived by happenstance for Lost Boys at Kakuma such as Jacob Deu, a slight young man who would one day hear Abraham Yel preach in Atlanta. His uncle walked into Kakuma on December 12, 1999, he said, with news that Jacob's mother, a sister, and a brother were in one of the camps in Ethiopia. Jacob's joy was tempered by the news that his father and younger brother and sister had been shot dead in the attack that had separated him from his family ten years earlier. Jacob absorbed the message like a body blow. He remembers sitting by himself and not saying much, friends putting a hand on his shoulder. Eventually he wrote his mother to say that he was alive and that he missed her. Her reply arrived weeks later, as word spread that the United States was considering opening its doors to southern Sudanese youth in Kakuma.

"Dear My Son Jacob Aweeng Deu," she began, "I greet you by the name of God almighty. I hope you are well as I am. We live in time of war and scattering places." She had advice: "Education is the way of the human being's life, but I have one thing to say. Don't go to USA because USA is so far with Africa. Follow your education here in Africa."

That would not be easy.

SELECTIVE COMPASSION

People have fled persecution throughout history, from the Jews and Moors expelled by Spain in the 1400s to Christians leaving Europe for the New World in the 1600s, but the idea that states should recognize victims of persecution as a group distinct from other immigrants is a relatively recent phenomenon. Until the twentieth century, most governments that had immigration laws and policies treated refugees such as Jacob, Peter, Daniel, and Marko the same as anyone else moving from one country to another. It did not matter whether someone crossed an international border to look for a higher-paying job, reunite with relatives, or seek shelter from repression. The concept of the refugee as someone in need of state protection began to take root in the early 1900s. It solidified with the mass displacements caused by World War I and the subsequent rise of the League of Nations, envisioned as a forum for collective approaches to global problems. Established in 1921, the league created an international organization devoted to addressing the refugee problem. It helped Armenians and Greeks leaving Turkey and Bulgarians who fled their country in the 1920s, but some European states prevented refugees from working or imprisoned them. By the time Adolf Hitler annexed Austria and Czechoslovakia in 1938 and early 1939 as a prelude to the German invasion of Poland on September 1, 1939, however, the League of Nations had withered into irrelevance and the world lacked an international body to deal with refugee flows.

Millions of people displaced during World War II received assistance from a new organization, the United Nations Relief and Rehabilitation Administration, created in 1943 to help people in territory liberated from the Axis powers. It distributed emergency food and medical supplies to people in China, Czechoslovakia, Greece, Italy, Poland, Ukraine, and Yugoslavia. By the war's end, in August 1945, the major Allied powers had agreed on a charter for the United Nations, a global organization that would try to maintain peace, resolve disputes, and foster international cooperation in addressing humanitarian problems, such as refugee crises. The relief and rehabilitation administration, together with a United Nations organization that replaced it in 1946, helped about 7 million people return to their native countries after World War II, but another 1 million did not want to return. Most were from parts of Europe that had fallen under the Iron Curtain of communist control after the war. The United Nations fed them while authorities in various nations wrestled with the question of their fate, conducting debates that drifted across the Atlantic and into the corridors of power in Washington, D.C.

Discussions in the U.S. Congress culminated in the Displaced Persons Act of 1948, the first federal law to recognize people fleeing persecution as a group separate from other foreign nationals seeking admission. It led to the arrival of a few hundred thousand of the 1 million European refugees and became the first of several refugee acts Congress would enact in the next thirty-two years in response to one crisis or another. The United States offered shelter to people fleeing repressive, communist governments in Cuba, Hungary, and Indochina in the 1950s, '60s, and '70s, a time when the United States was locked in the Cold War against the Soviet Union. Refugees languished around the world, including millions from war-ravaged African nations, but the United States administered its resettlement program with a kind of selective compassion that rewarded people fleeing communist control. For most of the Cold War, in fact, federal law defined a "refugee" as someone fleeing a communist government or a repressive Middle Eastern regime. Admitting people escaping communism, the theory went, would expose the cruelties of communist rule and celebrate the virtues of American democracy. It also might embarrass and discredit American adversaries and facilitate the formation of opposition groups in exile. So while Congress doled out opportunities for new lives to a select few of the world's refugees, the vast majority worldwide had no chance of coming to the United States. Enemies of Fidel Castro were welcome, but no one saw much value in letting in survivors of a war in faraway Sudan even though that country would displace more people than any other in the late twentieth century.

In 1980, Congress conducted a wholesale revision of U.S. refugee policy. The Refugee Act revised the definition of "refugee" to conform to a view embraced by the United Nations: a person who has left his or her country and cannot or does not want to return because of a credible fear of persecution based on race, religion, nationality, political opinion, or membership in a social or ethnic group. The law abolished the preference for refugees from countries in the Soviet bloc and Middle East, at least on paper, and cleared the way for the admission of a limited number of refugees from other parts of the world. The president would set a limit each year on the number of refugees who could enter the United States. He also would specify how many could come from each region of the world. The goal was to inject humanitarian concerns into the debate about which few of the world's refugees the United States would resettle, but foreign-policy priorities continued to guide admissions. Nearly 80 percent of the 1.8 million refugees the United States admitted from 1982 to 2002 came from traditional U.S. enemies or countries in which the United States had intervened militarily—Vietnam, Cambodia, and Laos (41 percent); the Soviet Union and its successors (29 percent); and Bosnia (8 percent).

A pattern of favorable treatment also played out in smaller refugee flows from Cold War battlegrounds such as Central America. From 1987 to 1990, as civil wars raged in Nicaragua, El Salvador, and Guatemala, countries with disastrous human-rights records, U.S. refugee policy tilted sharply in favor of Nicaraguans. The federal government granted refugee status to eleven hundred Nicaraguans from 1987 to 1990, compared with fifty-four Salvadorans and no Guatemalans. It was no coincidence that Nicaragua's Marxist government was embroiled in a bloody war with a guerrilla army subsidized by the U.S. treasury. The United States government had an interest in highlighting human-rights abuses by the Marxist rulers in Nicaragua. By contrast, the rulers of El Salvador and Guatemala were right-wing military men fighting guerrillas who had visions of communist rule. The United States heavily subsidized those rulers, just as it armed and trained the *contra* rebels in Nicaragua. Were the United States to accept refugees from El Salvador and Guatemala, it would be tacitly admitting that labor-union organizers, journalists, and other critics of the power structure sometimes were kidnapped, tortured, or executed by government forces in El Salvador and Guatemala. Accepting refugees from Nicaragua exposed the devastation its Marxist rules had wrought, but Washington looked the other way when confronted with evidence that allies in El Salvador and Guatemala had trampled human rights in wars with leftist fighters. This kind of calculated sympathy unfolded on a larger scale in decisions made on requests for asylum, granted to foreign nationals who arrive on U.S. soil and decline to return to their native countries for fear of persecution. Immigration judges granted asylum to tens of thousands of Nicaraguans; they routinely rejected claims from Salvadorans and Guatemalans.

It was a small example of the kind of favorable treatment of one nation or another that is woven throughout the nation's complex and labyrinthine immigration laws, dating to the Chinese Exclusion Act of 1882, which barred Chinese laborers from entering the United States. In 1924, in response to massive immigration from eastern Europe, Congress created a quota system that ensured a flow of immigrants from western Europe and closed the door to most people from countries in southern and eastern Europe. That system remained in place until 1965, when Congress exchanged it for one that favored foreign nationals wishing to come to the United States to work or rejoin relatives. That tilted the scales toward immigrants from Asia and Latin America. The next year, the Cuban Adjustment Act granted legal status to any Cuban citizen who arrived in the United States, a sweeping amnesty for people who otherwise would face detention and deportation as illegal immigrants. The goal was to punish the communist regime of Fidel Castro by siphoning off some of Cuba's best and brightest citizens and also to encourage the formation of opposition groups. Refugees from another Caribbean nation with a poor human-rights record, Haiti, often cite the favorable treatment meted out to Cubans to contrast the reception that greets them. The federal government tends to view Haitians fleeing persecution as economic migrants even though it knows that Haitians have been imprisoned and killed for their political views. Immigration authorities in the United States have detained and forcibly returned thousands of Haitians who came to the United States, including many who risked their lives to come here on rickety boats, an approach that has triggered complaints of racial discrimination, indifference, and double standards.

Many of the world's refugees leave their native countries and end up in camps run by the United Nations High Commissioner for Refugees (UNHCR). It provides food and shelter to millions of refugees around the world, from countries such as Afghanistan, Bhutan, Iraq, Liberia, and Sudan. Its overriding goal for most refugees is to help them return to their native countries, and millions of refugees do go home, usually after some measure of stability is restored. After a United States–led military campaign dislodged the Taliban regime in Afghanistan in the fall of 2001, for example, at least 1.8 million Afghan refugees returned home from refugee camps in Pakistan. A second option, used less often, is "local integration," in which the UNHCR helps refugees settle in a country near their own—if it can find a country willing to take them permanently. The third option, and the one most unlikely for the majority of refugees, is resettlement in the United States or another Western country. Ten nations consistently ran resettlement programs in the late twentieth century—Australia, Canada, Denmark, Finland, the Netherlands, New Zealand, Norway, Sweden, Switzerland, and the United States—but the United States resettled far more than the other nine nations combined. After the terrorist attacks on September 11, 2001, the United States temporarily suspended its refugee-resettlement program, resuming it with increased security measures that significantly slowed the flow of refugees. While the United States resettles more refugees than any other Western country, several other nations spend more, proportionately, on aid to refugee-assistance organizations. Figures from 2003 ranked the United States eleventh on a list of nations ranked by per-capita contributions, behind Norway, Luxembourg, and Finland but ahead of Japan, Canada, and the United Kingdom. As for who gets in, the nationalities of refugees resettled in the United States began to change in the late 1990s. There was a shrinking pool of refugees in the former Soviet Union, Cuba, and Vietnam, and the Cold War's end led to arguments that refugee policy should put more of an emphasis on humanitarian concerns. That raised the possibility of more difficult and time-consuming visits by U.S. officials to remote refugee camps in places that rarely made headlines. It opened the door to a small but growing number of refugees stuck in desolate camps around the world, like the one in Kenya where so many Lost Boys were coming of age.

THE LEVEL OF RESPONSIBLE PEOPLE

One of the first people in the United States government to think of opening the doors to Lost Boys fell into his position quite by chance. The State Department gave Mike O'Keefe a dull office job in the mid-1990s, but the department moves foreign-service officers around every so often, so O'Keefe was not surprised to learn in 1997 that his job duties were changing. He would become the refugee assistance officer for the Horn of Africa. Based in Washington, O'Keefe would travel occasionally to Djibouti, Eritrea, Ethiopia, Kenya, and Somalia to evaluate federally funded programs in refugee camps and make recommendations about which refugees the government might consider for resettlement. It was a welcome reprieve from the office for a man who had fallen into the foreign service almost by coincidence.

He was born and raised in Portsmouth, New Hampshire, and re-turned after a short stint in the Air Force to become a high-school history teacher. O'Keefe had politics in his blood and won election at the age of twenty-three as one of about four hundred members of the New Hampshire legislature. After the school where he taught developed a

Model United Nations club, O'Keefe used his political ties to set up a trip for the students to meet the U.S. ambassador to the United Nations. O'Keefe remembers the ambassador making small talk, saying he had always wanted to be a teacher. That's funny, O'Keefe responded. He had always wanted to be a diplomat. Then why not take the foreign-service exam, the ambassador asked. Three years later, after passing the exam and background check, O'Keefe quit his job at the school (he had become the principal) and joined the foreign service. He moved his wife and three children from New Hampshire to Botswana, in southern Africa, where he served as American consul. Later came posts in Korea and as an editor of an intelligence report delivered at 6 a.m. each day to the secretary of state. The 1997 transfer meant travel back into the real world. O'Keefe's first trip as refugee assistance officer for the Horn of Africa came in 1998. He would visit Somalia, Djibouti, and Ethiopia and tour two refugee camps in Kenya. He had heard of a group of unaccompanied Sudanese boys in one of the camps, Kakuma, and made a point to meet them.

The first thing he noticed when he got to the unaccompanied mi- nors' section of Kakuma was how clean it looked. The second thing he noticed was that nobody asked how they could get to the United States. That was unusual. He had worked with refugees in Botswana and was accustomed to refugees in camps peppering him with two questions: How could they receive more food? And how could they go to the United States as refugees? On this trip, several Somalis were practically begging for resettlement. They thrust into O'Keefe's hands notes that were varia- tions on a theme: Help me. The camp is dangerous. Let me go to the United States. O'Keefe said he sensed a difference with the unaccompa- nied minors from southern Sudan. They asked how they could receive more education. They also wanted to know what he thought of the pros- pects for peace in Sudan. When did he think they would be able to go home? Nearly all the minors were in school, but they had no idea what they would do after graduation. Kenya would not let them work. If they went back to Sudan, they risked conscription by the rebel army or injury or death in a government attack. No country in East Africa would ac- cept them as permanent and legal residents. After school, they had few options except to stay in the camp and wait for a change that might never come, a condition O'Keefe worried would only lead to trouble. Already an air of unpredictable danger swirled around the place. There was always the prospect that tribal rivalries would erupt into violence, Dinka versus Nuer. It had happened several times. More worrisome to O'Keefe were reports that SPLA soldiers came to Kakuma to recruit or kidnap potential soldiers. Some unaccompanied minors told O'Keefe it had happened a few days before he got there. Some friends, they said, had been knocked unconscious and spirited off by rebels in the middle of the night. "Life had dealt them an extremely bad hand, but they had persevered," O'Keefe remembers thinking. "While they were in the camp, they learned everything they possibly could."

O'Keefe told a colleague he thought they would be good candidates for resettlement in the United States. There were obstacles, but the timing seemed fortuitous. For one thing, the State Department had just started designating groups of African refugees for resettlement, as it had often done for groups in other places. It had just identified a group of Rwandan couples in which one spouse belonged to the Hutu ethnic group and the other to the Tutsi group. The couples had fled to a refugee camp in Tanzania after majority Hutus in Rwanda went on a genocidal killing spree in 1994, hacking, shooting, and burning more than eight hundred thousand members of the minority Tutsi group. The designation of Hutu-Tutsi couples as a group of special concern to the United States meant that refugees in such mixed marriages could get an interview with the INS to determine whether they qualified as refugees to be resettled in the United States. The designation of a group of African refugees at least raised the possibility of other African groups receiving the same treatment.

O'Keefe's visit to Kakuma also coincided with another phenomena that would pave the way for resettlement. It had to do with political pressure in the United States. For years, the Congressional Black Caucus had complained about the low number of African refugees the United States admitted. In the year after the passage of the Refugee Act in 1980, about 1,500 of the 231,700 refugees the United States said it would resettle were African. The proportions remained about constant into the mid-1990s, but they began to change amid complaints from the Black Caucus and a growing interest of the Clinton administration in Africa. Two Democrats on the caucus, Representative John Conyers Jr. of Michigan and Representative Melvin L. Watt of North Carolina complained in a 1997 letter to Clinton that "59 percent of all slots go to Europeans, while only 9 percent go to Africans" even though Africa is home to as many or more refugees than any other continent. They said "one would expect to see refugee resettlement allocations roughly proportionate to the refugee burdens in the world" and that it was "unconscionable" that was not the case. Partly as a result, the ceiling for African refugees climbed from seven thousand in 1998 (11 percent of all slots) to twelve thousand the next year (16 percent). The ceiling would go up for the next several years, until twenty-five thousand of the fifty thousand slots in 2004 were set aside for Africans (an additional twenty thousand slots were available for use in any region in a crisis). Even though the trend was just beginning to assert itself in 1998, when O'Keefe visited Kakuma, everyone knew the emphasis was shifting away from large groups of refugees in communist-bloc countries toward smaller groups in more remote locations.

After visiting Kakuma, O'Keefe and a colleague stopped in Nairobi to discuss the Lost Boys with representatives of UNHCR. Many United Nations employees opposed resettlement. So did some members of a Swedish organization that had worked with the Lost Boys for several years. Its employees told O'Keefe they suspected many Lost Boys had relatives who were still alive in Sudan. They said it would be wrong to ship young men to America and preclude any chance they might have for reuniting with parents or siblings. They also said it made no sense to remove young men from their traditional culture and drop them into a world of Madonna and MTV.

In the summer of 1998, a delegation from Lutheran Immigration and Refugee Service and the United States Catholic Conference visited Kakuma. As the sole agencies in the United States that resettle refugee children who arrive without parents, the agencies had a natural interest in the southern Sudanese boys and an expertise in the issues they faced. A conference the Lutheran group had helped plan months earlier in Washington, D.C., had brought together key players in the refugee-resettlement world to focus on the dwindling numbers of unaccompanied refugee minors the United States was resettling. In the 1980s, the State Department had opened its doors to thousands of refugee children without parents—mainly boys and girls from Southeast Asia who had lost track of their parents in war and its aftermath—but by the late 1990s the federal government was resettling very few unaccompanied children. Spurred by the conference, experts from the Lutheran and Catholic organizations spent ten days in Kakuma trying to determine whether the United States should resettle some of the unaccompanied Sudanese minors and, if so, how such a program would work.

Another group interested in the Lost Boys' fate, a U.S. advocacy organization called Refugees International, cited culture as a justification for resettling the Lost Boys. In September 1998, Refugees International said in a report that most Lost Boys did not fit the traditional Dinka or Nuer roles of a young man's place in society. Separation from relatives meant they grew up with a limited education on cattle herding, the traditional skill that defines men as competent and whole in southern Sudan. The minors also lacked cows or money to pay a dowry, so marriage seemed out of the question. In addition, many had not undergone the ritual scarification that marks a Dinka boy's passage into manhood.

Had war not separated them from relatives and forced them from home, the boys most likely would have welcomed the scarification celebration that traditionally accompanied the initiation of Dinka males sixteen to eighteen years old. It has traditionally been a time, Francis Deng writes, when "beasts are sacrificed and other rites of spiritual fortification are performed. No one sleeps" the night before the ceremony, "for excitement is high and the sounds of drums and songs fill the air. . . . Early in the morning, the operation begins. In their order of seniority or birth and lineage, the to-be-initiated lie on the ground to receive seven to ten deep and well-ordered" cuts in the forehead, "the bloodiest and most painful operation in Dinka society." Young men lie still as blood runs down their faces. If they flinch, the lines will be crooked and everyone will know. Women and girls surround the young men and "run wild screaming with joy; men chant their special verses of valor; both men and women running and jumping in a special ballet known as *goor*. . . . The initiates themselves, still and serene, first attempt to chant their boastful words of courage, but soon pass out from excessive bleeding." Most unaccompanied minors left home years before they would have been initiated, so few had the traditional mark of a man. Combined with their lack of experience herding cattle and inability to pay a dowry, Refugees International said, the men were "ill-equipped for integrating into the Dinka and Nuer societies that shun them."

By the time of that report, Jacob Magot, Peter Anyang, Daniel Khoch, and Marko Ayii had been in Kakuma for more than six years. Several thousand in the original group of about 10,500 had left, though precise counts were difficult to obtain because people came and went almost every day. Some ventured back into Sudan, trying against the odds to find relatives. Others tried to make it on their own in the underground economy in Nairobi, though nonprofit organizations paid to send a few to school there. Still others joined the SPLA in the fight against what they saw as northern domination. Echoing the stories that O'Keefe had heard when he had first visited Kakuma, Refugees International reported that "SPLA commanders regularly enter the camp, 80 miles from the Sudanese border, to recruit." The report's author shared O'Keefe's view that the Lost Boys faced a bleak future in Kakuma. "Because of their unique background and their long history as an exploited population," she wrote, "we believe that a limited number from this group should be eligible for resettlement."

O'Keefe was making the same argument in Washington, though some colleagues questioned whether it made sense for the United States to take young men so far from their culture. Others had heard that many of the southern Sudanese youth entered Kakuma in 1995, '96, or '97. They may have experienced horrors of their own—that's not uncommon in southern Sudan—but they were not in the group of unaccompanied minors that trekked toward Ethiopia in the late 1980s. Some people came to Kakuma in the mid-1990s after hearing they could go to school there. O'Keefe and others continued to talk about the possibility of resettlement, but the idea did not gain real momentum until a change in leadership brought in a new principal deputy assistant secretary of state for population, refugees and migration.

Alan Kreczko knew very little about refugees. He admitted it. He was a State Department lawyer known for his work in the 1980s on the Arab-Israeli dispute. Kreczko had accompanied President Ronald Reagan's special envoy to the Middle East on many missions of shuttle diplomacy, including one to Khartoum. Later he had worked as one of four deputy general counsels for the State Department and, from 1993 to 1998, as the legal adviser to the National Security Council in Clinton's White House. Now he was making decisions about refugees. Subordinates kidded their boss because he had never set foot in a refugee camp. O'Keefe ran into Kreczko in a hallway after a meeting one day and offered to accompany him to real refugee camps in the Horn of Africa. It would be a way for Kreczko to get his feet wet and learn more about the program. Kreczko had a wife and young children, so he didn't want to be gone too long, but he said it sounded like a good idea. O'Keefe arranged a trip to camps in Kenya and Ethiopia, taking pains to ensure their visit to Kakuma was especially productive.

O'Keefe and Kreczko arrived from Nairobi to as much of a dignitary's welcome as can be expected in a place where people are on the verge of starvation. O'Keefe remembers a few hundred refugees lining the runway, singing and pounding drums as the visitors climbed down onto the tarmac. A young girl presented Kreczko with a bouquet of flowers. Later, O'Keefe and Kreczko went to a part of the camp where Lost Boys lived. About three hundred Lost Boys huddled around the dignitaries as a few others performed a play that told the story of why they had to leave home without parents. They gave Kreczko paintings that depicted various scenes in the communal life of a group that had more or less been together since columns of boys began arriving at the camps in Ethiopia around 1987. One painting showed attackers burning a village while boys with cattle watched from afar. Another showed boys trying to cross a river while soldiers shot at them. Later, while walking through parts of Kakuma, Kreczko was struck with the resourcefulness of some Lost Boys. They had received vegetable oil in tin cans from the United States Agency for International Development and found uses for the cans long after they were empty. Several young men were cutting up the cans to make shingles. Others carved old tires into shoes—they even offered Kreczko a pair. And all of them, it seemed, wanted to talk about continuing their studies. At the end of their second day in Kakuma, O'Keefe and Kreczko got into a Land Rover and rode back toward the United Nations compound.

"What can we do for these kids?" Kreczko wanted to know.

"Well, you know, they'd probably be a good P-2 group," O'Keefe responded, using State Department lingo for a group designated for possible resettlement.

"Yeah," Kreczko said. "Why aren't we doing it?"

Back in Nairobi, Kreczko met with representatives of UNHCR. What did they think of the idea of the United States opening its doors to some of the Lost Boys? They raised the same concerns about cutting young men off from traditional culture. The Swedish nongovernmental organization repeated its concerns, but Kreczko returned to Washington determined to pursue resettlement. He asked around, brought it up in meetings. Eventually someone from the State Department called to ask the opinion of Deng, the foremost Dinka scholar and a widely respected historian and diplomat whose office walls display photos of him with Bill Clinton, Kofi Annan, and King Hussein of Jordan. He had mixed feelings. On one hand, Deng said, resettling Lost Boys would give them an unexpected opportunity to receive an education and earn money to support friends and relatives in Africa. It might also prepare a generation of architects, engineers, teachers, and leaders who might fill the void and help rebuild southern Sudan in the event of peace. On the other hand, Deng worried that resettlement might offer false hope and set a precedent. More Dinka might leave squatter camps in Khartoum, Deng worried, to go to Cairo to present themselves as refugees in need of resettlement in the United States. Others could conceivably make their way to western Europe and ask for asylum. There was no guarantee that southerners would succeed—chances were, they would fail—but he said increased flows in either direction could mean fewer recruits for the SPLA, and that, in turn, could tip the scales in favor of the government. If enough southerners chased futures outside of Africa, southern Sudan would be drained of the educated, professional classes who were to hold power in the New Sudan.

Even so, in 1999, the State Department announced plans to resettle a group of about thirty-three hundred Lost Boys who were in Kakuma. In addition, several hundred boys under the age of eighteen would also be eligible for resettlement if a UNHCR consultant judged it to be in their best interests. To filter out people who came to Kakuma for an education and did not share the group's common story of dangerous wandering, the State Department defined the group to include only those who arrived at Kakuma before 1995 and who lived in the camp without parents. Being a member of the group did not mean a ticket to the United States. It simply got someone an interview with an INS officer in the camp. The INS would judge whether a person had a well-founded fear of persecution based on his race, religion, nationality, political opinion, or membership in a social or ethnic group.

Before the interviews began, word got back to refugee-resettlement officials in Washington that many of the young men were being coached on what to say. Some Lost Boys were telling others they should tell the story of being in the field, tending to cattle, when attacking militias killed their relatives, the story of having to walk in the wild to survive. That clearly happened to some boys who later wound up in Ethiopia, but the State Department was well aware in 1999 of accounts that the SPLA trained child soldiers in Ethiopia in the late 1980s and early '90s. That did not make the refugees any less eligible for resettlement, but there was a perception in Kakuma that it might. An official in the refugee admissions program at the State Department traveled to Kakuma just before the INS interviews and urged the Lost Boys she met to ignore whatever advice they had received and "just be honest." Nevertheless, after the INS began questioning the young men, the refugees seemed "very uncomfortable" talking too much about what happened in Ethiopia. They told nearly identical stories about being forced from home by attacks around age six, seven, eight, or nine. The uniformity made it virtually impossible to tell how many Lost Boys actually left home under such circumstances, but did it really matter? No one disputed that these children were separated from parents or that thousands had died of starvation, disease, or animal attacks while trekking from southern Sudan to Ethiopia and then back into southern Sudan and into Kenya. If the United States was looking for a group to welcome on humanitarian grounds, the Lost Boys were perfect candidates.

In the aftermath of the Vietnam War, the United States resettled minors who had been separated from parents during the chaos and vio-lence that gripped so much of Indochina in the 1960s and '70s. In addi-tion, about fourteen thousand Cuban children arrived without parents on American shores from 1960 to 1962 in a program dubbed Operation Peter Pan, arranged by the State Department and the Catholic Church. The Cubans, ages five to eighteen, were sent by parents who feared their indoctrination in communist schools, but they arrived knowing that their parents were alive. They were generally from the middle and upper classes in Cuba. Unlike the Lost Boys, they generally had not endured traumatic months of wandering and arrived in south Florida very famil-iar with indoor plumbing and electricity.

To prepare the Lost Boys for the modern world that awaited, aid workers in Kakuma conducted cultural-orientation classes to give them a crash course in modern American life. The courses were taught by employees of the International Organization for Migration (IOM) such as Sasha Chanoff, a soccer enthusiast from Boston who discovered a pas-sion for refugee work after graduating from Wesleyan University in the mid-1990s. He volunteered and later worked for an agency that helped refugees find jobs. Intrigued, he volunteered with another agency to learn more about resettlement. Sasha started playing soccer with refugees. In 1998, when he heard the State Department was looking for people to go to refugee camps in Africa for five weeks to teach courses about American culture, he leaped at the chance and was enchanted by people in countries such as Ivory Coast and Kenya. The next year, Sasha got a full-time job in Africa with the IOM, an organization that conducts cultural-orientation classes, sets up medical examinations, and makes travel arrangements for refugees bound for the United States. He traveled around the continent with other IOM staffers, visiting the camps in which a few refugees were packing bags for America. So he spent a lot of time at Kakuma in 2000, passing around ice to give Lost Boys an idea of what winter felt like. One man asked whether the coolness would kill. Sasha tried to answer questions about how men find brides in the United States. He told his students that Americans "equate wealth with money," and he showed them one-dollar bills and five-dollar bills.

It was during these sessions that most Lost Boys received copies of

Welcome to the United States: A Guidebook for Refugees, a spiral-bound volume with the Statue of Liberty and the U.S. flag on the cover. "The United States is a large, diverse country, so generalizations about it are difficult to make," the book said. "It contains within its borders enormous contrasts in geography, a wide range of climates and a great diversity among the people who call themselves Americans. Americans are of many different racial and ethnic backgrounds, and they hold a variety of religious beliefs and values. Consequently, much of what you have heard about America may not be true for you."

The book said each refugee would be assigned to a resettlement agency that would give him some clothes and help him find a job and a place to live. The agency also would teach him to use public transportation and study English if needed:

> When you first arrive in the United States, there will be a place ready for
> you to stay. You can expect that the initial accommodation will be furnished
> with necessities and will probably be in a working-class neighborhood,
> racially and ethnically mixed. . . . One of your first goals after arriving in
> the United States will be to find a job. While you may receive some help
> from employment services which have been established to help refugees find
> jobs, your personal efforts and attitude are even more important. Employ-
> ment is not guaranteed by the government or your resettlement agency. You
> will be competing with others for the same jobs, so it is essential to develop
> a positive attitude and demonstrate that you are ready to go to work. . . .
> As your English skills improve through study and informal contacts with
> other Americans, your chances of moving to a better, higher-paying job also
> improve. Staying on the first job at least six months is an important step in
> creating a good work history. It is also important that you try to use English
> as much as possible, at work and elsewhere in the community.

Readers learned that "all communities have fire departments and emergency medical services" and that, in an emergency, "the telephone number to dial in most areas of the United States is 911." The book explained that people in the United States need a driver's license to legally drive a car and that breaking certain laws, such as the one against driving under the influence of alcohol, could result in the loss of a license, fines, and time in jail. Page thirty-four covered auto insurance. Page forty had a photo of the newspaper classifieds, an ad for part-time kitchen help circled in dark ink. Several pages later came a description of gross pay, deductions, sick leave, and retirement plans, valuable information that nevertheless overwhelmed many of the Lost Boys. Most had never ridden in a car, let alone considered the need for a driver's license. Most had never read a newspaper, and so the concept of classified ads floated in an abstract realm. For young men who had never worked in a wage economy, talk of salary deductions and benefits may as well have been written in Latin. The guide was full of nuanced observations, but many refugees, so eager for an education, could not glean from it a clear sense of whether they would be enrolled in school.

"Once you are settled into the community, you will learn more about the educational opportunities available," it said. The book said they would "probably have little opportunity for higher education during your first year in the United States," but it also mentioned General Education Development (GED) classes.

In the fall of 2000, aid workers began stapling white sheets to bulletin boards in the camp. The sheets listed refugees' names and the U.S. cities that would become their new homes. Walking to the board became a ritual for several hundred Lost Boys. After word spread that more sheets were up, young men walked to the board to search for their name. Abraham Yel, the ordained deacon who led church services in the camp, saw his name on the board after several trips. A camera crew from *60 Minutes II* captured his reaction. "I don't know much about America, but only one thing," Yel told CBS. "I like America because you think of others. You don't think of yourself."

The first flights left Kakuma that fall. Lanky men in khaki pants or dark slacks and untucked button-down striped shirts or short-sleeved pullovers boarded an airplane for the first time in their lives and were carried up on the first leg of a three-day journey to the United States. Others followed in the coming months. By the time Jacob, Peter, Daniel, and Marko saw their names on the board, they had watched hundreds of southern Sudanese refugees leave Kakuma.

Their last days in Africa passed in a blur. Marko bought a pair of acid-washed blue jeans for the journey. Jacob said good-bye to a girl-friend, his younger brother, and two sisters. Peter collected letters from friends in Kakuma addressed to Lost Boys already in the United States. He promised to mail them after he arrived in Atlanta. Daniel walked to the Holy Cross Parish one last time, to say good-bye.

On Saturday, July 14, 2001, the day before they would leave behind all that they had ever known, Peter and other Lost Boys on the way to the United States met with Dinka elders, who pleaded with them to behave well and study. Most importantly, the elders implored, they must remember the people they were leaving behind.

"So when you are there in the United States, you have to remember your land, your land is still in need of you. And when there is any support that is needed, you have to support us," one man told them. "You should not forget that also you are from Sudan, and whatever activity is going on in Sudan is also paining you. Don't think that you are in United States and you forget the war in Sudan. The war that is going on in Sudan is also affecting even people who are in United States. If you go to United States and do well, I think our relationship with USA will be good and that will bring a good relationship between us and United States. But if you do badly, then we shall have no link with the United States at all."

He said those going to the United States would help in the future. "The level you have reached is the level of responsible people. What we want to tell you, these people who are going, is don't forget people left behind. Don't forget southern Sudan. Don't forget your country."

The next day, at two in the afternoon, Jacob, Peter, Daniel, and Marko settled into seats in a two-propeller airplane on a red-dirt runway. Someone showed them how to buckle their lap belts. Then, after some waiting and final checks, the engines roared to life and the airplane began to move, slowly at first and then faster, the camp passing before them outside small windows. It picked up speed and seemed to get louder and then suddenly they were off the ground, looking down at human figures that soon enough looked like ants, the maze of mud huts in the refugee camp spread out beneath them.

Among the few possessions Jacob carried was a small blue date book, compact enough to fit in a pocket. On page eighty-two, in the box for

Sunday, July 15, 2001, he wrote, "Journey from Kakuma to Nairobi. Dpt time: 2:00. Arrival time: 4:15." Another plane took them from Nairobi to Brussels, Belgium, and then on to New York. Agencies that were coordinating their travel put them in a hotel overnight.

About midnight, Jacob lay in a hotel room, too excited to sleep. "There is a reason for the existence of everything," he thought. "There is a reason for me to be in the United States, but I do not know it. So I must ask God." He tried to envision his future, whether and when he would return to a land that he and others referred to as New Sudan. Jacob said he "asked God to help me know what is my potential in the United States." He lay there and prayed for several minutes. Then, in the darkness of his hotel room on his first night in the United States, he sat up in bed and scrawled in that blue day book,

> What have you plan for me?
> What are going to be my achievements here in US?
> What is my future and what am I going to be in NS [New Sudan]?

ARE Y'ALL RESETTLING ANY OF THESE GUYS?

The next day, an airplane flew Jacob, Peter, Daniel, and Marko from New York to Washington. They waited in the airport for a connecting flight that would deliver them to Atlanta. People coming and going from this city to that could not help but give them a second glance, these men with the darkest skin you could imagine and arms that dangled almost to their knees, tall and thin, wide-eyed and out of place. A polite woman struck up a conversation as they waited in the airport in Washington. She offered them some chocolate. Jacob had heard of chocolate but had never tasted it. He put a bite into his mouth, swallowed, and then felt light-headed and faint. His stomach roiled. The woman asked where they were coming from and where they were going. Were they students? They had gotten that question a few times already, though a growing number of Americans seemed to know something about them. In comparison to most refugees, the Lost Boys of Sudan were acquiring a kind of celebrity status in the spring of 2001.

Most Americans could not find Sudan on a map and had no idea of the depths of suffering there, and the arriving refugees provided an entree into a world that would have otherwise remained hidden. It helped that the Lost Boys spoke an archaic, stilted version of English; this somehow had the effect of charming Americans. To many, they sounded quaint. It also helped that most of the young men were polite and eager to learn, qualities that Americans in their late teens and early twenties often were perceived to lack. Here was a group of young men who had been separated from parents and cast into a precarious existence where they had watched friends die, who seemed to have been plucked from another era and dropped into the hustle and bustle of contemporary America. Their story piqued people's curiosity. Many Americans would describe seeing or reading a news account about the resettlement effort and feeling stirred to action as they rarely had been before.

One news story that left an impression aired on the CBS program *60 Minutes II*. It began with video from Sudan—a tank firing, refugees walking—as a narrator told the story. How boys were tending cattle when attackers struck. How they walked away from home for fear that returning would mean death. How this pattern of attack and flight repeated itself in isolated villages until streams of boys flowing east grew into rivers. How they walked barefoot, with no parents to protect them. How they spent four years in Ethiopia only to be expelled and driven to the banks of the Gilo River in May of 1991. "If you don't know how to swim, then you remain in that water," a refugee named Zachariah Magok told the CBS newsman, Bob Simon. "We saw so many people who were just floating in the river."

"Dead bodies?" Simon asked another Lost Boy, Joseph Taban.

"Dead bodies, yes. Floating on the river."

The segment returned to Simon's conversation with Magok. "About how many did you see?" Simon asked.

"One thousand to two thousand were died in that river."

Simon sounded incredulous: "One thousand to two thousand died in that river?"

"Yes."

Simon told how survivors walked back to Sudan and then to Kenya. "Last year, the U.S. decided that enough is enough," Simon said. "If any group could be described as your tired, your poor, your huddled masses yearning to breathe free, it was these Lost Boys from the south of Sudan."

Simon interviewed Sasha Chanoff, the man from Boston who taught cultural-orientation classes. "They feel that education will speak on behalf of them where their parents can't," Chanoff said. "So they have a saying. It's actually a very important saying that they have: 'Education is my mother and father.'"

The segment showed a plane landing on a dirt runway, lines of slender, beaming men waving good-bye. It followed Taban to Kansas City, Missouri, and told of his dreams of saving money for medical school. "How many hours do you want to work every day?" Simon asked.

"I want to work for sixteen hours."

"Excuse me?"

"Sixteen hours."

"That's a lot," Simon said.

"Not a lot to me."

"Why do you want to work sixteen hours a day?"

"I need to have money so that I go to school," he said. "I need to work hard so that I go to school."

The segment also featured Abraham Yel Nhial, the deacon. Simon called him "Abraham the Preacher Man."

"From what he's heard, America is a good place to go on preaching the gospel," Simon said. "He hopes to get there."

Abraham showed Simon the Bible he had carried since his days in Ethiopia. "I have been called a Lost Boy, but I am not lost from God," he said. "I am lost from my parents."

A national audience also met the Lost Boys of Sudan on April 8, 2001, a Sunday, when a story ran in the *New York Times Magazine*. It appeared under the headline, "The Long, Long, Long Road to Fargo" and these sentences: "This is snow. This is a can opener. This is a cereal box. This is a life free from terror." The writer, Sara Corbett, wrote about the adjustment of a group of Lost Boys in Fargo, North Dakota. She described their arrival in the airport, surrounded by "a swirling river of white faces and rolling suitcases, blinking television screens and telephones that rang, inexplicably, from the inside of people's pockets." She visited one apartment of young men on their first morning in the United States. They were reluctant to eat food in their kitchen because they were "uncertain for whom it is designated" and because, having been raised on a gruel of boiled maize, they did not know what to make of a box of Corn Flakes and so circled it "as if it were a museum piece or something that, improperly touched, might explode."

About five hundred of the thirty-eight hundred Lost Boys brought to the United States were under eighteen. The federal government put them with foster families because they were not adults according to U.S. law. Many were terrified to learn that, having arrived in an unfamiliar world, they would live apart from the brothers and colleagues who had been with them for the last dozen years. One of the minors noted that, in American homes, "everybody disappears into their rooms" at night. "Being alone," he said, "makes me think about what's going on in Sudan." Corbett interviewed one set of foster parents in Fargo—"a smiling, earnest couple named Wayne and Carol Reitz." At night, Mrs. Reitz said, the family "occasionally heard mournful singing coming from his bedroom, but bound by politeness and maybe a hint of fear, they left him undisturbed."

Among the hundreds of thousands of people who read those words that day was a woman from Atlanta named Susan Gordon. She and her husband, Kevin, a computer consultant, were on an airplane, flying back from a wedding in Chicago to their home in suburban Atlanta. Susan had worked for years as a computer consultant with one of the big accounting firms and then as a systems analyst at another corporation, but had decided to stay home after she married Kevin and moved to Atlanta in 1993. She and her husband attended a Methodist church in Decatur, a leafy hamlet with a downtown peppered with gourmet coffee shops and trendy restaurants a mile or two east of Atlanta's city limits. Susan had for several years busied herself with volunteering. She donated her time at places such as the Ronald McDonald House and Grace Academy, an after-school program for poor children affiliated with Grace United Methodist Church in Atlanta. She sat on the airplane that Sunday, captivated by the story in the *New York Times Magazine*, and felt, she would later say, "the hand of God working." She never had thought of working with refugees, had rarely thought of refugees at all, but landed in Atlanta with a conviction to try to meet some of these Lost Boys of Sudan. Her heart, she would say, was "literally breaking for these guys."

The next morning, Susan picked up the phone and called the Atlanta office of Lutheran Ministries of Georgia (later renamed Lutheran Services of Georgia), one of the agencies that, according to the magazine article, was coordinating the arrival of the Sudanese refugees. "Are y'all resettling any of these guys?" Susan asked. "Do you need volunteers?"

They did need volunteers, it turned out, and Susan found herself two weeks later at a conference table at Lutheran Ministries with several refugee-agency employees and two other women. One was Dee Clement, the former exercise physiologist who already was bouncing from apartment to apartment to offer company and advice to the young men from southern Sudan. Dee had been around refugees since 1975, when she was a twenty-one-year-old graduate student who earned spending money checking in tennis players at the courts of a private club in north Atlanta. Dee struck up a friendship with two coworkers who cleaned the swimming pool. They were Vietnamese men about her age who had lost track of their families during the fall of Saigon. The United States resettled them in an airlift that offered fresh starts to hundreds of thousands of South Vietnamese. Before long, the men were coming over to Dee's house to teach her and her mother to cook Vietnamese food. She invited them over for Christmas dinner—Dee didn't realize they were Buddhist—and developed a friendship that would span the next twenty years.

In the mid-1990s, Dee and other members of her church helped two families of Bosnian refugees find furniture, secondhand clothes, and televisions. When one of the women got pregnant, Dee took her to one garage sale after another. A few years later, in 1999, Dee sobbed and sobbed while watching television images of Kosovar refugees. When her husband told her to stop crying, she looked at him and asked, suddenly, whether she could go to Macedonia and work in the camps. She did not know what she would do, she said, but maybe her experience treating neck and back injuries and relieving chronic back pain could help. She knew it sounded absurd—massage therapy in a refugee camp—but it was something; it was a start. Maybe she could divert attention from the raw suffering and death that seemed to pulse through the television screen and into her living room. Dee called the Atlanta office of the International Rescue Committee and posed to the director the same question she had to her husband: Can I go to Macedonia to work in the camps? The director told her that several hundred Kosovar refugees were coming to Georgia. He gently suggested she forgo a trip to the Balkans and channel her energy instead into working as a volunteer with the new arrivals. She got off the phone and began calling furniture stores to plead for surplus chairs, tables, and chests. In the next few months, Dee became intimately involved in the lives of Kosovar refugees, taking them to doctor's appointments and grocery stores, helping parents enroll children in school. She kept it at, too, volunteering over the next few years with refugees from Afghanistan, Bosnia, and Iraq, a commitment that meant frequent trips to Clarkston, the town just northeast of downtown Atlanta where nearly one in three people is a refugee. She was there one afternoon, having just delivered clothes to a few women from Congo, when in the parking lot of an apartment complex she bumped into a resettlement-agency caseworker she knew. The caseworker told her about two refugees from southern Sudan he had just left in their apartment. These guys have nothing, the caseworker said. Nothing. The caseworker suggested Dee visit them, and there she was, a few minutes later, knocking on their door. She found them inside in white shoes with red stripes and gray sweatshirts that said "USRP." Dee introduced herself, told them she was there to help and that she would return with something for them. Their apartment had no furniture—the resettlement agency had not yet supplied it—and she raced home and called neighbors to say, in a tone of breathless urgency, as if her house was in flames at that very moment: "I need clothes and shoes right now!" She returned to the apartment later with donated clothes, collected from neighbors in a ritzy Atlanta neighborhood, and was in the kitchen with one of the refugees not too many weeks later when she peered into the dishwasher and spotted a loaf of bread on the bottom rack.

Dee and Susan met that day in the offices of Lutheran Ministries of Georgia with a third volunteer, a woman named Cyndie Heiskell, an administrator at a private Christian school in Atlanta that her family ran. Cyndie, who had volunteered with Vietnamese refugees in the early 1980s, said she had known about the Lost Boys of Sudan for more than eight years. She first saw them, she told people, in a dream that returned on several nights. In it, she said, she saw a line of hundreds of African boys in tattered clothes, walking in a far-off wilderness, desperate. There were no adults or girls. Just a column of boys beckoning to her from the subconscious. Cyndie remembers waking up in bed, distraught, feeling an overwhelming impulse to help.

Cyndie would say years later that the dream had recurred several times by the day in 1992 that she found herself in the waiting room of a doctor's office. Thumbing through a copy of *Life* magazine, Cyndie browsed past stories about the riots in Los Angeles triggered by the acquittal of white police officers charged with beating black motorist Rodney King ("Three Days That Shook America—A Vision of Terror") and past the ad for the all-new Buick Skylark ("A lasting impression for the nineties") but stopped suddenly at page fifty. There Cyndie saw a color photo of bedraggled boys walking in a line through an African forest. "Hunted by lions and hyenas, living on leaves and bark, swarms of boys wander the wilderness in a nation ravaged by a long and bloody civil war," the text said.

Cyndie said she believed the children in the photo were the ones she had seen in her dreams. She had not known, she would say, that the Holy Spirit could talk to you in a dream, but how else to explain her dream and the photographs in *Life*? Cyndie asked a receptionist if she could have the magazine. She returned home and kept it on a table in her kitchen for the next eight years.

During that time, she confided the story to friends. She concluded that God had planted the dream in her mind and had revealed to her the story of the Lost Boys because he meant for her to do something about their suffering. She tried. She was no expert in the Sudanese war—who was?—but she knew more than many Americans. Church groups and missionaries had made presentations at her school and church about the famine in the Horn of Africa in the mid-1980s. In fact, she knew an

Ethiopian preacher in Atlanta well enough to ask him about the Lost Boys of Sudan she read about in *Life* magazine. He told Cyndie that several thousand boys had recently crossed into northern Kenya and that the United Nations High Commissioner for Refugees had built a camp for them at a place called Kakuma. The preacher happened to be planning a trip to that very camp. Cyndie set out to raise money he could deliver, a small but tangible way of helping those boys who she felt so desperately needed her help. Their story touched her in a way no other news account had. She could not understand why the newspapers and television news programs in the United States were not paying more attention to the story. It was as if she apprehended something that everyone around her ignored or did not understand. Cyndie would tell friends over the next several years that she felt guilty for not doing more, as if she were ignoring a calling from God. Eventually, she said, she came to believe she could help by praying, and so she did. She may never have met them were it not for a chance encounter at North Avenue Presbyterian Church in Atlanta one day in early 2001. She went there to hear a missionary speak about reconciliation—he talked specifically about reconciliation between Dinka and Nuer rebels who had fought a bloody internecine war in southern Sudan in the early 1990s. After the presentation, she told him she had been praying for many years about an unusual group of refugees from southern Sudan. Had he ever heard of the Lost Boys of Sudan? Not only did the missionary know about the group, he told Cyndie a few thousand were coming to the United States. Her heart raced. Cyndie interpreted the coming of the Lost Boys to the United States as a confirmation of all she had believed since the spring of 1992, that God had spoken to her in a dream, chosen her for a role in the lives of young men she did not even know. The missionary steered Cyndie to a web site for World Relief, a refugee-resettlement agency. There she learned that World Relief was resettling several Lost Boys in Atlanta and that the agency needed volunteers to work with this unique new population. Cyndie called the agency and asked whether any of the young men from southern Sudan had been resettled in Atlanta yet. Years later, she would cry when she recalled the reply: "The first two came yesterday, and they need a mother."

Cyndie brought them pencils, paper, and a Bible. She asked about their lives and one of the roommates got so emotional in recounting his experiences that he pulled a shirt up over his head to hide his face. As more Lost Boys arrived, Cyndie found herself shuttling between apartments in Clarkston "from sunup to sundown" to attend to their needs and fulfill one of her own, a mothering impulse that found an outlet at work, surrounded by schoolchildren, but not at home. Like Susan and Dee, Cyndie had no children of her own. All three became fiercely protective of what they perceived to be the refugees' best interests. The more they got involved in the young men's lives, however, the more disillusioned they grew with the agencies that had resettled them.

Agencies supply kitchen staples to new arrivals, for instance, and Cyndie was outraged to learn that Lutheran Ministries was supplying Lost Boys with out-of-date pork from a local food bank. Cyndie was also aghast after visiting an apartment rented for four Lost Boys. You had to walk through standing water, she said, to get to the squalid apartment. She decried a "flippant attitude" from some resettlement-agency workers who seemed to resent her concern. She also rebelled against what she saw as the agencies' desire to control volunteers: "They want to tell you exactly what to do and what not to do."

Cyndie suspected she might have found an ally when she saw another middle-aged white woman step out of a Ford Explorer one day in the parking lot of an apartment complex where several Lost Boys lived. White, middle-aged, middle-class women were rarities in the complex, home mostly to refugees and young African American men or couples, and Cyndie soon was chatting with Dee Clement, who seemed as driven as she by the need to spend time with the Lost Boys. Later, after Susan Gordon read about the resettlement in the *New York Times Magazine*, all three women went to a conference room at Lutheran Ministries for a meeting about the needs of this group.

Afterward, Cyndie took Susan to an apartment in Clarkston to introduce her to some refugees. Susan recalled docile young men who wowed her with cheerful dispositions despite overwhelming needs. Her husband was in Denver on business, so Susan came home to an empty house. She said she sank into her living-room sofa and sobbed as she thought about the young men from Sudan.

This was happening all over the United States, mainly because of widespread news coverage of the resettlement effort. Newspapers such as the *Philadelphia Inquirer* and the *Houston Chronicle* covered the story. The *Boston Globe* sent a reporter to Kakuma. Papers often printed the phone numbers of resettlement agencies along with the stories. Many Americans who would become involved as volunteers did so after reading about them in a newspaper or magazine or hearing their story on TV. After reading a story in the *Atlanta Journal-Constitution*, one woman raced to Wal-Mart to buy $239 worth of mops, brooms, razors, shaving cream, soap, toilet paper, paper towels, and sidewalk chalk. Others offered their time as volunteers and mentors. Stories were told and retold in dozens of newspapers, and, in the fall, Tom Brokaw narrated a one-hour special on *Dateline NBC*. Most refugees arrive in the United States without such fanfare, mainly because most do not come as part of such an unusual group. Many come to rejoin relatives who already have been resettled, but the media has shone its spotlight before on groups of refugees offered shelter by the United States, including the Vietnamese, Bosnians, and Kosovars.

Dee was just one of thousands moved in the late 1990s by television images of Kosovar refugees. Resettlement agencies in Atlanta were deluged with phone calls then, too. They prefer volunteers offering whatever help is needed, with whatever group of refugees needs assistance, but often find themselves talking with people who want to help, say, Bosnians and only Bosnians, or Sudanese and only Sudanese, the groups they had seen on television. The agencies had to be careful. One resettlement director in Atlanta recalled a farmer who called during the Kosovar crisis in 1999. He wanted two women to come help with farm work and who knew what else. A few others seemed to be fishing for servants or maids. So the antennas were up when people in metro Atlanta started calling in the spring of 2001. Agencies conducted workshops to teach recruits how they could provide help beyond what the refugees already received.

The State Department guarantees that each refugee resettled in the United States will receive certain help for one month, but most refugees receive aid for a few additional months through one of two primary assistance programs. The rationale for providing assistance is that refugees come to the United States with nothing and need some financial help to become self-sufficient. Unlike immigrants, who choose to come to the United States, often for a better job or to rejoin relatives, refugees typically are people who were forced to flee home. The level and duration of assistance a refugee receives after the first month depends on which of the two federal assistance programs he or she is enrolled in by the resettlement agency. In Georgia, most refugees participate in a program that pays the rent and power bill through their fourth month in the United States. Then they are on their own except for public assistance programs, such as food stamps, that are available to anyone who meets income and legal-residency requirements.

Nationally, the State Department has contracts with ten nonprofit organizations that receive federal money to resettle refugees through about 450 affiliate offices in cities such as Atlanta. The State Department pays resettlement agencies to provide services for thirty days to all refugees resettled by the United States. Resettlement agencies must meet new arrivals at the airport and provide them with safe and sanitary housing. They are required to provide groceries or a food allowance to cover the first two or three weeks, "appropriate seasonal clothing," job training, and transportation to job interviews. Agencies also are responsible for furnishing a refugee's apartment with items that include beds, drawers, a kitchen table with enough chairs for everyone in the apartment or house, a couch, one lamp for each room without an overhead light, one place setting of silverware for everyone in the apartment, pots and pans, an alarm clock, lightbulbs, dish soap, laundry detergent, trash bags, toilet paper, shampoo, soap, toothpaste, and a toothbrush for each person. If needed, agencies provide pocket money during the first month. They also are required to help refugees apply for a Social Security card and, if needed, cash and medical assistance and food stamps. In addition, the agency is required to explain personal and public safety, the local health-care system, public transportation, and the availability of public support programs.

After the first thirty days, most refugees receive additional help through one of two main federally funded assistance programs. Roughly 60 percent of refugees nationwide receive Refugee Cash Assistance. Under that program, the federal government provides a monthly payment to the refugees for up to eight months, though the aid typically ends after a refugee goes to work. For a single person in Georgia, Refugee Cash Assistance paid $155 a month in 2003. A similar program, Refugee Medical Assistance, provides some health-care coverage for up to eight months, but most of the Lost Boys resettled in metro Atlanta received assistance after their first thirty days through the federal Matching Grant program, administered by the federal Office of Refugee Resettlement, part of the U.S. Department of Health and Human Services.

The Matching Grant program, designed to encourage self-sufficiency within four months, bars refugees who participate from receiving other forms of federal welfare assistance. As the program's name implies, the federal government awards matching grants to resettlement agencies. For every two dollars the government provides, the resettlement agencies are to chip in one dollar in cash, goods, or services (the guidelines say at least 20 percent must be in cash). The money pays a refugee's rent and power bill for three months. Also, resettlement agencies provide refugees with two hundred dollars a month in pocket money through their fourth month in the United States. They also provide financial incentives to attend classes and go to work—several Lost Boys who were resettled in Atlanta received about $150 to go to computer and English classes and another $300 for transportation and uniforms after they found a job. Resettlement agencies agree to provide job counseling and take refugees to interviews, if necessary. As a condition of receiving the grant money, agencies also agree to offer English classes or refer refugees to agencies that do.

Guidelines govern the work of resettlement agencies that receive money through the various programs, but the level of service any one refugee receives can vary depending on his resettlement agency. A handful of Lost Boys resettled by a small agency in Atlanta complained that it provided them twenty dollars each for food in their first week in the United States but promptly subtracted ten dollars for clothing even though the State Department funnels money to resettlement agencies to provide clothes. Two Lost Boys resettled by the same agency said they were taken from the airport to an apartment with no furniture. They said a caseworker put them in a hotel for a few days and then moved them into a furnished unit. When Dee Clement came by to introduce herself as a friend and volunteer, she was alarmed to find six young men in an apartment and only a head of cabbage in the refrigerator. She complained to the men's resettlement agency and received twenty dollars to buy more food.

For refugees who come to the United States to rejoin relatives, there is less need for help from a volunteer. In those cases, the relative in America—agencies call him or her an "anchor"—usually agrees to meet the new arrival at the airport and provide entree into the community by explaining the grocery store and emergency phone numbers and by helping the newcomer find a place to live. It's a different story for refugees who have no family members awaiting them. Resettlement workers call them "free cases" and try to match them with Americans willing to help. Some agencies find church congregations willing to help refugees acclimate. Members of a congregation are told to help for three or four months. Other agencies recruit volunteers from the general public. What a volunteer does depends on the amount of time he or she has and the refugees' needs. One volunteer may explain how to establish phone service and drive people to the grocery store. Others may give cooking lessons or take refugees to the bank to open checking and savings accounts. News accounts of the Lost Boys' coming to Atlanta and to the rest of the United States swelled the ranks of volunteers, and resettlement agencies found themselves answering more and more phone calls from people eager to help these Sudanese teenagers and young men. It did not take long for a pattern to emerge.

For one thing, most of the volunteers were women. They tended to be in the middle or upper class, professional women or the wives of doctors or executives. There were exceptions, of course, but many volunteers were suburban women in their forties and early fifties with no children of their own. Some saw in the Lost Boys an opportunity to nurture and, at the same time, become acquainted with someone with dark skin, a real person from Africa. Many lived in mostly white neighborhoods and had little contact with African Americans, a common pattern in the American South that cultivated, for some, a fear of the unknown, shaped and refined by whispered rumors and television stereotypes. Volunteering with the Lost Boys allowed them a safe adventure with people who were so different yet, much to the relief of the volunteers, not so different as to prevent acquaintance. There was an aura of excitement, the promise of a delightful excursion from the ho-hum routine of an air-conditioned world with few surprises. Most Lost Boys spoke English, after all, and tended to worship in a Christian church. Some women who volunteered would talk breathlessly at first about meeting the refugees, as if they had gone to the moon. Here finally, it seemed, was an adventure, exotic but safe. Yet it would be wrong to say that the women volunteered for primarily selfish reasons. In the next two years, many would invest hundreds of hours and up to several thousand dollars of their own money to shepherd the Lost Boys into American life. They would be the ones to determine whether the young men got the education they craved. And if they were at times pushy and protective, well, the refugees seemed willing to accept that as part of a bargain that delivered them a guide. Most volunteers went through a brief orientation and were matched with an apartment with four, five, or six Sudanese youth, but Dee, Susan, and Cyndie, much to the consternation of resettlement agencies, were freelance volunteers who did not align themselves with any agency and instead moved from apartment to apartment, offering help to whomever needed it.

The independent volunteers were hard-charging women who approached their tasks with a missionary zeal. They became unabashedly aggressive advocates for whatever needs they perceived among the Lost Boys of Sudan. The Atlanta director of one resettlement agency later would acknowledge their good intentions but also remember women who were accusatory, pushy, and demanding. "I've never been spoken to the way those women spoke to me," she would say. "They were hostile." Some hardcore volunteers also were quick to suspect that resettlement agencies were not doing enough. One was appalled to find that a resettlement agency had included Sara Lee coffee cake among the provisions in one apartment. She tossed it out because she "wouldn't let them eat all those preservatives and crap." She reported finding an inordinate amount of butter and sausage in another kitchen. Incensed, she split the butter among several apartments, threw away the sausage, and complained to the national office of the agency that supplied the food.

Another volunteer zeroed in on what she saw as financial impropriety after she got to know some Sudanese refugees resettled by Lutheran Ministries of Georgia. The agency was obliged to provide spending money to each of the refugees it resettled for four months, but, instead of giving a refugee his entire monthly allotment in one sum, Lutheran Ministries was distributing it in weekly payments. Refugees resettled by other agencies were getting their monthly two hundred dollars all at once, while those resettled by Lutheran Ministries received the money in fifty-dollar increments. A volunteer who thought refugees were getting just fifty dollars a month through Lutheran Ministries—rather than fifty dollars a week four times a month—was so convinced that someone was embezzling money that she phoned a prosecutor in the DeKalb County district attorney's office. He promised to investigate if she uncovered evidence of wrongdoing, but the volunteer realized later that the young men had been getting the full amount in the end. The agency directors did not question the motives of the volunteers, who were doing what they thought was in the refugees' best interests. But one of the agencies, the Christian Council of Metropolitan Atlanta (later renamed Refugee Resettlement and Immigration Services of Atlanta), distributed a sheet entitled "*Dos* and *Don'ts* of Refugee Resettlement," which summarized, under the heading of "Don't," some concerns that other agencies had about a few volunteers. The sheet warned people to avoid "the trap of giving as a form of self-gratification" and urged them not to "keep the refugee dependent on you. Remember your goal is to assist them in becoming self-sufficient." There was also this: "Don't smother them or try to possess them. They have been making their own decisions for years." Some of the volunteers could have used such admonishment, but their possessiveness would eventually pale in comparison to that of other American women in Atlanta who were yet to emerge as self-anointed guardians.

Some volunteers, meanwhile, said that agency caseworkers did not spend enough time with some of the young men. The agencies responded by saying the volunteers might be unaware that caseworkers handle 125 cases or more in a year. Most caseworkers are former refugees who understand the refugee experience, but a controversy dogged at least one Atlanta caseworker. Some volunteers said he was too harsh with the Lost

Boys, too demanding. They suspected he was short with them because he was Muslim and the Sudanese refugees were Christians. One volunteer described him as lazy. "The less they have to do, the happier they are. I think it's an Arab thing," she said. The caseworker's boss said she questioned some of the refugees assigned to the caseworker. Did they feel comfortable with him? she asked. Sure, they said. They liked him. They called him Uncle.

The caseworker who met Jacob, Peter, Daniel, and Marko at the airport, Mathew Kon, was a Dinka from southern Sudan, like the majority of Lost Boys. He would emerge as a problem solver for the Atlanta Lost Boys in the next two years, someone to call if you had questions about car insurance or a power bill. Volunteers like Mathew, Cyndie, Dee, Cheryl, and Susan would field dozens of questions about the mysteries of everyday life: What could be done about a cordless phone that did not work? How did one get rid of roaches in the kitchen? There were larger questions, too: Why did people drive everywhere in Atlanta? Why were there so few Americans on the sidewalks? The volunteers eventually would talk about whether and how the refugees could pursue their education, but there was a more immediate concern. Before the refugees in apartment 40-G could talk seriously about going to school, they had to figure out how to pay the rent. Like so many refugees who came before them, they had to find a job.

Separated from parents in the swirling chaos of war, in the late 1980s boys from several parts of southern Sudan walked hundreds of miles toward the promise of safety in Ethiopia. Thousands died along the way. Reporters and relief workers dubbed survivors the Lost Boys of Sudan after the Peter Pan characters who are cast without parents into the world of adults. © Wendy Stone/Corbis. Corbis DWF15-257640.

The four Lost Boys who arrived in Atlanta on United Airlines flight 1905 on July 18, 2001, were guided into everyday life in the United States by Mathew Kon, a fellow southern Sudanese who worked as a caseworker at the Atlanta office of the International Rescue Committee, a nonprofit refugee-resettlement agency. Seen here *(from left)* are Kon, Marko Ayii, Daniel Khoch, Jacob Magot, and Peter Anyang. Photograph courtesy of Jacob Magot.

Mathew Kon explains how to use the Atlanta transit system. Photograph by John Spink for the *Atlanta Journal-Constitution*.

An American volunteer delivered an electric typewriter to the young men of Apartment 40-G at Clarkston's Olde Plantation Apartments shortly after their arrival. For young men who prized education above most everything else, this instrument of the written word was something worth getting excited about. Jacob Magot types as roommates *(from left)* Peter Anyang, Daniel Khoch, and Marko Ayii look over his shoulder. Photograph by T. Levette Bagwell for the *Atlanta Journal-Constitution*.

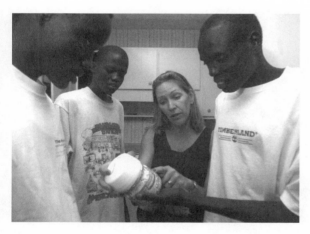

Peter Anyang pointed to a container of orange powder, uncertain of its purpose. "It is written here, 'Tang,'" he said, "but we do not know if it is healthy." Dee Clement, an American volunteer, explained. Photograph by T. Levette Bagwell for the *Atlanta Journal-Constitution*.

Two weeks after arriving in Atlanta, Peter Anyang and his roommates went to the home of Cheryl Grover, a real-estate consultant who volunteered to mentor them. Peter said that the grass and trees in the suburbs reminded him of southern Sudan. Photograph by Mark Bixler.

When Cheryl Grover first took several young men to Lake Lanier near Atlanta, they asked whether crocodiles or hippopotamus lurked in the lake. The last time they had been near such a large body of water, while crossing the Gilo River from Ethiopia to Sudan in 1991, hundreds of boys had been killed by crocodiles or sucked under by a raging current, never to surface alive. It took little time at Lake Lanier for the young men to relax. Shown here are four of the six young men who were roommates in Apartment 40-G: *(from left)* Daniel Deng, Jacob Magot, William Dut, and Daniel Khoch. Photograph courtesy of Jacob Magot.

A week after arriving in Atlanta, Jacob Magot received a broom and a bucket with a bottle of Pine Sol from the International Rescue Committee. He also received a dictionary and a GED study guide, tied together with a silver ribbon by an IRC worker. Photograph by John Spink for the *Atlanta Journal-Constitution*.

The federal government paid the rent and power bill for four months. Then the refugees were essentially on their own. A job developer with the International Rescue Committee, Ben Cushman, helped Jacob Magot prepare for an interview at the Discovery Channel Store at Lenox Mall, an upscale shopping center in Atlanta. Jacob got the job. Some days he worked there for several hours, caught a few hours' sleep, and then rode a bus to an overnight job stocking shelves in a department store. Photograph Charlotte B. Teagle for the *Atlanta Journal-Constitution*.

Jacob Magot was so dedicated to his education that he often
would fall asleep studying a GED guide after working
overnight. He received his high-school diploma in July 2003,
at the end of his second year in the United States. A few hours
after graduation, he reported for duty at a security-guard job,
worked overnight, and arose the next morning to attend class at
a community college near his home. Photograph courtesy
of Jacob Magot.

Daniel Khoch grew frustrated fast in Atlanta. Well-intentioned Americans kept talking about GED classes that never materialized. He left Atlanta about five months after arriving in search of a better future in South Dakota, a trip that would eventually lead to a classroom in Iowa. Photograph courtesy of Jacob Magot.

Daniel Khoch was the first of the young men in Apartment 40-G at Olde Plantation Apartments to find his way into a classroom. He followed his dream of becoming a priest to Divine Word College, a Roman Catholic seminary with about one hundred students in Epworth, Iowa. Photograph by Clint Austin for the *Atlanta Journal-Constitution*.

Peter Anyang started classes at Georgia Perimeter College in the spring of 2003. Some days he went to class from 8 a.m. to noon, slept for two hours, and then went to work from 3 p.m. to 11 p.m. He hoped to study computers and business. Photograph by Mark Bixler.

Marko Ayii found work in a meat-packing plant about thirty-five miles south of Atlanta. He left around 5 a.m. and returned exhausted around 7 p.m. After many months of this grueling routine, shared by several of his roommates, Marko went to live in the Atlanta suburbs with Carolyn Geddes, a semiretired travel agent who became his legal guardian so he could go to high school. Marko started his junior year in August 2004. Photograph by Mark Bixler.

BODY LANGUAGE IN THE WORKPLACE

Thirteen days after arriving in Atlanta, on a Tuesday, Jacob rode a bus to
the offices of the nonprofit International Rescue Committee. He got off
the bus and walked into the Kensington Office Park off Memorial Drive,
a complex of two-story office buildings labeled "A," "B," "C," and "D."
He followed a sidewalk to building A and opened a door on the ground
level. In the room he had entered was a yellow Post-it note stuck to the
wall that said "wall" and another on the window that said "window."
Jacob sat at a table with an Iranian family of three and an Iraqi man. In
the center of the room stood an American woman in her early thirties
named Robin Harp. She worked for the IRC, helping refugees find jobs
and looking for employers willing to hire refugees.

When she learned of this group of Lost Boys bound for Atlanta,
Robin and her coworkers counted on a relatively easy time finding jobs
for these men who spoke English and seemed so eager to work. It was
true that most Lost Boys lacked experience working for wages, so job
developers would have to be creative when they helped the refugees
fill out resumes that asked about previous work history. Yet jobs were

plentiful in Atlanta in early 2001, as the resettlement agencies were preparing for this new population. Robin and her coworkers in the employment program hoped to steer the Lost Boys into cleaning jobs in places such as universities and hospitals on the rationale that such jobs were stable, paid decent wages, and were less likely than manufacturing jobs to be affected by layoffs in the event of a recession, which was appearing more likely with each passing day. Still, around March 2001, the job developers were having little trouble placing Lost Boys in Atlanta in jobs that paid seven to eight dollars an hour. By August, though, it seemed that the available jobs were paying only six to seven dollars an hour. With the economy sputtering toward recession, employers were getting choosy. Hotels that once hired refugees with no experience as maids suddenly demanded housekeeping experience.

Robin stood in the middle of the room that Tuesday with a three-ring notebook in her hand. She glanced down occasionally to remind herself of points to cover in the basic employment orientation. "In the United States," Robin began, "there is an attitude that if you're healthy and you're capable and you can work, then the government should not give you money and you should work."

Jacob nodded.

"Your first job will be difficult and you probably will not like it," Robin said, "but remember, it's just a starting point." She said they would most likely start work during their second month and that they could expect to earn about $6.50 to $7.00 an hour. An IRC job developer would take them from business to business so they could fill out applications and get to interviews. She passed around a sample application, from Waffle House, noting that "just because you fill out a job application does not mean you get the job."

She urged them to make eye contact during interviews. "Show that you're interested in what the person says even if you can't understand everything the person is saying," Robin said. "You should wear the very best clothes you have to the interview. You should not talk about your personal problems. In American culture, one of the most important things in a job interview is the handshake." Robin strolled around the room, shaking hands with everyone in the class. She held out her hand for a refugee who grasped it limply. "More firmly," she said.

He squeezed.

"Good." She shook hands with Jacob and the three Iranians and the man from Iraq. She told them to be gracious to interviewers. "After it's all over, before you leave, say 'Thank you,'" she said.

Robin reminded them that their first job would not be easy or fun. "You may have to ride up to an hour and a half to the job and an hour and a half back. Keep in mind, the first job is a starting point just so you can meet expenses," she said. "We expect you to take the first job that's offered to you or that we find for you. Do you know what 'fired' is?" she asked.

"Yes," Jacob replied. "It is to be dismissed."

She passed around a sheet that said: "Top 5 Ways to Get Fired: Body odor or lack of cleanliness; tardiness, missing work, or not calling in when sick; not trying to learn English; working too slowly; and showing little interest in the job. You also have to remember that it's very hot in the summer in this part of the country. It's very important before you go to work each day to take a shower and wear clean clothes," she said. "Americans are very sensitive to the way things smell." Robin dealt with companies that hire refugees and knew that body odor was one reason companies cited for firing refugees. "Deodorant is something that is very important for Americans to wear every day. It smells kind of sweet. You put it under your arms," she said. "Wear it every day." Once they got a job, Robin said, they should make certain they understood how often they would be paid.

In the meantime, they would receive spending money of two hundred dollars a month for their first four months in Atlanta. Jacob, Peter, Daniel, and Marko sent most of the money back to Kakuma, to help Sudanese refugees still there. They would talk about how little food refugees received in the camp, what bleak futures awaited those who were not bound for the United States. The threat of violence enveloped the camp, they said, and people who got sick had a hard time getting medicine and treatment. Refugees in Kakuma could use money for trips to Nairobi to go to hospitals, make long-distance phone calls, or buy food. The Lost Boys in apartment 40-G did not say they felt guilty at having been plucked from windswept desolation and delivered to America, but they did not have to say it. The words of a Dinka elder, spoken the day before they left Africa, echoed in their minds: "What we want to tell you, these people who are going, is don't forget people left behind. Don't forget southern Sudan. Don't forget your country."

And so Jacob, Peter, Daniel, Marko, John, and William took the first two hundred dollars in spending money they received from the International Rescue Committee, marched to a money-wiring business, and sent it to people still in Kakuma. They did that after receiving two hundred dollars the second month, too. The IRC was using money from the federal government to pay their rent and power bill and giving them tokens for public transportation. They had few other expenses. They ate once a day, usually rice or chicken with slices of bread and a glass of water. Most days they passed in their apartment reading donated books or hanging out in apartments of others from Kakuma. Cheryl Grover donated a computer and showed them how to use it. She taught them about the Internet and established free e-mail accounts for them. They spent several hours at her house one day for a course on sending and receiving messages.

"Today I am learning how to write an Email and trying to send you this letter to see if I know how to do it myself," Peter wrote in his first message. "John, Jacob, Marko and William are doing different things on the computer too. Please write and tell me how it look like so that I can improve next time. Thanks you very much."

Marko was more succinct: "I am learning in computer in Mrs. Cheryl home today and good-bye."

Their minds were crowded with life lessons as they waited to work. They would learn something from Cheryl or Dee and then spread the word when talking with other Sudanese. Or they would hear something from friends about life in the United States and ask an American friend about it the next chance they got. Most often they compared notes about jobs. They had so absorbed messages of self-reliance, given by players at several steps along the way from Africa to Atlanta, and of the need to support their kinsmen who stayed behind, that their sense of pride and self-worth was tied up in this desire to live up to the pressure they felt to hurry up and find a job. So Jacob, Peter, Daniel, and Marko were excited the day they went to Mathew's office to apply for Social Security cards.

"We were told that we need Social Security to work," Daniel said. "Is this true?"

Yes, they were told.

"We were told that you must wait three to four weeks to get the Social Security. Is this true?"

Yes.

"That is a very long time," Daniel said.

Soon enough, the IRC matched them with a job developer. Jacob and his roommate from the same region of southern Sudan, John, were paired with Benjamin Cushman, a man in his mid-twenties who had worked in Africa in the Peace Corps and who dressed smartly in khakis, button-down shirts, and ties, a rare look in the more casual world of refugee resettlement. Jacob and John called him Mr. Benjamin out of respect for the power he wielded. They had been told they could look for a job on their own, but in practice they had no conception of how they might do this. They knew by reading the book they each received, *Welcome to the United States: A Guidebook for Refugees*, that skilled-labor and professional jobs usually required formal training and a college degree, and so were beyond their grasp. "[E]ntry-level jobs," the book said, "are those which require little training or experience, such as hotel housekeeper, restaurant helper or factory worker. They usually pay an hourly wage and don't require a high level of English. Many refugees work in these jobs while studying English or learning other skills."

Mr. Benjamin reinforced this point. Like Robin, he told Jacob and John to expect to start in a job that required little experience or training. He took them to a grocery store to fill out applications to work stocking shelves or bagging groceries. Then it was off to a hotel to follow up on the possibility of a job stocking refrigerators, but there was some confusion, and by the time Jacob and John arrived, the positions already had been filled. Peter, Daniel, and Marko were going through the same drill. They completed applications and went home to wait.

After a few weeks, Jacob came to a conclusion about employers in the United States. "When they say they will call you," he said, "we know we will not get the job. It means they will not call you." After six weeks, he began to worry. "Here in America, it is through jobs that you can make your life to be very successful, but if you have no jobs, then you cannot make it," Jacob said one afternoon. "I don't know whether I will make it . . . but I am trying if possible."

Other southern Sudanese youth around the country also faced a bumpy ride on the road to work. One young man in Louisville, Kentucky declined to work in a cafeteria on the grounds that it was "women's work," but Jacob could not wait to go to work. He figured the first job would be a paycheck, not much else, but that a college education would open the door to more fulfilling work later. "The problem that will lead me not to get a better job is because I have no skill, and it is through college that I will get that skill," he said. "And the jobs will help me to help my people back in Africa." He and his roommates appreciated the help paying the rent and utilities, but they were beginning to realize how much everyday necessities cost. "Things are very expensive. It is something which affects every citizen here in America," Jacob said one day. "If one gets a job, one can be like everyone else." He noticed that the Americans around him somehow seemed to manage. If they could, he figured, he could, too.

Jacob and his roommates were picking up clues about America every day that they waited for the phone to ring with a job offer. After Cheryl helped them establish phone service, John emerged from the apartment one day to announce, "I have learned to use telephonic communication." Peter rode in a car past the Clarkston campus of Georgia Perimeter College, a school with a large international population. "One day, we shall go to that college," he said. An American friend drove him, Jacob, Daniel, and Marko to Pizza Hut for their first taste of pizza. They were stymied by the options at the soft-drink fountain machine. Would it be Pepsi or Mountain Dew? Orange Slice or Dr. Pepper? The young men did not ask how to conjure ice and soda from the machine but watched others before them press clear red plastic glasses against a lever that sent ice tumbling through a black funnel. Their eyes followed glasses move to one of eight levers dangling beneath a plastic nozzle. Push the lever and out comes a drink. Easy enough. Later, at a table, after the pizza arrived, Jacob, Peter, Daniel, and Marko hesitated. The others watched as Jacob cut a piece with his fork and knife and held it in front of his mouth, steam rising.

He put it in his mouth and looked down at the table, chewing slowly. He raised his head and said, "This is good." The others followed his lead. They ate one slice each.

Peter picked up a bottle of grated mozzarella. "What is this?" he asked.

"Salt," Jacob said.

"Sugar," Daniel said.

Told it was a kind of cheese you could sprinkle on food, Peter nodded and replaced it. Jacob stirred his Orange Slice with a straw and Daniel asked him in Dinka why he was doing that. Peter and Marko laughed, as if stirring one's drink with a straw might be some breach of protocol. "It is my own way," Jacob said. "If I stir my drink it does not matter." He pointed to a jukebox. "What is this machine?" he asked.

Another time, they rode with a friend toward downtown Atlanta, awed again by the cars and trucks. They were everywhere. Jacob worried that "an accident will happen if there is an impatient driver." No one seemed to walk in Georgia. The young men peered through the car windows at all the traffic and at some of the billboards they had seen as Mathew drove them from the airport on their first day in Georgia. The highway took them to the edge of downtown, within sight of that cluster of buildings reaching like fingers toward the sky. They followed smaller roads, under a bridge or two and up a small hill, into the heart of downtown Atlanta. After the car stopped, Jacob, Peter, Daniel, and Marko spilled out into a parking lot just as a train whistle pierced the afternoon. They heard a low sputtering rumble, like thunder, the combined sound of car and truck motors revving or idling, this gear shifting and that brake squealing. The sound of a siren grew louder and louder and then suddenly diminished. A recurring staccato blast reminiscent of machine-gunfire whipped down a sidewalk, but men and women in business clothes walked on, unfazed, and the roommates traced the sound after a moment to a man who wore faded blue jeans and an orange vest over a white T-shirt. He grasped a motorized drill in both hands. It vibrated wildly and expelled puffs of smoke as it chewed asphalt around his feet. A smell like gasoline drifted toward them in the parking lot as they craned their necks upward to see dozens of buildings a hundred times their height. Their gaze went first to the back of a ten-story red brick building directly in front of them. Dozens of silver-colored pipes snaked up it, humming as if alive and coughing out wisps of white smoke. Two rust-colored staircases zigzagged down, from the top of the building to street level, where a sign said "Checks Cashed" in yellow and, below that, in red, "24 Hours." Jacob followed the stairs with his eyes and laughed at the idea that people actually lived and worked in a building in the sky. Marko absorbed the scene in silence, staying close to Daniel. Peter turned to the right to see another building rising into the sky. This one was sleek and modern, with windows of dark glass between beige ledges. He looked in another direction and there, through an alley, he saw that round glass building with "WESTIN" written at the top.

All around them were buildings they had seen from the air, when the United Airlines jet descended through clouds on a brilliant summer afternoon to reveal miles of green trees that define Atlanta from the air. They walked down Marietta Street a few dozen yards and Jacob stopped and pointed and laughed again. He chattered in Dinka with his roommates and they followed his gaze to a four-story parking garage, a building where, from the street, you could see rows of cars parked on each level, trunks and rear lights facing the street. The young men laughed at the thought of a house for cars and trucks. They asked about passageways inside the building that allowed cars and trucks to move up and tried to understand why anyone would build something to store cars. Another marvel awaited across Cone Street, an imposing tall building made of glass that reflected clouds passing overhead. Jacob knew of buildings of stone and wood, but who would have thought that someone would have constructed a building from glass?

"I was really pleased and I was really a little bit confused about the tall buildings," he said later. "I was really surprised with how they came up with the technology to build that big, big, big building out of glass. I could not imagine how was it possible for man to come up with that decision, to build a tall building. It is something very, very, very nice about America, that one can get that knowledge to do such things."

American life raised a thousand questions for the four men. They heard that nearly half of all marriages end in divorce. How was that possible in so prosperous a land? They also had heard that sometimes in the United States that men go with men. They doubted at first it was true, but the rumors were confirmed when a friend reported seeing a man dressed as a woman on a MARTA bus. "He wore short white pants and had applied some chemicals here," the friend said, moving his hands in circles in front of his cheeks. "He was wearing the woman's shoes and he had applied the lipstick. He was having a ring in his ear. And the hairstyle identifies him as a woman. And the way he moves is like a lady."

They saw more men than women on public transportation and concluded that more women owned cars. Why was that? And why did they see so many people in the United States who were overweight? They had heard that something called the Olympics had been held in Atlanta a few years before they arrived. Was that some sort of play? They waited for answers while they waited for employers to call. There would be plenty of time to figure out modern America, but they would be in trouble if they did not find a job. Jacob, Peter, Daniel, and Marko had each filled out several applications and had been told to wait for calls that never seemed to come. So Jacob was thrilled when Mr. Benjamin phoned six weeks after his arrival to say there were some openings at the Discovery Channel Store, a shop that sold telescopes, books, videos, games, and toys such as remote-control hovercraft. The store needed part-time help through the winter holidays. A manager would interview Jacob about 2 p.m. on the first Friday in September.

Jacob tried to remember what Robin had said: Wear your best clothes, make eye contact, sound interested. And the handshake—that was important. They couldn't forget to give a firm handshake. On the morning of the interview, Jacob awoke early and dressed in tasseled black wingtips, khaki pants, and a dull blue shirt with a navy tie that had red polka dots, donated clothes he received through the IRC. He tucked his Social Security card into a manila envelope with Form I-94, the official record of his legal arrival in the United States. It took a few years for refugees to receive the green cards of legal permanent residents—they could not apply until they were in the United States for one year and then faced waits that varied from a few months to two years, depending on how short-staffed and overworked the local INS office happened to be when they applied. Jacob and his roommates would need to produce the I-94 at job interviews to verify their eligibility to work, so they kept it in a safe place.

Jacob rode a bus to the MARTA train station, where he met Mr. Benjamin and another job developer named Valerie. His roommate, John, would interview, too, and the four rode on the east line in the middle of the day to downtown Atlanta, where they got off and boarded another train headed north. They rode in silence for a few minutes. Then Valerie turned to Jacob. "You look very nice," she said. "I don't think I've had another client wear a tie for a job interview."

"Thank you," he said, smiling.

The train stopped at Lenox Mall, a sprawling three-story magnet for the well-to-do that also attracts legions of teenagers and twenty- and thirty-somethings who drift through the atrium as if they were models on a runway. In addition to the bookstores common to most malls, Lenox had a store that offered rare first editions and antique maps that fetch up to twenty-five thousand dollars. This was a place with mannequins the color of peach and milk chocolate lavished in furs and jewelry in well-lit displays behind glass, a place where doctors' wives in tennis skirts drift toward the nail salon in the middle of the day and pause afterward for a rewarding cappuccino. It was a place to see and be seen, a mall whose customers would not be surprised on occasion to see in person the sculpted athletes, actors, or models who grace their television screens and magazine covers at home. In the tony Buckhead section of north Atlanta, not far from the governor's mansion in one direction and dance clubs in another, flashy Lenox is more Crate and Barrel than Sears and Roebuck, more Williams-Sonoma than Montgomery Ward. It exudes an aura of wealth and hip sophistication obvious even to someone who has spent most of life clinging to survival on one meal a day of mashed-up grain in a refugee camp. "Somebody who is not a millionaire cannot come and buy something here," John said as he walked through the mall, spellbound by mannequins with pouty lips and stylish scarves.

Jacob's eyes darted right and left, from the ground level up to the second floor. So many corridors invited customers with tempting displays.

"It will be confusing if one is to get a job here," he said. "If I come alone, how will I find the way I am to go to my workplace?"

Mr. Benjamin led them through the glamour to a bench near a Starbucks in the middle of the mall. He went into the Discovery Channel Store, chatted with the manager, and returned with two applications. He and Valerie helped Jacob and John supply their names, addresses, and dates of birth. (Each used January 1 as his birth date, as most Lost Boys did. The United Nations had assigned them that "birthday" because most had no idea of their actual dates of birth.) Then they sat on the benches and waited, middle-aged women flowing past them in ankle-length skirts and business suits, cell phones pressed to their ears. The manager strode to the benches and asked Jacob to follow him into the store. They were gone for about twenty minutes. Then the manager reappeared with Jacob and summoned John inside. Jacob looked serious and contemplative at first but beamed after the manager went back to the store. "I told him I am hardworking, punctual, willing to work," Jacob said. "We were told in the job interview you have to sell yourself, to talk about yourself. I told him that I'm punctual and very cooperative. I told him, 'I can cooperate with you and do my job here in the company.'"

After John came out, he smiled, too. The manager had told them this was just a preliminary interview and that they might be called back for a second interview with the district manager. Though he said before the interviews that the store had openings for salesmen, stockers, and packers, he said afterward that there was actually only one opening, a part-time position that would last through the winter holidays. So Jacob and John left confused about what jobs actually were available and whether they had a shot at filling them. Nevertheless, it had been their first interview. That was an accomplishment.

"He asked me do I like to work on a team," John said.

"That question was asked of me, too," Jacob said. They walked a few steps more. "It will be really exciting if they accept me to work here."

SEPTEMBER 11, 2001

Four days later, on September 11, 2001, an airplane smashed into one of the towers of the World Trade Center in New York. A fireball engulfed several floors and sent thick, black smoke pouring into the New York skyline. Then another jet slammed into the other tower on live TV. The roommates of apartment 40-G watched with the rest of their new countrymen as both towers collapsed in a sickening cloud of gray smoke. They, too, heard news reports on television describe an explosion at the Pentagon and then the crash of another airplane in Pennsylvania. What was happening? They had come to the United States to escape war and seemed as shocked as everyone else that bloodshed on such a scale had followed them across the Atlantic. Many of the Lost Boys in Atlanta reacted to the attacks with a weary speculation that perhaps they would never escape brutality and killing, no matter where they went. Born and raised amid war, maybe they were destined to grow old surrounded by the threat of death. They also shared an almost instant fear with other immigrants and refugees that the attackers would turn out to be citizens of a country other than the United States and that Americans would regard noncitizens in their midst with suspicion and hostility. The fears heightened twelve hours after the attacks, when four thugs shoved a Lost Boy named Simon Machar against a wall in Clarkston and said, according to his recollection, "You killed our people in New York. We want to kill you tonight." Simon said one attacker with a knife tried to cut him. He said the blade sliced his shirtsleeve but did not break the skin. A Lost Boy in a nearby apartment heard the commotion and told the attackers he had a gun. He really held an electric hair clipper, Simon said, but the attackers did not know that. They ran. Simon ducked into his apartment, but the men returned and smashed his living-room window with a rock and wooden plank.

Word of the attack raced through the community of Lost Boys. Several displayed U.S. flags in their apartment windows. Led by Abraham Yel, the deacon who led church services for them each Sunday, many contributed five dollars each to a collection for the relatives of victims in New York, Washington, and Pennsylvania. They gave the money to the Red Cross, the same organization that had helped them years earlier by providing them with water and other assistance as they had walked from Ethiopia to Sudan and then on to Kenya.

As it became clear that Islamic militants in the al-Qaida network had carried out the attacks, the refugees from southern Sudan were quick to point out how intimately they understood the depth of a new suffering in the United States. They would say that the September 11 attacks were like what had been happening in southern Sudan for more than ten years, that forces of radical Islam had killed and maimed hundreds of thousands of people in Sudan, too, even if few people in the United States seemed to know. They did not mean to minimize the tragedy of September 11 but they wanted to call attention to a suffering that had plagued their native land ever since the resumption of civil war in 1983.

Fighting broke out after a few years of rising tension between north and south. The government sent more northern soldiers into southern Sudan, and they came with disdain for the local population. Douglas H. Johnson, an author and historian, writes that "harassment of civilians became common" and that "shooting of civilians was frequent" in rural areas. Sensing problems, an Army battalion composed of southern soldiers refused an order to move into northern Sudan. In May 1983, the Sudanese military attacked Battalion 105 at Bor. The northern government also reneged on a pledge and imposed *shari'a*—Islamic law—on the entire country, including non-Muslim regions of the south. In 1986, as fighting raged in southern Sudan, a new leader took power in Khartoum. He was Sadiq al-Mahdi, grandson of the Mahdi who had led a revolution to expel foreign powers from Sudan in the 1880s. He shifted strategy to rely less on the Sudanese military and more on proxy fighters. He did this by arming tribal militias in regions bordering southern Sudan. As a result, there was a sharp increase in militia attacks on southern villages in 1987 and '88, particularly in the Bahr El-Ghazal region. Militias slaughtered men and women, burned homes, stole cattle, and enslaved an untold number of southerners. The attacks separated thousands of boys from their families and forced them on journeys that would end, for survivors, in Ethiopia. By 1989, though, Sadiq al-Mahdi was negotiating a possible peace deal with rebels when hard-liners in the military deposed him.

They installed in his place General Omar Hassan Bashir, a strongman who charted the nation's course by the compass of Islamic fundamentalism. People who renounced Islam or committed adultery faced execution. A government *fatwa*, or religious decree, said "Zionists, crusaders and arrogant persons" were to blame for the war and that Muslims who doubted the wisdom of *jihad* would "suffer torture in hell for eternity." The lurch toward radical Islam was coordinated from behind the scenes by a fundamentalist political organization, the National Islamic Front, led by a shrewd and charming lawyer named Hassan al-Turabi, educated at the Sorbonne and Oxford. His party got less than 20 percent of the vote in a 1985 election, but other forces lacked power to stop the coup. The ascension of radical Islam in 1989, analysts concluded, meant the war would almost certainly grind on.

After Bashir took over, human-rights groups said his regime tortured opponents in secret "guest houses" around the capital. "Even the director of the government antiquities department was locked up, reportedly because he found more Christian than Islamic ruins," Scott Peterson writes. The government banned political parties, trade unions, and independent newspapers. It outlawed groups such as the Sudan Bar Association and the Sudan Human Rights Organization. Authorities granted themselves the right to detain anyone they saw as a threat to political or economic security. Moderate Muslims and non-Muslims were fired from government jobs—about 120 judges and twenty thousand civil servants were dismissed. Most were replaced with Muslim fundamentalists. New penalties called for the amputation of limbs, flogging, crucifixion, stoning, and beheading. The changes alarmed policymakers in Washington at a time when militant Islam had emerged as a major concern.

Unlike most Arab states, Sudan joined Libya, Jordan, and Palestinian leader Yasser Arafat in siding with Iraqi dictator Saddam Hussein in the 1991 Gulf War, triggered by Iraq's invasion of Kuwait the year before. Also troubling to the State Department was a visit of the Iranian president to Sudan in December 1991. During the trip, Bashir told a radio audience that the 1979 Islamic Revolution in Iran, led by Ayatollah Khomeini, "carried hope to Muslims and encouraged us to declare an Islamic revolution in Sudan."

This kind of talk appealed to the adherents of radical Islam. And since the government of Sudan allowed any Arab to enter the country without a visa in those years, Khartoum became a popular destination for extremists who would use their time in Sudan to plot attacks against the West. Peterson writes that "Khartoum hosted every conceivable resistance group or guerilla force—just about anyone who might be or was branded a 'terrorist' by the U.S." Abu Nidal, mastermind of a ship hijacking in which gunmen killed a wheelchair-bound American tourist, lived in Khartoum. So did Illich Ramirez Sanchez, better known as Carlos the Jackal, the Venezuelan-born terrorist who claimed credit for killing ninety-three people. Representatives of groups such as Hamas, Hezbollah, and Palestinian Islamic Jihad, considered terrorist groups by the U.S. government, also operated in Sudan. Hundreds of Iranian Revolutionary Guards were on hand to "advise" the Sudanese military, but more ominous for the United States was the arrival of a man who would spend the next decade orchestrating attacks on Western interests around the world.

Osama bin Laden arrived in Sudan in 1991. The Saudi millionaire had gone to Afghanistan in the early 1980s to become one of the leaders of Arab volunteers fighting Soviet invaders. He arrived in Sudan with four wives, several children, and "Afghan Arabs," fighters from Arab countries who had followed him to Afghanistan to fight the Soviets. In Sudan, bin Laden "established a construction company, farm and tannery in Khartoum and became closely associated with the Sudanese government. Bin Laden and his men were ensconced in a large house, which was heavily guarded by well-armed men and off limits to outsiders," writes Donald Petterson, former U.S. ambassador to Sudan. Bin Laden forged links in Sudan with Islamic extremists from Egypt, including leaders of a group responsible for the 1981 assassination of President Anwar el-Sadat.

The al-Qaida network felt compelled to act when U.S. Marines landed in neighboring Somalia in 1991. After the Somali government collapsed and was replaced by famine and anarchy, bands of wild-eyed young men from rival clans, some stoned, prowled the streets in open four-wheel-drive vehicles with machine guns mounted on top. Islamic fundamentalists in Sudan scoffed at the assertions of President George Bush that he had sent the Marines to Somalia for humanitarian reasons. They saw an America eager to exert control in a region with oil, a colonial power with designs on Sudan and Yemen, bent on checking the advance of an Islamic "revival" in Khartoum. If Bush would send his powerful military into Somalia, Turabi and bin Laden argued in Khartoum, what would stop him from citing humanitarian reasons to send troops into southern Sudan? Not long after al-Qaida religious advisers called on Muslims to attack Americans in Mogadishu, al-Qaida associates blew up a hotel there, killing an Australian tourist. A bin Laden associate traveled to Somalia early in 1993 to arm and train an Islamic militant group in Somalia as well as a militia controlled by a Somali warlord, Mohammed Farah Aideed, who had evolved into an American target after attacking United Nations troops in June 1993. He was reported to be receiving assistance from the Sudanese government. An American military operation to capture two of his aides, led by U.S. Army Rangers and Special Forces on October 3, 1993, led to what was then the longest firefight involving U.S. troops since the Vietnam War, a battle that killed eighteen Americans and hundreds of Somalis.

By the time of the battle in Mogadishu, bin Laden and his associates in Sudan had leaped to the attention of counterterrorism authorities in the United States. Several Sudanese nationals were charged and later convicted in a plot to blow up the United Nations and several landmarks in New York. The United States accused two Sudanese diplomats at the United Nations of helping the conspirators. Increasing ties between Sudan's leaders and violent extremist groups led the State Department to add Sudan in 1993 to a list of nations that sponsor terrorism, with Cuba, Iraq, Iran, Libya, Syria, and North Korea. In addition to stigmatizing the regime, it disqualified Sudan from nearly all U.S. economic and military aid. It also prevented most American companies from doing business in Sudan. Economic conditions worsened as the international community isolated Sudan. The United Nations imposed economic sanctions after Khartoum refused to extradite suspects wanted in a 1995 assassination attempt on Egyptian president Hosni Mubarak. As time passed, the Sudanese government increasingly recognized the liabilities that came with being seen to support terrorism. Desperate for foreign investment, particularly to help it develop oil reserves in the south, Sudan cooperated with French authorities in the capture of Carlos the Jackal. The government of Sudan also expelled bin Laden in May 1996. He moved to Afghanistan and became a household name after Western intelligence sources blamed him and his al-Qaida network for the 1998 bombings of U.S. embassies in Nairobi, Kenya, and Dar es Salaam, Tanzania. Those attacks killed 224 people and injured more than 4,000. In retaliation, President Bill Clinton ordered a cruise-missile strike on a pharmaceutical factory in Khartoum said to be producing nerve gas. Two years later, bin Laden was suspected in the bombing of the USS *Cole* off the coast of Yemen, an attack that killed seventeen U.S. sailors.

And so when it became clear that bin Laden and al-Qaida were behind the attacks on September 11, 2001, many southern Sudanese refugees empathized with America's raw pain. Some thought Americans might pay closer attention to what had been happening in Sudan for the previous several years. They would tell anyone who would listen horror stories of the kind described in a 1995 United Nations report by Gaspar Biro, the U.N.'s special human-rights representative for Sudan. He found that "thousands of civilians are reported to have been killed in deliberate and indiscriminate attacks, including aerial bombardments on civilian targets by government forces." He said "Muslims and Christians alike have been killed in these attacks or summarily executed. Others are reported to have lost their lives as a result of brutal torture in secret detention centers run by the security organs or in military barracks."

The report describes one of many aerial attacks: "[O]n 21 June 1995, an Antonov aircraft operated by government forces dropped 22 bombs on Regifi and surrounding villages starting at 9 a.m. Six civilians were killed and 12 others seriously injured. Eyewitnesses reported that the bombardment was concentrated on a densely inhabited area, indicating an intent on the part of the government to terrorize the civilian population and to force people to flee the area."

The report quotes a forty-two-year-old man detained by the government: "I was arrested on 10 January 1995 and released in March 1995. That was after a long period of torture. The torture was applied to many parts of my body, including the head, the eyes and the genitals. During [my] detention, my wife was compromised by members of the Sudanese security, then she became pregnant. They have used many instruments, such as electric chairs. Many Sudanese political detainees have died inside these detention centers without the knowledge of their relatives."

His body corroborated the account: "Puncture wounds, which the victim explained were caused by nails being driven into his arms and the soles of his feet, were clearly visible. . . . Numerous burn marks were also seen on his torso. The victim's eyes were inflamed and blood-shot from gas that had been sprayed into his eyes during his detention."

The report and several others detailed the abduction of women and children in Sudan, particularly in the south. Investigators said "reports were received from all over southern Sudan on the abduction of men, women and children by the government of Sudan army, the Popular Defense Force, government-armed local militias and groups of mujahidin fighting the war in southern Sudan on the government's side." Some women "are used as wives by the soldiers," a witness reported, while children "work in the fields or as servants." Other children, including southern refugees in northern cities, were rounded up and sent to "special camps" where "they are ideologically indoctrinated" and "non-Muslims are forcibly converted to Islam and have their identity changed by being given Arabic names." The report said some were "trained by the military in order to be sent to southern Sudan to fight the war."

Despite this report and many others like it, the Islamic fundamentalists who ran Sudan insisted that the Western press and power structure played up reports of human-rights abuses in Sudan. In 1993 Turabi told a *Baltimore Sun* reporter, "[T]he problems are exaggerated." He said "Americans don't know much about the world" and that gullible newspapers in the United States did not do their homework. "If someone tells them something, they publish it. There are no massacres," he said. "These are just tribal fights. It's not serious." On another occasion, Turabi told journalist Scott Peterson that the "Islamic resurgence" in Sudan "was part of an unstoppable, worldwide awakening, and secular Arab governments, such as Egypt's, had reason to fear. 'Yes, we're fighting a jihad, and we've always been fighting a jihad in the Sudan. . . . Did the West develop democracy without violence?'" Turabi said the government wanted "to plant a new civilization in the south."

There was no shortage of carnage in Sudan in the 1990s, not only from fighting between north and south but also as a result of a fracture in the southern rebel forces. In 1991, the Sudan People's Liberation Army split along tribal lines. Dinka fighters led by Colonel John Garang and Nuer fighters led by Riek Machar often attacked not only each other's forces but also civilians of the rival ethnic group. A British ethnologist who studied the Nuer in the 1930s said "there has been enmity between the two peoples" for "as far as history and tradition go back." After the split in the SPLA, Nuer raiders stole Dinka cattle and killed Dinka civilians, most infamously during a 1991 battle that came to be called the Bor Massacre.

"Nuer warriors marched on the Dinka heartland at Bor and Kongor to recapture lost cattle, chanting their battle cry: 'We will make you Dinka drink your blood!'" Peterson writes. "The raiders killed so many that the death count was stopped after reaching 2,000. People were speared and shot, bound with ragged belts and knotted cord, strangled and burned. Three boys were tied to a tree and clubbed to death. Men were castrated and disemboweled." Dinka soldiers under Garang's command retaliated: "Near Bor, one group of 19 Nuer men were tied up in a cattle shed and speared to death." Garang's troops killed forty people waiting for food in an attack on a feeding center run by the United Nations. His Nuer rivals killed patients in a leprosy hospital.

Complicating the picture were dissident SPLA commanders like the one whose forces attacked civilians in an incident detailed in the United Nations report:

> The most serious incident took place in Ganyiel region on the night of 30 July 1995, when a large group of men from Akot, approximately half of them wearing uniforms and carrying weapons, some with radio sets and walkie-talkies, attacked at 3 a.m. two villages, Manyal and Guk, situated northwest of Ganyiel. Later the attackers split into three groups and continued the assault on villages east-south-east and south of Ganyiel. According to information provided by a local chief, 210 people were killed, out of whom 30 were men, 53 were women and 127 were children. Seven children were reported missing; since their bodies were not recovered in the following days, it was believed that they had been abducted. Eyewitnesses reported that some of the victims, mostly women, children and the elderly, were caught while trying to escape and killed with spears and pangas [a weapon similar to the machete]. M.N., a member of the World Food Programme (WFP) relief committee at Panyajour, lost four of her five children (aged 8–15 years). The youngest child was thrown into the fire after being shot. D.K. witnessed three women with their babies being caught. Two of the women were shot and one was killed with a panga. The babies were all killed with pangas. A total of 1,987 households were reported destroyed and looted and 3,500 cattle were taken.

The September 11 attacks generated a flood of news accounts about al-Qaida and Islamic extremism, and that in turn led to a mild increase in interest in Sudanese fundamentalism and its civil war. Bookstores reported brisk sales of books about Islamic extremism and terrorism. Headlines about shark attacks and extramarital affairs between congressmen and interns gave way to ones about the devastation in New York and Washington and the "war on terrorism" promised by President George

W. Bush. The United States attacked Afghanistan three weeks after the terrorist attacks, swiftly dislodging the Taliban rulers who sheltered bin Laden and ran a state based on an archaic and fundamentalist interpretation of Islam similar to that espoused in Sudan.

Back in the United States, fallout from the attacks touched virtually every aspect of life. Police were everywhere, it seemed, guarding bridges and water-treatment plants, towing suspicious cars. A country still reeling from the killings also was on guard against threats that loomed just out of sight. A new phrase—*homeland security*—entered the national vocabulary. Flights were grounded for several days and resumed only after a new vigilance asked passengers to arrive two hours before their flights were scheduled to leave. Guards confiscated pocketknives and knitting needles. And the heightened suspicion of foreigners that several Sudanese refugees envisioned became a reality.

Immigration authorities rounded up at least eight hundred noncitizens, mainly from Arab and Muslim nations, in the months after September 11, 2001. Most were held for violations of immigration law, such as overstaying a visa, that had once been largely ignored. None was charged with a crime related to terrorism. The government held many in secret and deported most. The number of illegal immigrants expelled to predominately Muslim countries in north Africa, the Middle East, and south Asia soared in the year after the terrorist attacks while the number of illegal immigrants returned to Mexico went down dramatically even though the majority of immigrants in the United States had come from Mexico. Meanwhile, FBI agents fanned out to question about five thousand foreign students, mostly Arabs. Congress ordered the INS to speed up development of a long-delayed online system to monitor foreign students. The agency also launched a controversial program requiring students, tourists, businesspeople, and other visa holders from two dozen mostly Muslim countries, including Sudan, to be fingerprinted, photographed, and questioned. Agents also dusted off an obscure law requiring noncitizens to tell the government of any address change within ten days of moving. Like many actions the immigration service took in response to September 11, the change-of-address requirement raised questions about whether it would actually do anything to keep the country safe from terrorists, particularly after it came to light that the INS was buried in change-of-address forms it lacked the manpower to review. So many forms had piled up that the agency shunted about 2 million of them, unread, to an underground warehouse in St. Louis. They sat there, gathering dust.

The terrorist attacks had a profound impact on the refugee-resettlement program. The State Department suspended it for several weeks after the attacks even though none of the nineteen hijackers who struck on September 11 entered the United States as a refugee. (Fifteen came into the country by obtaining tourist visas at an American embassy or consulate abroad, three posed as businessmen to receive business visas, and one received a student visa to study English in Oakland, California.) Noncitizens enter the United States by a variety of means, but the majority are tourists, students, or businesspeople who receive visas to come for a few weeks or months and return home. Others come in as legal permanent residents, typically to begin prearranged employment or reunite with a relative. Refugees make up a relatively small number of the noncitizens who enter the United States each year, but the refugee program was the only avenue of legal entrance into the United States that closed after September 11. It resumed with enhanced security measures that slowed the flow. The new regulations said that a maximum of thirty-five refugees could travel on any one flight and that airplanes carrying refugees had to land in one of five U.S. cities. The government also required more-thorough background checks, called Security Advisory Opinions (SAOs), for refugees from more than two dozen countries with links to Muslim extremists. The FBI and CIA would have to issue SAOs on any foreign national from those countries, which were not identified publicly but were generally understood to encompass countries in the Middle East, south Asia, north Africa, and the Horn of Africa. Taken together, the temporary suspension and increased security measures meant longer waits for refugees bound for new lives in the United States. It also led to a sharp decline in the number of refugees the United States resettled. From October 2001 through September 2002, the State Department resettled just 27,100 of the 70,000 refugees it said it would accept, fewer than in any year since the program had started in 1980 and fewer than the previous low of about 62,000, in 1983. In the next budget year, ending in September 2003, admissions were low again—28,148—but the number climbed to about 52,000 in the budget year that ended in September 2004.

Officials at the Immigration and Naturalization Service, later abolished and subsumed within the mammoth Department of Homeland Security, also worried about the dangers INS officers might face in distant refugee camps. The agency was particularly worried about security in Kakuma. Acting on a threat it said it received that al-Qaida might target American interests in Kakuma, the INS would not send officers to the camp for several months in 2002 and 2003. That meant longer waits for refugees in line to be interviewed by an INS officer who would decide whether they had a fear of persecution that would allow them to be resettled in the United States. About one hundred of the thirty-eight hundred Lost Boys of Sudan were stuck in Kakuma, waiting for an INS interview, after the terrorist attacks. For those already in the United States, including the young men in apartment 40-G of Olde Plantation Apartments in Clarkston, the months after September 11, 2001, were frustrating and uncertain for different reasons. They felt increasing pressure to go to work and find some way to enroll in school. Consumed by the idea of day-to-day survival, they would not realize for months that September 11, as terrible as it had been, had produced the best chance in eighteen years for peace in Sudan.

CHASING THE WIND

For the first two months that Jacob, Peter, Daniel, and Marko lived in Georgia, they spent very little money. Their resettlement agency gave them two hundred dollars a month in spending money, but the roommates sent the money to Kakuma to help others in their group who were left behind. They had questions at first about whether bandits would attack, but they soon came to feel safe for the first time in their lives. Though they heard police sirens every now and then, there was no thought that violence lurked in Clarkston the way it had in southern Sudan, or in the camps in Ethiopia and Kenya. Once they relaxed, the young men of apartment 40-G felt the giddy elation of exploration, the thrill of discovering an alternate way of living. They saw tall buildings and highways alive with cars and trucks. Invisible signals beamed television programs into their apartment for free. And what an apartment it was—solid walls and a roof and windows that opened and closed and toilets that flushed and water in a sink and a tub with water that came out hot or cold depending on which way one turned the faucet.

One night, a friend took the four of them to an Atlanta Braves baseball game at Turner Field. They had never heard words like *bat*, *base*, or *home run*, much less *sacrifice fly* or *fielder's choice*, and so they explained the game in much more literal terms: A man with the stick tries to hit the ball. He runs toward a small white square and hopes to arrive before the ball, but he can't hit the ball just anywhere. It has to go between white lines on either side of the field to count. And if he hits the ball and it is caught before it hits the ground, he has to let someone else try to hit. That's called an *out*. It can also be achieved by swinging at the ball and missing three times.

Marko laughed at the arcane and seemingly contradictory rules. Daniel and Jacob leaned back in their seats, chuckling, slapping their hands on one another's knees and pointing. Peter shook his head with a broad grin, transfixed by the spectacle of thousands of people watching men under floodlights perform some obscure ritual. A middle-aged couple sitting in front of them that evening overheard the refugees trying to make sense of the game and was intrigued by the thought that there existed people who spoke English—a peculiar brand of it, anyway—and yet knew nothing of this great pastime. It was as if they had fallen from the sky. The couple turned to ask where the young men were from and Peter said Sudan, a country in Africa. They made small talk with Jacob, Peter, and Daniel, but Marko just smiled and nodded, too unsure of his English. The woman rose between innings and returned with a tub of popcorn and four Cokes for them.

A half-hour later, in the eighth inning, when a man with a stick hit the white ball so far that it went into the seats, everyone in the stands leaped up as if on cue, pumped their fists in the air, and screamed in happiness and joy. The refugees sensed what was expected and they stood up, too, and started clapping. Then something happened that set off spasms of uncontrollable laughter. Suddenly, way up above left field, on the highest level of the stadium, streaks of red and green and yellow fire rocketed up from a giant, well-lit plastic Coca-Cola bottle to explode in a colorful mosaic against the night sky. At first Daniel and Jacob flinched. Marko and Peter stopped clapping and stood frozen, staring, mouths open, hands in front of them in the act of applause, held apart a foot or so. The sound was hard to place. Like the crack of a rifle, maybe, but louder. Something like bombs exploding, but that wasn't it either. Everyone around them was still cheering. Somebody whistled. The fire-spewing Coca-Cola bottle was not a source of danger but rather something for amusement and delight. Fireworks, they were told. They come from the bottle after a man with the stick hits the ball so hard that it does not land until it is over the seats. Marko and Peter clapped again. Daniel looked at them with a smile of incredulity followed by peals of laughter. Now they were all pointing and laughing. Jacob doubled over, clutching his stomach and laughing. A giant plastic Coca-Cola bottle that sent colorful explosions into the sky. Who could have imagined it?

The baseball game was a rare diversion from days in apartment 40-G. They were waiting to work. Job developers told them companies did not seem to be hiring as often as they had been just a year earlier, when the entire country had been riding a wave of economic prosperity. The mood had shifted. The developers seemed exasperated even as they told newly arrived refugees to hang in there, something would turn up. So the roommates slept late and watched *Divorce Court* in the afternoon.

"We are worried," Jacob said two months after he arrived in Atlanta. "It is getting now a long time without a job." Soon he would receive his third two-hundred-dollar check for spending money from the International Rescue Committee. This time, instead of sending the entire amount back to Kakuma, Jacob planned to spend some of the money on himself, to save some cash, just in case, and buy tokens to get around now that his public-transportation allotment had run out. Each roommate paid about $126 toward the $755 rent for their three-bedroom apartment. They paid forty dollars a month for the phone, which worked out to about six dollars a person, as long as no one made long-distance calls (they bought international calling cards for that). Mathew, their caseworker, also had told them they would pay for the lights in their apartment, and air conditioning in the summer and heat in the winter. Jacob felt guilty as he left to get his third check for two hundred dollars. "This amount, I think, I will not send to Kakuma," he said.

A few weeks later, much to everyone's relief, the phone started ringing with job offers. William went to work at a health club. He cleaned the men's locker room and swept up in the common areas. John bagged groceries. Jacob and Peter were hired at Target, a department store. They worked the night shift, unloading trucks and putting linens on shelves in the housewares department at three in the morning. The Discovery Channel Store also hired Jacob to work a few days a week. He fell into an exhausting routine. Jacob worked at Target from about 10 p.m. to 6 a.m., then he rode the bus home, slept for a few hours, and left in time to be at work at the Discovery Channel Store by 2:30 p.m. He worked there until the store closed at 9 p.m. and took a bus to Target to start the cycle over again. Sometimes Jacob fell asleep on the bus rides from one place to another, but he said he needed the money. He and his roommates were proud to work. They took their responsibilities seriously and felt a small infusion of power when they received a paycheck. Yet it took very little time for them to start feeling overwhelmed, guilty, and pressed for time.

People stuck in refugee camps often see resettlement in the United States as the most ideal of all possible outcomes, even thought it is highly unlikely for any given refugee. Aid workers report a widespread vision of the United States as a place where "the streets are paved with gold," an idea that is especially prevalent in remote parts of the world where people have little access to international, independent sources of information. Many Dinka refugees who remained in Kakuma sometimes would leave to go to Nairobi so they could call a friend among the Lost Boys resettled in the United States. They would swap news about friends and relatives on both sides of the ocean and then, inevitably, ask for money to buy this person food or that person medicine. The phone rang most often in apartment 40-G in the middle of the night. Peter knew how hungry they were, that their needs were not invented, but he was coming to a sobering realization: He and the others supported themselves on jobs that paid six to eight dollars an hour in a country where everything seemed to cost a fortune. The streets, it turned out, were not paved with gold, but that was hard to explain to people in Kakuma. What did people in the camp know about paychecks and rent and light bills? So-and-so is sick, they would say. The rations are late again.

One day, without telling his roommates, Peter called the phone company and changed their telephone number. If people in Kakuma did not know their number, he reasoned, the phone would not ring so much. "It can give you a hard time thinking about it," Peter said.

Julianne Duncan, an anthropologist and child-welfare expert from Washington state who had interviewed Lost Boys in Kakuma, had predicted that those who were resettled in the United States would have such reactions: "As with other refugees, they may experience an increase in guilt, as they have so much better conditions than those they have left behind." For about twenty years, Duncan steered refugee children into foster care and helped them enroll in school in Seattle and Tacoma. The United Nations High Commissioner for Refugees hired her as a consultant to conduct "best interest assessments" for Lost Boys who were under eighteen. She tried to interview six children a day, asking for their names, ages, and hometowns and about the events that separated them from their parents. Her job was to determine whether resettlement in the United States would be in the best interest of a particular child. She screened 1,125 children and recommended resettlement for about 70 percent, though some who were approved were not actually resettled. Dozens had turned eighteen by the time flights began leaving Kakuma. That made them too old to travel with the minors, and no one had thought to move their names to the list of Lost Boys over eighteen being resettled, so they were stuck. Among the 30 percent for whom Duncan discouraged resettlement, a leading reason was that they lived with an older uncle or other close relative not being considered for resettlement. In such cases, Duncan advised against breaking up families.

Duncan found "significant symptoms of mental health distress" and said in a report that "virtually all were experiencing symptoms of unresolved trauma" and anxiety, though few felt depressed or guilty. She and three child-welfare experts who worked with her were impressed that the refugees were "so well socialized." They attributed this to a "small but effective group of adult caretakers who have been watching over the children since they streamed into the camps in Ethiopia between 1987 and 1991. The caretakers number about 100 for the approximately 12,000 children. . . . They have instilled the children with a vision of their self-worth and have given them a way to understand their role as contributors even if the usual social structure (as members of families) is closed to them."

The young men impressed Duncan. "We found that the population had considerable strength and resiliency," she said. "The major protective factors were belief in God, desire for success in education and desire to be helpful in the future.

"Based on our years of work with refugee unaccompanied children, we usually expect about six months of euphoria followed by depression," Duncan said. "After nine to twelve months, we expect the child to reach a level of stability which will carry him/her through to self-sufficient adulthood in the United States."

Though the findings were from a study of those Lost Boys who were under eighteen, Duncan's forecast could easily have applied to all thirty-eight hundred refugees, not just the minors. So would other predictions: Many probably would feel survivor's guilt. They would find themselves shopping at grocery stores overflowing with fruits, vegetables, milk, and bread even as friends in Kakuma stood in line for rations. Also, "since school has been such a major factor in maintaining their hope in life, we would expect anxiety and disillusionment about schooling to contribute to anxiety and depression."

Several months after the United States began putting into foster care the first of roughly five hundred minors among the thirty-eight hundred Lost Boys, Duncan interviewed several of them to see how her predictions compared with their experiences. "Initial reactions were indeed euphoric," she reported. "Children reported having a feeling of safety for the first time within their memories. Many reported having good dreams of their mothers and few reported any bad dreams or nightmares. Most did connect with supportive religious communities." She found refugees still "devoted to their schooling," still "eager and active participants in church activities," and "appear[ing] to find solace in their religious beliefs." They approached "interactions with strangers with openness and trust."

Even so, some refugees were "beginning to have nightmares, intrusive thoughts and other symptoms of post-traumatic stress. Some of the symptoms are serious enough to interfere with learning." Thoughts drifted to Africa. "Inability to communicate with Kakuma was extremely frustrating and some children experienced anxiety attacks about those left behind."

A survey turned up sadness, loneliness, and occasional "anger out-bursts in the face of frustration." As predicted, "survivor's guilt is rampant and is resulting in emotional outbursts." Some who were "nice and gener-ally respectful of authority" were nonetheless "very needy of adult atten-tion and are sometimes unable to wait their turn," an attribute Duncan chalked up to years without parents.

"In thinking about the group as a whole, we must note that most were separated from their mothers when they were about four to seven years old, and have not had a true parental figure since that time. Thus, much of their neediness, even demandingness, may be the pent-up de-mand for the mother they have not had," Duncan said. "Now that they are safe, they are deeply distressed by the fact that nothing anyone can give them can make up for the mother love that they want."

To cope, many Lost Boys relied on their Christian faith. "Belief in God and participation in religious activities are strong protective factors against some psychological distress," Duncan wrote.

In Georgia, a congregation of Lost Boys worshipped every Sunday afternoon in a room at the Clarkston Community Center, an old high school that was saved from demolition after protests in the mid-1990s. Months into the resettlement, their congregation found a champion in Elizabeth Roles, who ran a refugee ministry at All Saints' Episcopal Church in downtown Atlanta. She had heard of a group of refugees con-ducting their own services at Jubilee Partners, a Christian welcome center for refugees on 260 acres in rural northeast Georgia. A few resettlement agencies in Georgia steer refugees through Jubilee Partners before putting them in apartments in Atlanta. Since 1980, twenty-five hundred refugees of various faiths from about thirty countries have spent roughly two months each at Jubilee Partners, receiving English lessons and tips on life in modern America before moving into everyday life. Abraham Yel, the pastor featured on *60 Minutes II*, spent a few weeks at Jubilee Partners with about a dozen countrymen. Jubilee's founder, Don Mosley, is a prolific speaker who has spoken to nearly two thousand church and civic groups about the plight of refugees from Central America and elsewhere, as well as about his belief that U.S. sanctions against Iraq in the 1990s contributed to the deaths of thousands of children by denying them medicines. Mosley so impressed a man from northern Sudan during one of his speeches in 2001 that the man visited Jubilee Partners and wound up talking with Abraham for several hours. They hit it off discussing the need for peace in Sudan. After several hours, the man surprised Abraham with a confession: He was closely related to Sadiq al-Mahdi, who as Sudanese prime minister in the late 1980s was the man Abraham blamed for the militia raids that killed some of his relatives and separated him from others. The man had another surprise. He said Sadiq al-Mahdi was in Washington, D.C., and that he could arrange for Abraham to meet him. A few days later, Abraham found himself in a hotel room with the man vilified by so many Lost Boys as a mass murderer. Abraham said he told the former prime minister how much their country needed peace, that he felt the suffering needed to end for north and south, Muslim and Christian. Sadiq al-Mahdi told Abraham he and the other refugees should be called "Peace Boys" instead of "Lost Boys." Their meeting did not stop the war, of course, but it underscored Abraham's desire to forgo violence and work for peace—a commandment, as he interpreted Christianity.

Back at Jubilee Partners, Abraham led Dinka-language worship services for Lost Boys who were at the center with him. That impressed Elizabeth Roles. She had volunteered at Jubilee Partners but had never come across a refugee group that met for worship services beyond ones offered to all refugees at the center. She told Abraham she would try to help him keep his church afloat after he moved to Atlanta. A few weeks later, after he had moved, he tried leading services at an apartment. Dozens of Lost Boys showed up. They spilled out onto a stairwell. Worried that neighbors would complain about noise or crowds, Roles set out to find a better solution and eventually thought of the old Clarkston High School, but the building was in sorry shape. Plywood covered one window and several ceiling tiles were missing. A nonprofit group reincarnated the building as the Clarkston Community Center and envisioned soccer fields, a convenient picnic pavilion, and meeting space for gardening clubs and scouting troops. That day seemed far off—the building was condemned except for an old classroom, a conference room, and an office. Still, Roles decided it would work. The price was right, too; the Lost Boys congregation could rent it for twenty-five dollars for each Sunday service. Roles used money from a refugee ministry's budget at her church. Abraham led his first service in the classroom in the summer of 2001, just a few weeks after Jacob, Peter, Daniel, and Marko had arrived.

The room had no stained glass, but sunlight streamed in through blinds on five tall windows facing the street. Chantlike hymns in Dinka and English echoed off the walls, and the hum of floor fans filled the room on summer and fall afternoons like the one in 2001 when Yel preached to twenty-eight southern Sudanese wearing khaki pants and blue jeans with green golf shirts, long-sleeved striped button-downs, and black T-shirts depicting professional wrestlers. Three young men in the front row beat drums and shook tambourines as Abraham led the congregation in Dinka hymns, voices rising and falling in a tempo that had been with them from those first days in the camps in Ethiopia. Abraham wore a black priest's collar and a white robe with a green sash descending diagonally across his chest, from his right shoulder to his left hip. He stood behind a folding table covered in white cloth at the front of the room. A cross rested between green candles in the middle of the table.

Abraham preached from First Corinthians, chapter 12. "'For as the body is one and has many members, but all the members of that one body, being many, are one body, so also is Christ.'" He told them they formed one body with many parts: "Whether Jew or Gentile, whether slave or free, we all belong to God. We all belong to one body, the body of Christianity, of Lost Boys, of New Sudan."

Duncan had noted that religion was one way the Lost Boys would sustain a sense of purpose and belonging in the United States. She said they would also continue to assert that their lives had meaning by pursuing the old dream of going to school: "Dedication to education as a means of gaining power to do good in the future continues to be an effective way to have meaning in the world."

Education. The word itself held an almost mystical appeal for so many of these Lost Boys of Sudan. Most of the minors Duncan surveyed were in high schools in the United States. The other refugees, more than three thousand teenagers and young men judged to be over eighteen, generally were too old to enroll in high school. They had to find a job and pursue an education after work. This came as a surprise to many refugees. They said over and over that they had thought they would go to school after they got to the United States. They were grateful for their new lives but could not understand why the government seemed to have brought them without a plan for their education. Instead, it seemed, they were shunted off to work in American factories, warehouses, and department stores with only vague promises that maybe someday they would receive an education. It disoriented Jacob, Peter, Daniel, and Marko and left them scrambling for some class, any class, to attend. Jacob and Peter attended pre-GED classes at the International Rescue Committee from 5:30 to 8:30 each Monday and Wednesday evening during their first few weeks. For a time, Peter attended an advanced English class at another Atlanta resettlement agency, where he studied alongside students from Afghanistan, Ethiopia, Nepal, Russia, and Togo. One night, his teacher tried to explain some of the nuances of American English. She had her students toss an inflatable beach ball around the room. They were to name a student, throw a ball to that person and then say one of the vocabulary words for that day's lesson. The student who caught the ball responded with a synonym. One student chose *creep*. He threw the ball to a woman who picked *crawl* as a synonym.

"Some words have negative connotations, like *creep*," the teacher said. "Does a baby *creep*?" Blank faces. "No," she said. "A baby *crawls*."

The lesson listed *settle* and *colonize* as synonyms, but the teacher told her students to ignore that. She had heard an earful in an earlier class from students whose native countries were conquered in the 1800s by powers such as Great Britain. Ask them what *to colonize* means and they would talk about having to leave home at the point of a gun. It had a pejorative flavor, while *settle* conjured images of a young couple, maybe, making a home near Mom and Dad.

On the night the class compared *settle* and *colonize*, however, Peter was on his way to work. He had attended regularly at first, but came less and less often as the weeks went on. One problem was that he had to leave class early to catch the bus that would take him to work on time, but more importantly, Peter couldn't see the point in throwing an inflatable ball around the room while trying to think of synonyms for words like *crush, cultivate, dictate, flaw*, and *harvest*. It didn't seem to get him any closer to his goal of studying computers or commerce in college.

Jacob had done so well in his pre-GED class that his teacher predicted he would be one of the first Lost Boys in Atlanta to pass the GED exams. Now he worked two jobs and got four or five hours of sleep many nights. He came home exhausted and tried to flip through a dog-eared study guide, but uncertainty gnawed at him. "The problem that I realize is time," Jacob said. "The work leaves me no time."

He and the others were puzzled and frustrated by what they perceived as a patchwork of classes, some at one agency, others at a community college and many, they suspected, that they did not even know about, each with seemingly arbitrary and capricious rules and deadlines. It would be an overstatement to say they were gripped by despair, but confidence ebbed. Daniel needed a GED diploma to get into seminary, but he wasn't going to get it if he spent so much time at work, serving food to students at Emory University. Peter seemed embarrassed to talk about his dream of college, as if it were absurdly unattainable.

Their despair contrasted with an optimism that spread through the community of Lost Boys in Atlanta after a woman with connections announced in the summer of 2001 that she would create a charitable organization called the Lost Boys Foundation. Mary Williams, informally adopted daughter of Jane Fonda, seemed to appear from nowhere as a savior. In time, though, many Lost Boys in Atlanta would come to feel used, embittered, and disappointed in her.

Mary went one Sunday to the Lost Boys' church service in Clarkston. She introduced herself to Abraham Yel after he preached and asked whether they might talk in private. The next day, Mary went to Abraham's apartment and told him she was creating a charity that would help Lost Boys receive medical care, find jobs and, most importantly, go to school. She said her foundation would offer GED-preparation classes and buy a community center where Lost Boys could study and worship—Abraham could even preach there. There was more. Mary said she was not going to limit herself to Atlanta. She planned to raise $10 million to provide services to all thirty-eight hundred Lost Boys resettled around the United States. After outlining her vision, Mary told Abraham that she wanted him to work with her. Having him on board would lend the foundation an air of legitimacy. After all, Abraham was widely respected. He was about to take a landscaping job that paid eight dollars an hour, but Mary said he would earn fourteen dollars an hour if he worked with her. After Mary left, Abraham called Dee Clement. She had been working with the Lost Boys in Atlanta longer than just about anyone else. Abraham trusted her. He told Dee what Mary said and asked her opinion. Was this woman for real? Could he trust her? Dee told Abraham that Mary's mother was a famous actress. That meant Mary had connections to the rich and powerful. Dee couldn't say whether Mary could raise $10 million, but it couldn't hurt that her mother was so well known. Abraham hung up the phone wondering about this woman who had come from nowhere with such ambitious plans. Who was she?

Mary was born in California to parents who were members of the radical Black Panther organization. Her mother, a welder, was left to raise six children after her father went to jail. Then her mother got hurt and lost her job. At age twelve, Mary met Jane Fonda at a theater camp the actress ran for children from various backgrounds. Mary returned home, but she and Fonda stayed in touch. Fonda offered to pay to send Mary to college if she made good grades. Finally, around the age of sixteen, Mary left her family to move in with Fonda. She completed high school and went on to study African American history and literature in college. Then came jobs at a California homeless shelter for the mentally ill, as an English teacher in Morocco, and as a health outreach coordinator in Tanzania. In Atlanta, she worked at the Centers for Disease Control and Prevention and the International Rescue Committee. Mary was raising money for the IRC when she first met the Lost Boys. She would say later that she expected the young men to be unruly and wild and was enchanted to discover polite young men who were eager to work and learn.

Mary quit her job with the IRC and went to work, along with Abraham, for an Atlanta nonprofit called Bridging the Gap, which worked with immigrants and refugees and trained police officers to work in foreign-born communities. Mary would coordinate youth programs and run a Lost Boys project at Bridging the Gap, funded by one hundred thousand dollars from the Fonda Family Foundation, until her Lost Boys Foundation got off the ground.

In the next year or two, she courted publicity and cultivated a very healthy public image. A front-page story in the *Atlanta Journal-Constitution* said Williams's program "could become a national model for groups eager to help Lost Boys adjust and continue their studies." The newspaper said the foundation one day "could pay nonprofits to help Lost Boys recover from psychological trauma, find a job and learn a little of everything, from what to do after a car wreck to why it matters in America to be on time." Even though resettlement agencies offered job placement services, English classes, and an array of other services, and even though a small army of committed volunteers was lavishing the Lost Boys with more assistance than many refugees receive, Williams insisted that they "need services above and beyond what the average refugee needs."

Later, *60 Minutes II* said the foundation was "dedicated to raising money for the boys' education." *People* magazine said it was "dedicated to giving the refugees free health care, helping them find employment and aiding in their adjustment to American life." The Lost Boys Foundation said it was "dedicated to provide funding for programs to help the young men" and that it would "assess the educational level of competence for each Lost Boy" and "prepare an individual program of study for each Lost Boy."

It sure sounded good.

Out of the spotlight, however, the young men from southern Sudan used very different language to describe the foundation. Mary's foundation had raised their expectations, they said, only to sputter toward irrelevance in their everyday lives. On the one hand, refugees would say, Mary and a few confidants arranged well-attended birthday parties and Thanksgiving dinners for the Lost Boys in Atlanta. The foundation matched refugees with volunteers who would be a major presence in their lives, helping the young men buy cars and understand auto-insurance rules or complicated medical bills, but many volunteers were helping the refugees before the foundation came along and nearly all of them eventually renounced Mary's organization and worked on their own with the young men. They said Mary and two companions at the foundation were overly controlling and seemed obsessed with public recognition and with pursuing book and movie deals, as if perhaps Mary saw the young men as a ticket to Hollywood. In fact, Mary eventually struck a deal with a respected author who planned to pen the life story of one refugee and donate proceeds to the foundation. She also succeeded in getting herself hired as a consultant on a feature film being made about the Lost Boys.

Her foundation also distributed money to a handful of refugees in Atlanta who enrolled in college, though that caused controversy because some Lost Boys in college said they had applied for the promised stipend but had been rejected for reasons they did not understand. One of two women who worked most closely with Mary helped about twenty refugees find jobs, but many refugees came to believe as time passed that the foundation lavished attention on a few young men while disregarding the majority. What they wanted most was an education, they would say, and they got into school almost exclusively through the efforts of volunteers working independently of Mary's foundation. In addition, many in the small circle of Lost Boys in Atlanta wound up with mixed feelings about what seemed most important to Mary—sharing their story with people in the United States. The foundation sent refugees to speak at places such as schools and churches—it occasionally paid them—but a speaker who had made about a dozen presentations said he had quit after one of three women who worked for a time for the foundation admonished him for talking about the political situation in Sudan. She essentially had told him to stick to a script. "They wanted me to talk about my miserable life as a Lost Boy," he said. Suspicion of Mary grew so deep that Abraham quit his job at the foundation and told Mary and her two coworkers that they were no longer welcome to address the congregation at church services he led for Atlanta Lost Boys every Sunday afternoon. Nearly all the volunteers most intimately involved in the lives of southern Sudanese refugees in Atlanta came to repudiate the foundation and form their own loosely organized group.

None of the distrust was apparent in the days after Mary opened her foundation office in downtown Atlanta, in a building that also housed a nonprofit that Jane Fonda founded. The building was on Auburn Avenue, in a part of downtown Atlanta that had once been the epicenter of a powerful black middle class, a neighborhood of shops and restaurants down the street from a church where the Reverend Martin Luther King Jr. had preached. Mary arranged Saturday-morning meetings that attracted dozens of volunteers with refugees. She also lined up speakers: Police urged refugees to wear seat belts, obey the speed limit, and dial 911 in emergencies. Immigration lawyers listed the kinds of crimes that trigger deportation. Doctors and dentists volunteered to provide medical screenings. But it took little time for tension to surface.

In the late summer of 2001, the actress Angelina Jolie, a goodwill ambassador for the United Nations High Commissioner for Refugees, met with a few dozen Lost Boys in Atlanta. She told them she would donate money to send a few of them to college. Jolie eventually contributed ten thousand dollars to the Lost Boys Foundation, but Williams announced at one of the Saturday meetings that she would use the money to provide GED-preparation classes for many instead of college tuition for a few. One refugee who had been in the audience that day said he had asked Mary how much money she had and how she was spending it. He said she had embarrassed him in front of dozens of friends by telling him she could see he did not trust her and that if he did not trust her, she could not change him or do anything for him. Other refugees were upset that the money did not pay to send young men to college, as they said Jolie had told them it would. Their frustration would only deepen. Not only did Mary not use the money to send young men to college, as some expected, she did not use it to provide GED-preparation classes, either. This deeply upset several Lost Boys. What they wanted above all else was to be in class. They felt as if they had been lied to, though Mary insisted she had said only that she would try to arrange a GED-preparation class and that she never made any promises. (The foundation never did buy a community center, but that seemed far less troublesome to the refugees.) Mary said the money from Jolie paid an instructor who taught composition to about a dozen Lost Boys in four or five sessions.

Meanwhile, some volunteers on an education committee established by the foundation offered to test Lost Boys to gauge their level of readiness for the GED exam. About thirty-five young men were tested, the foundation said, but only half that number ever got their results. The reason: foundation volunteers close to Mary said they could not find refugees to give them their scores. That highlighted two problems. For one thing, the foundation's office was in downtown Atlanta, an hour-long bus ride from Clarkston. Nearly all the refugee-resettlement offices and most agencies that serve refugees were located in or near Clarkston, within walking distance or a short bus ride from the apartments where so many refugees lived after first arriving in Georgia. Second, volunteers who would later sour on the foundation, such as Dee Clement and Susan Gordon, had much closer, day-to-day contact with the refugees than did those who would continue to support the foundation. How could an organization not find the very refugees it purported to serve? Yes, many of the young men from southern Sudan worked odd hours and often left their apartment to visit a friend's apartment, but fifty to seventy of them met for church each Sunday. Besides, if volunteers like Dee and Susan could find a young man they were looking for, why couldn't foundation supporters?

Before he became disillusioned, Abraham Yel was one of several featured speakers the foundation used successfully to tell the Lost Boys' story. Abraham made one of many speeches in the summer of 2002, this one at a small white wooden house on Roland Street in Clarkston from which a nonprofit ran an after-school program for refugee children. On this day, about sixty children sat in chairs in a semicircle under a towering oak tree with limbs that swayed in a gentle breeze. Abraham wore gray slacks and a gray sports coat over a beige button-down shirt with an open collar and spoke in his slow, steady style.

"The war started in 1955," he began.

Abraham held the children rapt as he retold the story of an attack on his village. He told them that militiamen killed his mother, two sisters, and one brother and that he left home with no shoes and no food. As he spoke, an airplane passed over them, high in the sky, its jet engines a low rumble, but none of the children looked up.

"Our own friends and brothers were eaten by wild animals."

A boy in the front row raised his hand. "How old were you?"

"I was seven years old," Abraham said. "Some of us were young like you guys here."

He told them about the days without food walking toward Ethiopia, how friends dropped over dead. About how they tried to squeeze moisture from tree roots. And how at times they drank their own urine.

"When I say no food, I mean no food," Abraham said. "You could not see a single bean."

He talked about the evacuation from Ethiopia in 1991, that day at the Gilo River.

"How did people escape the crocodiles?" one boy asked.

"People who were unlucky to be grabbed by a crocodile, that was the end of their life," Abraham said. "You think, 'Why not me?'"

As for the future, he repeated the mantra, "Education will save us. It will save our country."

In addition to arranging talks to community groups, Mary seemed to always have her eye on raising money. She was in her office one afternoon when she got a call from someone at another foundation, this one founded by Manute Bol, a Dinka and former professional basketball player who is famous among southern Sudanese. The caller wanted to talk about the possibility of contributing money to the Lost Boys Foundation so one of the young men from southern Sudan could go to college. Mary slipped flawlessly into a comfortable role, charming and polite, laughing agreeably at all the right spots.

"Oh, that's amazing!" Mary said. "That's so great." A pause. "Actually what the guys need is the GED. I think your money would be better spent establishing classes for the GED. The money that it would take to send a guy to college could let fifty guys get a GED."

The conversation shifted quickly.

"We are going to do a six-page spread in *People*," Mary confided, beaming. Another pause. "The guy who did *Training Day* is doing a film," she said. "He's already hired a director."

Mary listened.

"So the guy who did *Hoop Dreams* is also interested in a film?"

They talked about an episode of the *Oprah Winfrey Show* that had aired the previous day. For a program about volunteers helping children, Winfrey interviewed an investment banker from Kansas City who was working with Joseph Taban, one of the Sudanese youth featured on *60 Minutes II*. The banker told how a friend had urged him to volunteer with refugees. "I thought he was going to ask me for a check," the banker said. "Had no problem. It was, 'Great. This will make me feel better.

I'll give him a check and then, you know, I'll be on my way.'" Instead, his friend had introduced him to fifteen Lost Boys and had shown him the segment from *60 Minutes II*. He recalled how the Lost Boys "were laughing, teasing each other as they saw each other on television. And I'm watching it in tears. And I was moved. And I left and said 'How much do you want?'" said the banker, who was busy with a full-time job, a wife, and five children. "He said, 'I don't want any money. Just take one of them on.'"

Mary told the caller she had not seen the show. "I heard he said 'I tried to give them money, but they didn't need it,'" she said. "Did he say that?"

He did say that.

"I could choke him," Mary said. "I could absolutely choke him!"

As time passed, a growing chorus of refugee voices bore witness to a gap between what the foundation promised and what it delivered. It was providing very few Lost Boys with "funding" or "educational opportunities," as it had said it would. The foundation had a corps of volunteers that invested countless hours in one-on-one mentoring sessions with Lost Boys, but one by one, most severed their ties with the foundation to work on their own until the foundation mainly amounted to three people, no matter how grandly it portrayed itself. Before disenchantment spread, though, the foundation tried to raise money by sending Abraham to make speeches. "I'm here on behalf of the Lost Boys Foundation," he would say. "We are raising money so that we can go to school."

As time passed, Abraham began to have doubts. "We are raising money," he remembers thinking, "but nothing reaches the boys."

Volunteers began to raise questions about money after Mary decided in the summer of 2002 to hire two colleagues. The plan was for her to receive an annual salary of fifty thousand dollars. An executive director would get seventy thousand a year, a program director, thirty-five thousand, high salaries for a start-up nonprofit, especially one dogged by questions about what it did with donations it received. As it turned out, the foundation did not raise as much money as expected, so its three employees made less than planned, but the intended salary levels struck many volunteers as much too high, especially when volunteers were the ones in the trenches, doing grunt work that made the most difference to the refugees. It also sent a message to some volunteers about Mary's priorities. An interior designer and day-to-day volunteer with Lost Boys, Janis Sundquist, said she was surprised by the intended salary levels because Mary kept telling her "we have no money for this, we have no money for that." She also said she asked for a copy of the budget and was told the foundation was not required to show it. A financial statement the foundation filed in 2003 showed that only $8,000 of $181,000 the foundation raised in 2002 went for "specific assistance to individuals," mainly assistance paying the first semester of college or help here or there with a medical bill, though the amount going for college scholarships increased after a news story raised questions. (About seventy-five thousand dollars of the money the foundation received came from the Fonda Family Foundation; another five thousand dollars from a foundation controlled by Fonda's former husband, Ted Turner. Most of the rest came in the form of small donations from individuals.) Abraham knew the amounts were small by the standards of most nonprofits in the United States, but small amounts could have made a big difference for the Lost Boys in Atlanta. A few hundred dollars here could have helped one man pay unexpected medical bills. A few hundred there could have sent one more young man to college. The foundation's financial priorities seemed especially out of whack compared with unpaid volunteers, some of whom spent thousands of dollars of their own money to cover medical bills, buy clothes, or pay boarding-school tuition for a Lost Boy's brother or sister in Uganda.

Abraham came to the bitter conclusion that people at the foundation were interested not so much in doing something good as in being seen to be doing something. "The Lost Boys Foundation promises but they don't do," he said. "There are a lot of things the boys have been promised, especially school. These are all lies."

As the realization grew that the 156 southern Sudanese in Atlanta had completed different levels of education, a fog of confusion descended on the young men in apartment 40-G. Friendly Americans flitted in and out with words of encouragement. Cheryl Grover assured them they would eventually get to school, but Jacob, Peter, Daniel, and Marko had a hard time seeing themselves in class. Dee Clement and Susan Gordon told them to hang in there, that it was only a matter of time. Slowly, each of the young men tried to devise his own plan for obtaining an education even as he poured himself into work.

Marko quit his job at a university cafeteria for a better-paying position at a meatpacking plant about thirty-five miles south of Atlanta. Conditions were rough. Marko complained of the bitter cold inside the meatpacking plant, said it made his chest hurt, and wondered whether it caused the white marks under his fingernails. But it was a full-time job at a time when many companies were laying off workers or shifting employees to part-time work. Not long after Marko signed up, Peter and two other roommates—John and William—also found jobs at the plant. They were soon on a grueling schedule. They awoke about 4:30 a.m. and took showers or splashed some water on their faces. They grabbed hats, gloves, and coats and trudged outside to meet a van that would take them to work. It picked them up at about five o'clock at a gas station near the apartment. Three Sudanese refugees already were in the van by the time it stopped for Marko, Peter, John, and William. It drove on to pick up a Somali man from another complex, then a Sudanese refugee who came to the United States after finding shelter in Egypt. Next came another Somali and an Ethiopian. Then it was off down Memorial Drive, past the Wendy's and Circuit City, left onto I-285 just before the DeKalb County Jail, and south for fifteen minutes to another interstate. They rode for another quarter hour on I-85 to go to work with other immigrants, mainly from Mexico. Their shifts usually ended around three or four in the afternoon, but the van didn't leave until six or seven. The refugees would wait in a break room unless the company offered overtime. When it did, they were more than willing to work. In one three-month period, John worked an average of fifty-five hours a week. He earned eight dollars an hour for the first forty hours and twelve dollars per hour of overtime that he worked. After he paid the rent and set aside some money for a car he hoped to buy, John wired money to relatives and friends in Africa; in those three months, he sent $940. The money went to a cousin in school in Kenya, a friend in Uganda, a cousin's wife in Kenya, and a sister he had not known was alive until a cousin found her in a refugee camp in

Uganda. Though the meatpacking plant was good for making money, it left little time for anything else. The same van that carted them south in the mornings carried Peter, Marko, John, and William north at night, stopping in front of their apartment in Clarkston at seven-thirty or eight. They climbed stairs, exhausted, shoveled in some food, and sank into the couch as roaches darted across the kitchen counter or up the bathroom wall. The pests were a scourge in many refugee apartments. One young man taped a note to the living-room wall as a reminder: "Kitchen and sitting room should always need to clean all the day. This is the only way of avoiding bad smell from the areas for sure. Dear guys, it is a very important point in our personal activities to have a good care of making cleaning throughout the week or weekend."

The refugees were accustomed to being cared and provided for by volunteers, as well as caring and providing for one another. Now they were, for the most part, on their own in a country with a grand tradition of individual achievement and initiative. Even as an aura of hopelessness replaced anger among many, an impulse toward individual action began to stir. Like so many of their fellow refugees, the young men in Apartment 40-G began to sketch out plans for themselves.

Jacob was the most determined. He would study for the GED exam after work and try to earn the diploma that would open the door to college. It would be difficult, but a friend had given him a GED study guide he often read before going to bed. Informed of the American tradition of a New Year's resolution, Jacob resolved to pass five sections of the GED exam and receive his high-school equivalency diploma by the end of 2002. That would prove to be more difficult that he imagined.

Peter settled into work at the meatpacking plant, sweeping meat off the assembly line floor for $8.45 an hour. He also wanted to save money to buy a car and go to college. How long it would take to save enough and how he would get into college were unclear. He was the oldest of the roommates in apartment 40-G and tried to project the dignified confidence of a decision maker, but, privately, when his roommates were not around, Peter admitted to feeling despair at working so hard for so long for so little money. He was not saving nearly as much as he wanted to. He wondered whether he would ever achieve his goals. "I feel like a man chasing the wind," he said.

Marko was floundering, too. He was the youngest of the six Lost Boys in his apartment, prone to broad electric smiles and doubling over in laughter. He often greeted strangers by patting them on the arm or back, beaming, but the meatpacking routine exhausted him. Though he looked and acted fifteen or sixteen, relief workers in Kenya had estimated him to be older. His legal documents said he was twenty-one when he came to the United States, too old for high school in Georgia. So Marko awoke with the others before dawn, rode to the meatpacking plant south of Atlanta, and returned late in the evening. He saw no alternative. "I am looking for the way to go to school," he would say, but he had no idea how he might find it. Marko had been in ninth grade in Kakuma, so there was no way he could study on his own and pass the GED exam. He worked and waited for something to change.

Daniel was restless. He was working part-time in a cafeteria at Emory University, making hardly any money. He craved a better job. Daniel's dream of becoming a priest also seemed to be in jeopardy. He could not go to seminary without a GED diploma and he could not figure how to get one. If he lacked a high-school equivalency diploma, he feared, he would be stuck in a dead-end job for the rest of his life. And then what use would he be in New Sudan? What would they say about this man sent to the United States with high hopes that he would receive an education? That he was a failure? One day in his apartment, a friend told him about a new round of classes meant to help Lost Boys prepare for the GED exam. Daniel was suspicious. The Lost Boys Foundation had talked a lot about helping the young men acquire an education, but all that talk never amounted to much. Why should this be any different? "These people are joking!" he yelled. "They're lying!"

Daniel had a friend from Kakuma in Sioux Falls, South Dakota. Conditions there sounded so much better. Several Lost Boys were in school. Others earned $10.50 or $11.00 an hour at work, more than most jobs in Atlanta paid to refugees who lacked skills and a high-school diploma. When he talked about traveling to South Dakota, Americans told him two things about the state: It was god-awful cold and it had very few black people. Nevertheless, Daniel was determined to look for a way to the classroom, even if it meant leaving Marko. They had been together almost every day since they had met in the refugee camp in Ethiopia in

1987, but Daniel was eager to improve his lot in life. Here he was in the vaunted land of opportunity, where you could go from place to place to chase your dreams. He told Marko he was only going to Sioux Falls for a few weeks, to visit. Marko told Daniel to call if he decided to stay longer; maybe Marko would move to South Dakota, too. Daniel promised to say so if his plans changed, but he told people who asked that he would be back. He had no way of knowing that during his trip across the United States, he would find himself pulled closer to the land he had left behind. He was about to find answers, to discover, at last, what had happened to the mother he had not seen in fifteen years.

CAN YOU NAME YOUR SISTERS?

On the day Daniel left for South Dakota, a cold morning in December 2001, five months after he had arrived in Georgia, he rose early to ride to the bus station with Dee Clement. She knocked on his door to pick him up and walked down to the parking lot with him. Daniel carried a duffle bag and backpack and wore a knit cap, heavy coat, and boots. His friend had told him he would need the winter gear in South Dakota. Marko followed him into Dee's car for the ride to a Greyhound bus station in downtown Atlanta. Dee lived in a neighborhood where homes fetched several hundred thousand dollars, a community of gated driveways and tennis courts. The bus station, she said, was in a place "where I'm typically scared to go, where I was looked at with glancing eyes like 'What are you doing here?'" A little nervous, Dee marched into the station with Daniel and Marko and took a seat. She used a yellow pen to highlight places Daniel would transfer buses. She tried to drum up conversation, to ask Daniel about the adventure soon to unfold, but he said little. She bought hamburgers for Daniel and Marko, but they did not eat. When an announcer called Daniel's bus, the trio rose and walked awkwardly toward a gate. Dee kept waiting for Marko to say something. She remembers seeing tears in his eyes. "Marko was incredibly distraught," she recalled later. "He looked like he was at a funeral."

Daniel was about to cry, too, but he did not. They stopped at a door to the walkways that led to the buses. Dee hugged Daniel and wished him a safe trip. Daniel said good-bye and told Marko, "You know, just forget about it. I will be coming back."

A ticket taker looked at Marko. "You can walk all the way down to the bus to say good-bye to your friend if you want to," he said.

They walked down in silence. Daniel carried a Walkman that Dee had given him and a carry-on bag she had packed with apples, prunes, energy bars, and a bottle of juice. They got to the bus and Daniel said good-bye to Marko again and Marko said good-bye to Daniel again. Then Daniel climbed up a few steps and walked down the aisle to a seat near the back. Dee followed him up the stairs and spoke with the driver. "Are you familiar with the Lost Boys of Sudan?" she asked.

"Yes."

"Well you have one," she said. "Could you please make sure that he doesn't get off in the wrong place?"

"Yes," the driver said. "I will look after him." The driver walked back to Daniel, looked at his ticket, and promised to remind him where to change buses. As the driver walked back to his seat, Daniel looked through the bus window and saw Dee with her arms around Marko's shoulders.

"I see in his face, he want to cry. Even me, I feel bad," Daniel recalled. "I saw Dee Clement talking with Marko and I didn't know what they were talking about."

What they were talking about was whether Marko wanted to stay there and watch the bus leave and wave good-bye. He said nothing, but he made no move to leave, either. So they stood and waited. When the bus rumbled out, Dee and Marko waved good-bye. On their walk back to the Ford Explorer, Dee put her arms around Marko. "Are you sad?" she asked. No answer. "Are you going to miss him?" Nothing.

"I felt like if he said anything, he would lose it," Dee said later. "He never said one word to me."

Marko remembered thinking about how often he and Daniel had been together since their time in Ethiopia. He admitted that he almost cried but did not.

Daniel had similar thoughts as the bus traveled north toward Tennessee under dull gray clouds: "It is really hard for somebody who's been living together ten years and he leaves there and then you go stay with other people. That would be lonely. So I miss Marko." As the minutes passed, though, he also acknowledged a sense of excitement. He remembers his surprise, upon crossing the state line into Tennessee, that no police officers or soldiers boarded the bus to review travel documents. Later, the sight of cows thrilled him. It had been so long since he had seen cows. They passed through Kentucky in darkness. He slept mostly but remembers a lake and a bridge. They rode on and on until Daniel saw flat fields and straight roads sprinkled with what looked like flour. He turned to a passenger beside him. "What's that?" Daniel asked.

"Snow," the man replied.

He arrived in Sioux Falls thirty-six hours after leaving Atlanta. His friend met him at the bus station and took him to his apartment, where Daniel would stay for the next few weeks. It would turn out to be a rough time. He spent hours talking with friends he had last seen in Kakuma, but they eventually went to work, leaving him alone in the apartment. Daniel asked about jobs at a meatpacking plant that paid several Sudanese refugees ten dollars an hour to process beef and pork, but there were no openings. He visited a refugee-resettlement agency in Sioux Falls to see whether a job developer could help him, but he was told that he did not qualify for services because he was a secondary migrant, someone who had chosen to try his luck in a city other than the one in which he had been resettled. If he was going to find a job, he would have to do it on his own. Daniel learned of some classes in Sioux Falls that prepared students for the GED exam, and he considered taking them, but he felt guilty to be living in an apartment without paying any share of the rent. How could he justify going to classes indefinitely while his friends worked? He could not live there forever without helping pay the rent and power bill. Having arrived full of hope, Daniel had sunk into depression by the time a woman named Tami Trussell knocked on the door.

Tami was a professional mediator with two daughters in their early twenties and a husband who ran a local bank. She was active in her church and had volunteered with refugees before. She first heard about the Lost Boys at a dinner party in honor of a Bosnian friend who had just become a U.S. citizen. A woman at the table was talking about her work with a newly arrived group of young men from southern Sudan. Tami and the woman got to talking, and soon she was bouncing from apartment to apartment in Sioux Falls the way Dee Clement, Susan Gordon, and Cyndie Heiskell were in Atlanta.

She remembers being struck when she first saw Daniel. He was sitting on a sofa, staring down at a Bible and a dictionary. He was reading the Bible and stopping to look up the definitions of words he did not understand. Tami was accustomed to Lost Boys who bounded up, pumped her hand, and told her how glad they were to meet her. Daniel forced a smile and shook her hand limply. "He just doesn't have any life in him," she remembers thinking.

Over the next few days, Tami took Daniel to Sam's Club to buy him some winter clothes and tried to pry him out of his shell. She was struck by his "tender heart" and empathized when he told her he felt like he was "never going to make it." Eventually, after Daniel told Tami he wanted to become a priest, she introduced him to a Catholic priest about to retire. Daniel told the man he had applied to go to seminary in Africa but that the resettlement began before he got an answer. He asked how someone could become a priest in the United States. Most seminaries required a high-school diploma or a GED, the priest said, but he knew of one that enrolled foreign students without high-school diplomas. Instructors there taught students English and helped them prepare for GED exams as a prelude to undergraduate work. The school was called Divine Word College in Epworth, Iowa—Daniel's strongest lead yet.

About this time, back in Atlanta, someone called apartment 40-G and asked to speak with Daniel. Marko answered. On the other end of the line was a man in Kenya who identified himself as Daniel's brother, Yel. Marko knew Daniel had heard nothing of his brothers, sisters, or parents since the day an attack had flushed him into the wild a dozen years ago. "If you are his brother, tell me your grandfather's name," Marko said.

"Akech."

He was right. Marko told the man to call back in a few days. He hung up and called Daniel in South Dakota. "I got your brother!" Marko said.

Daniel thought Marko was joking. "I thought that my brother is not alive," he said later. "I told Marko, 'What do you mean? There are so many men named Yel. Maybe it is not my brother.'"

Marko told him the man had known the name of Daniel's grandfather, and, a few days later, the phone rang in Daniel's apartment in South Dakota. A man in Kenya was calling to say he was Daniel's brother, Yel, but that he could not have an extended conversation until he went to Nairobi. For that, he needed money. Daniel sent him one hundred dollars and waited.

When the phone rang again a few days later, the man named Yel told Daniel he had arrived at Kakuma in December 2001, about the time Daniel had left Atlanta for Sioux Falls, South Dakota. Daniel wanted evidence that this voice on the phone really belonged to his brother. "Can you tell me my nickname?" Daniel said.

"When you were small, they called you Alek," the caller said.

No one had used that name in so many years that Daniel had nearly forgotten about it. When he heard it, he said, he knew. Still the questions came. "Can you name your sisters?" Daniel asked.

"Akuol, Thuol, Adhel, Auyen, and Akuot."

Daniel said nothing. "I felt like crying," he said, "but I adjusted myself not to cry."

Yel told Daniel that after he had arrived in Kakuma, he had sought out others in the camp who were from his village. Yel met a man in Kakuma who told him he looked like a friend who had gone to the United States. Not only did they look alike, but they were from the same village and had the same number of siblings. The friend encouraged Yel to call Daniel.

Yel asked Daniel not just to name his brothers and sisters but to list them from eldest to youngest. Daniel did. Yel asked where their parents were. Daniel had planned to ask Yel the same thing, but it was obvious his brother knew no more than he did. Their minds went back to the day outside church that they had heard the sound, as Daniel put it, of the "plane they use to bomb the people." Yel and Daniel had bolted in different directions in a rush to escape. Each had hoped the other had fled with their parents, or at least knew what had become of them, but Yel and Daniel realized as they spoke that they had taken separate paths away from home. Yel said he had walked aimlessly for a while before meeting other people fleeing attacks. They had walked east for months, toward Ethiopia, on a journey as deadly as the one that Daniel had taken. Yel had arrived at the Panyido refugee camp, which eventually would count ten thousand unaccompanied minors along with about sixty-six thousand other refugees, nearly all from southern Sudan. He never knew his brother was less than thirty miles away, among two thousand unaccompanied boys in the Dimma refugee camp.

Daniel also never knew, until his phone conversation with Yel in the winter of 2002, that he had another name.

Many southern Sudanese refer to each other by traditional names, using their Christian names mainly with Americans or other Westerners. People from Daniel's village had called him Kuol for as long as he could remember, but he had never known why. Maybe it was just a nickname. His formal name was Khon Khoch. (He chose the name Daniel after he was baptized in 1993). Yel had news about his brother's name. He told a story about their mother's despair at having given birth to four girls in a row with no boys. She and her husband wanted a boy, Yel said, so elders summoned a traditional healer. He performed some kind of ceremony. Sure enough, the story went, their mother became pregnant and gave birth to a boy. Under the traditional Dinka naming system, the child would have acquired a first name of his own and taken as his second name the first name of his father. For example, Deng writes, "Kwol, son of Arob" would be known as "Kwol Arob." The Dinka have no direct equivalent to the last, or family, name in the Western system. In fact, according to Francis Deng, "there is no precise moment when a child is named, nor is there any designated person who selects the name. Several days after birth, suggestions for names begin. The result becomes more a matter of which name catches the popular ear than it is a matter of formal choice." Some Dinka receive names that relate to "events or circumstances surrounding conception or birth. For example, I was named 'Mading' because a bull of that name was sacrificed on my mother's marriage and people prayed that her firstborn would be a son. Being her firstborn, I was named in honor of the bull. To give other examples: *Monyyak*, 'The Man of the Drought,' was given to a child born in a severe drought; *Monylam*, 'Delivered by Prayer,' was given to a child born after a difficult labor necessitated sacrifice and prayers."

It gets complicated because Dinka boys sometimes are called by a nickname when they are young, or by a name that refers to the color of a particular ox. Yel told his brother that people called him Kuol because the name Khon Khoch was borrowed from the traditional healer as a way of paying tribute to his supposed powers to conjure a male child. Furthermore, Yel said, Daniel had been baptized when he was five months old. His parents had chosen the Christian name Gabriel, though they rarely called him that. So Daniel Khon Khoch came to believe that his real name was Gabriel Kuol Akech, Akech being his father's first name.

His parents could clear up the confusion, of course, but who knew whether they were even alive? Though Daniel had always longed to know what had become of his mother, it had never seemed practical to think that might happen. Then again, it had never seemed practical that his long-lost brother would call, either. Emboldened by the contact with Yel, Daniel let himself wonder whether it might be possible to find news of his family. A friend and fellow Lost Boy in Michigan told him that he had found his own mother by calling Dinka exiles in Khartoum, where millions of internally displaced southern Sudanese live, often clustered next to others from their hometown. Now that the refugees were in the United States, calling Khartoum was easy. All you needed was a few bucks for an international calling card. Daniel bought a few of those cards and wired money to a friend who agreed to ask around among Dinka refugees in Khartoum. The goal was to find people from the same village as Daniel. It was a long shot, but at least there was some chance to find out what had happened to Daniel's mother, Manyuon Mon Achol, rumored to have left Modhol around 1988 for some part of the capital.

Daniel waited.

The longer he stayed in South Dakota, the worse he felt for living there without paying rent. There had been a time when Daniel thought of suggesting Marko might follow him to Sioux Falls, but now it seemed absurd. Follow him to what? A town of snow and ice without jobs? At least in Atlanta, Marko was making money. Broke, Daniel packed his bags and said good-bye to Sioux Falls. The Catholic priest who had told Daniel about the seminary in Iowa gave him money for a bus ticket. He left South Dakota in the first week of February 2002 and rode south, calling Marko during a stop in Kansas City to say he was coming home. After the bus pulled into downtown Atlanta at 3 a.m. during a rare southern night of snow, sleet, and ice, Daniel picked up a pay phone and called Dee Clement. "Can you come get me?" he asked.

Half awake, Dee tried to think straight. "Who is this?"

"This is Daniel."

She paused. "Does this mean you're at a bus station?"

He was, he said. Dee lay there for a minute, groggy and frustrated. She had not known Daniel was coming back. She knew her husband would not want her driving into downtown Atlanta in a storm in the middle of the night, but he was out of town. If she didn't pick up Daniel, she wondered, who would?

"Okay," she said. "Just a minute. Let me get dressed."

The next day, Marko gave Daniel some MARTA tokens so he could get around. Daniel was back in apartment 40-G, broke and living again in an apartment without paying his share of the rent. Marko asked his manager about jobs at the meatpacking plant, and before long, Daniel was getting up before dawn to ride with other refugees in a company van to a dangerous, loud plant almost as cold as South Dakota. When he told friends about finding his brother after so many years, he learned he was not the only person reconnecting with relatives.

Abraham Yel knew of several members of his congregation who were finding out after so many years what had become of their parents. The discoveries brought a mix of good and bad news. Sometimes refugees in the United States reconnected with parents and siblings whose fate they had never known, but other times, Abraham said, a man would work the phone network only to be told, "Oh, we are sorry, but everybody in your family is dead."

So there was some precedent for what happened to Daniel when he trudged into his apartment on the evening of July 12, 2002. His roommate Kuan Tong was waiting for him. Kuan had moved in a few weeks earlier, after he had injured his arm falling off a bicycle and could not keep his job loading and unloading boxes for a moving company in the Atlanta suburb of Sandy Springs. Since he could not work, he could not pay his former roommates his share of the rent. His roommates had suggested he find somewhere else to live, so Kuan moved in with Daniel. Older than many Lost Boys, Kuan was one of the few southern Sudanese in Georgia with the deep scarification marks on his forehead from the traditional Dinka initiation that Francis Deng describes as "the bloodiest and most painful operation in Dinka society." Three or four thick scars danced from the nape of his neck toward the crown of his skull and then down again, to a series of Vs on his forehead, one inside another, markings of a ritual that has become far less common as the modern world encroaches on tradition in southern Sudan.

On this night, Kuan had a message. A friend had called Daniel from Africa with stunning news: he had found Daniel's mother alive, in a settlement just south of Khartoum. He left the phone number for the apartment where Daniel's mother was staying. Daniel raced to a grocery store to buy three ten-dollar phone cards and marched back into the apartment. He sat alone in his bedroom and picked up the phone as Marko listened in the living room, a receiver pressed to his ear. Daniel dialed the numbers and waited.

It was 5 a.m. in Khartoum when a woman's voice came on the line. "Who is this?" she asked.

Daniel said he was her son.

"No," she said. "It's not you." Suspicious, she asked the name of his older brother.

"Yel," Daniel said.

She started to cry. "Why have you forgotten me?" she said. "Where have you been for this time?"

Daniel let her talk. "I was about to cry," he recalled later, "but, really, I didn't cry."

He told her to be patient and tried to explain what had happened that Sunday after mass, how he had been playing soccer when the attack began. "I just ran away alone. You cannot blame me," he told her.

Later, Daniel's mother told him that his father had gone missing shortly after the attack that had flushed Daniel from home. She said two sisters had been shot to death years ago. Two other sisters, though, were alive and living with her. Another sister was married and living somewhere near their village in southern Sudan. A rush of conflicting emotions washed over Daniel. He would later find it difficult to put into words except to say how happy he was to have found his mother after all these years. "I thought that I was left alone," he said.

A few nights later, Marko had a dream. He was walking into his village, he said, a grown man coming home for the first time in his life. He saw his "age mates," boys who, in traditional peaceful times, would have been organized into a group that would sing together and tend cattle together and one brilliant day lie in a line on the ground together and endure deep cuts in the forehead as a moving mass of girls and women chanted and sang of the young men's valor and courage in a scarification ceremony that would mark their glorious transition into manhood. In the dream, Marko was much older than he had been when he had left home, but it did not matter. His age mates smiled; they recognized him. Marko saw his brother and sister. He was eager to greet them and they were eager to greet him. He kept walking, floating almost, wanting to believe but cautious, guarded. Then he saw his mother and his father, arms wide, inviting. He was laughing now, that uninhibited, radiant laugh of ineffable joy. His mother and father, at last. He walked toward them with his own arms outstretched. Then something roused Marko from sleep. He sat up in bed in the darkness and felt "annoyed and unhappy," reminded of an emptiness that could not be denied. There were no sounds. After a minute, Marko lay back down and rested his head on the pillow. There was no sense brooding. He had to go to work in the morning. He closed his eyes and drifted back to sleep.

THIS IS YOUR FUTURE

The desire for an education still burned strong in Jacob Magot. He had come to the United States expecting to work but also to study. That had proven difficult. When Jacob attended GED-preparation classes at the International Rescue Committee in the first weeks after he arrived, he had made an impression on the instructor, Adrian Jelks, a woman in her early thirties. She had been part owner of a bar in Atlanta called the Righteous Room, but had quit to do something she felt would make a difference. Adrian had taught refugees from Afghanistan, Bosnia, Iraq, Vietnam, and the former Soviet Union and had helped them prepare for high school or college. When the Lost Boys of Sudan were brought to Atlanta, she taught a GED prep class at the IRC offices off Memorial Drive, a short bus ride from the apartments in Clarkston. Jacob's nimble mind impressed her so much that she told him she expected he would be one of the first of the southern Sudanese refugees in Atlanta to earn his high-school equivalency degree. Then Jacob started working at the Discovery Channel Store during the day and Target at night. Suddenly he did not have enough time to take classes, but he did not give up.

To receive a GED diploma, students must pass five tests covering different topics—math, social studies, science, writing, and literature. Students could score anywhere from 200 to 800 and needed a minimum score of 410 on each section to pass. After he started work and stopped attending classes, Jacob went with Daniel, Peter, and dozens of other Lost Boys to take a pre-GED test at the Lost Boys Foundation in downtown Atlanta. Instructors said his score would indicate how prepared he was for the actual test and show the areas on which he needed to focus. Like Daniel, though, Jacob said he was never able to find anyone at the foundation who could tell him his score. Another time, he took a GED practice test at a community college in Clarkston. He had to read three passages and answer seventeen questions, but the passages were so dense, so hard to understand. Like most other Lost Boys in the United States, Jacob spoke a literal, archaic English. The GED test was full of mysterious words and phrases, everyday American English and slang that perplexed him. Jacob was still struggling to understand one passage when an instructor told him time had expired.

"When we came here, we had our own expectations, to go to school," Abraham Yel said. "We were discouraged because the Americans had their own expectations for us, to enroll us in work and make money."

Some frustration was rooted in a misunderstanding among the young men from southern Sudan of what awaited in the United States. The federal government resettles refugees with the expectation that they will be self-reliant after receiving financial assistance for a few months. That means they are expected to work. Most agencies offer English classes and information about how a refugee can receive a high-school equivalency degree or enroll in college or a technical school, but the cold reality was that work left little time for school. That was hard for many southern Sudanese to swallow. The importance of an education had been drilled in so deeply, from such an early age, that their failure to study exerted tremendous pressure. The resettlement agencies tried to accommodate their yearning to study, but they had other refugees to consider, too, and they could not possibly tailor a solution that would meet the needs of all 156 Lost Boys in Atlanta. Some worked one job, some worked two. Some worked in the mornings, others at night. It had been easier in Kakuma to craft a collective solution. It was easy enough there to offer classes in the morning for refugees who cared to attend. What else did they have to do? In the United States, though, the understanding began to dawn on many of the young men from southern Sudan that a collective approach to their problems was not on the way, that they would have to fashion their own plans to receive an education.

Peter had finished high school in Kakuma and wanted to go to college. Marko, years younger, was still in high school in Kenya when the United States flew him to a new life. The age assigned him by relief workers made him too old for high school in Georgia, but he doubted he could pass the GED exams. He longed to go to high school. Daniel was thinking more and more about the seminary in Iowa, but Jacob had committed himself to passing the GED by studying on his own.

So one Thursday morning in the spring of 2002, Susan Gordon drove him from his apartment to the city of East Point, about five miles south of downtown Atlanta. He would sit for three of the five GED exams at the Fulton County Schools Staff Development Center, a two-story brick building near Atlanta's airport. Susan and Jacob arrived about 8:15 and talked for ten minutes while sitting on a concrete picnic table just outside the front door. "You can take MARTA home, okay?" Susan said.

Jacob nodded.

"If you can't figure it out, just call me."

"All right."

"I'll have my cell phone on."

"Okay."

"Good luck, sweetie," Susan said.

"Oh, thank you," Jacob replied.

Jacob strode into the building and walked down a corridor with walls of cream-colored cinderblock. He turned into a classroom and sat in a desk in the front row, right in the middle. A booklet stared up at him. He had been waiting for this. "Georgia Department of Technical and Adult Education," the cover said. "Tests of General Education Development." With a pencil, Jacob darkened bubbles that corresponded to the letters of his name and numbers that matched his Social Security number. Then he sat there and waited. In the class with him were about two dozen students, mainly African Americans in their late teens or early twenties. There was a young woman with short blond hair tucked into a blue bandana, another with a cigarette tucked like a pencil behind her ear. A man in baggy blue jeans and a gray T-shirt looked at the clock. A woman sauntered in wearing a white skirt so light and so tight that her pink underwear leaped out as if part of the outfit. One man yawned. Two women in the back whispered into cell phones. After they hung up, the only sounds were of someone unwrapping a candy bar and someone else unzipping a purse; beneath the hush was the dull distant roar of airplanes taking off and landing. An administrator marched in at 9:10 with instructions to get out photo identification and line up at the door. She would call each of their names, check IDs, and usher them into another room where they would actually take the test. She called each name like a drill sergeant, lowered her eyes to check the ID, and pointed out the door with her left hand. "Barnesworth. Green. Hamilton. Howard. Jackson. Johnson. King. Mitkin. Magot."

Jacob presented his state-issued ID card, waited for her nod, and followed other students into the hallway and then left into room 103, the classroom where he would take the social studies, science, and literature-interpretation sections of the GED test. Jacob sat next to the woman with the blue bandana. He folded his hands in his lap and waited for the room to fill. He glanced down; social studies was first. He waited. After three or four minutes, the woman who had checked his ID entered room 103 and stood up front, under a clock with black numbers on a white face and a ticking red second hand. "This is your test," she said. "This is your future."

It was 9:25.

"You may begin."

That afternoon, Jacob would remember being astonished at how quickly the woman in the blue bandana finished the test. The students had an hour and fifteen minutes, but she put her pencil down after half an hour. Jacob could "only figure she was randomly assigning probabilities," by which he meant she must have been guessing. As for his performance, he did not want to say much about it. The social studies and science portions went well, he said, but literature interpretation was a killer. Jacob was not too sure about that section.

Literature interpretation was emerging as a stumbling block for many Lost Boys. For one thing, they complained, there was not enough time. For another, they had a tough time understanding cultural references in poetry and essays. It seemed so different from the English they learned in Africa. One afternoon, John perched himself on the edge of a sofa in the living room of apartment 40-G, just under a map of the world tacked to the wall, and squinted at a reading-comprehension passage in a GED-preparation book. In the passage, one person was describing his job search to a friend. He had scoured the "classifieds" but wanted a job that was more than "a box in the newspaper." John rarely saw newspapers and did not know what the "classifieds" were. He spoke an English that let him convey complex thoughts in a simple, straightforward language, but U.S. slang bewildered him. The passage that referred to a classified ad as a "box in a newspaper," for example. How could he possibly understand that? He had never even seen a classified ad.

He read another practice essay question aloud.

"Is it advantageous or disadvantageous to have a pet?"

John raised his head and stared at the wall on the other side of the room, seeming to mull over his response.

"What is a pet?" he asked.

Despite obstacles that seemed overwhelming, dozens of the southern Sudanese in Atlanta received a morale boost in the spring of 2002 when John Garang, leader of the rebel Sudan People's Liberation Army, visited the Carter Center in Atlanta. Dozens of young men who had once been known as unaccompanied minors broke into song when they caught sight of him. Later, they listened as Garang shared his views on the prospects for peace.

"The Lost Boys—now found I should think—I wish you well and please do pursue your education however difficult it is," Garang said. "I was in this country myself. I used to wash dishes at Grinnell College. I worked on farms. I worked in a bottling company. I worked in the Minnesota Conservation Department . . . to make money to go to school." He reminded them of their role after the war. "So whatever difficulties you are facing, you must overcome them and educate yourself so that you have something that you came here for—when you return home, you return with something, some skill that you have acquired."

Garang thanked volunteers in the United States who were helping them: "Please continue to take care of them and to look after their welfare so that they are able to acquire an education. This is the primary reason for which they came. Most of them wanted an education and I'm sure most of them would want to go back. This is the land of opportunity. Give them that opportunity."

Susan Gordon and another volunteer, Linda Amick, wanted to do that. They were among several volunteers who felt with the passing of several months that the refugees would value help pursuing their education over a cooking lesson or an outing to the zoo. And so in the summer of 2002, about a year after Lost Boys began to arrive in Atlanta, they were becoming more and more consumed with directing the refugees toward a school. Susan and Linda, like other volunteers, had abandoned hope that the Lost Boys Foundation would help the young men pursue their educations. After all, the foundation had made a splash by promising GED-prep classes that never materialized. It said it would test each refugee and tailor him an individual plan of study, but that did not happen, either. Frustrated, Susan and Linda decided to act on their own to get some of the young men into high school and college. Linda told Susan they should start with "the low-hanging fruit." What she meant was that they should identify refugees who had finished high school in Kenya and help them, if they were interested, apply for financial aid and admission to a community college. For several weeks, Susan went from apartment to apartment, asking whether any of the refugees had finished high school. Several had. She brought them to Linda's house, where they applied for financial aid and admission to college with Linda's help. In this way, the first of several Lost Boys in Atlanta enrolled at Georgia Perimeter College, a two-year school within walking distance of the apartments in Clarkston.

Susan and Linda also hoped to help some of the young men who had not finished high school in Kenya. In the summer of 2002, they told several Lost Boys, discreetly, that they may have stumbled upon a path that could get some Lost Boys into Open Campus High School, a second-chance school where most students are eighteen to twenty years old. The school had about 950 students but no sports teams, clubs, or cafeteria. It attracted students who had dropped out of high school at age sixteen or seventeen only to realize after a year or two that a diploma actually was of some value in the world. There were also young men and women who had spent four years in high school but still needed to pass a class or two to graduate. The school's "Statement of Understanding," which every student was required to sign, noted that success at the school "depends largely on the student's maturity level, self-discipline and a strong desire for a quality education." Classes lasted an hour and forty minutes, more than twice as long as in a traditional high school. The idea was to cover material as quickly as possible so students could receive diplomas and get on with life.

A few people had thought of Open Campus as a possibility for the Lost Boys, but there was a general understanding that people over the age of twenty could not enroll. One Sudanese man who did attend classes at Open Campus was nineteen, but most Lost Boys in Atlanta had been assigned ages that made them older than twenty. Several months after the resettlement, Adrian Jelks, the education worker at the International Rescue Committee, was on the phone with a guidance counselor at Open Campus, chatting about the possibility of enrolling another student. At one point, she was talking to herself, really, reciting a mental checklist of the requirements.

"Of course, they must be under twenty," Adrian said.

"No," the counselor said. "We have two forty-year-old women here."

Adrian perked up. Contrary to popular belief, it turned out that the school occasionally did enroll older students. If a student was twenty or older, he or she had to meet the principal but could enroll if the principal did not object. Suddenly, Open Campus seemed like a possibility for some Lost Boys in Atlanta. Susan and Linda told Adrian they wanted to try to enroll some refugees, but Adrian worried about overwhelming the school. She urged them to keep it small. As the next registration approached, Susan and Linda spread the word to eight refugees. They said they took pains to explain that it was not a done deal—they still had concerns about the age requirement. They tried not to raise hopes only to dash them, as they felt the Lost Boys Foundation had done. "We can't promise you anything, but we will try," Susan remembers telling them. "We don't want to disappoint you again."

Despite the efforts at secrecy, people affiliated with the Lost Boys Foundation caught wind of the plan. They would later say they "felt betrayed" by volunteers who had not so long ago aligned themselves with the foundation. The executive director of the foundation, a woman named Barbara Obrentz, came to the Lost Boys' church in Clarkston to make an announcement on the Sunday before Open Campus would open its doors to register new students. Susan Gordon was in the audience. So were a few other volunteers, including a computer-network engineer named Neal Kelley. Barbara began by saying she knew how badly many of the Lost Boys wanted to go to school. She said that she understood that some volunteers might already have been talking about Open Campus but that the Lost Boys Foundation was taking over—she even had a sign-up sheet. Susan saw Barbara's speech as consistent with a desperate need to control anything relating to the Lost Boys in Atlanta. She seethed. Susan said later that she was mainly upset because the foundation had promised something that was not at all a sure thing. Abraham was angry, too. "They were upset or jealous," he recalled later. "If the volunteers are finding a way for Lost Boys to go to school, the foundation will want to take it over to make it look like they are providing services."

After Barbara's presentation, she got an earful from several volunteers as a crowd of Lost Boys looked on. "I said, 'Do you know what just happened? You just announced something that is not certain,'" Neal Kelley recalled. "'You guys have a huge public relations problem. People don't trust you.'"

The result of the confrontation was that everyone said they would try to work together. Barbara and a colleague at the foundation tagged along the next day, to the first step of registration, as Susan arranged for eight young men to have self-recorded transcripts from Kenya evaluated. A week later, Barbara's colleague at the foundation showed up at the second phase of registration and watched as Linda and another volunteer guided young men from table to table in the school gymnasium. Linda waited for the other shoe to drop, for someone to say that the refugees were too old to go to Open Campus, but it did not happen. One refugee after another listened as an administrator explained the attendance policy—students could miss no more than five classes during the nineweek term. They nodded when told that the school required "clear plastic or mesh book bags." At another table, they signed up for classes. And then that was it. They were in.

Word spread about Open Campus. As the students settled into classes that taught math, science, and English, the high school seemed with each passing day like a solution for a group that had for the most part been running into obstacles that had kept them from school. Not all refugees could attend, though. The big drawback was that refugees enrolled in Open Campus could not continue working jobs that required their presence in the morning or early afternoon. Many found jobs that let them work in the afternoon or at night, after classes. To pay the rent and buy groceries, they also relied on money they had saved or, more commonly, on roommates who were working. The Lost Boys had lived as a group for more than a dozen years, so it was not unusual for one refugee to pay another's share if the other had a good reason not to be working, and everyone understood how important school was. Some refugees at Open Campus took too many classes and ended up dropping one subject to avoid failing, but on the whole Open Campus was an option with wide appeal.

Two months later, another group registered at Open Campus. First they met the guidance counselor for an orientation. Four Lost Boys went to the school on a Wednesday morning and settled into blue plastic chairs around a wooden table. A poster on one wall asked "Where Am I Going?" above images of a factory worker, a rancher, a judge, a banker, an accountant, and a veterinarian. On another wall, beyond the army recruitment poster and rows of college catalogs, a poster demanded "How Will I Get There?" A few inches to the right, a long rectangular wall hanging repeated the phrase "I think I can" fourteen times above this line: "Positive thinking is half the work." There were more volunteers than refugees in the room. Linda Amick and Susan Gordon were there, along with two women from the Lost Boys Foundation. There was a young woman named Tiffany Byers, a management consultant, and Bill Morgan, a retired businessman, each of whom mentored one of the young men enrolling at Open Campus. They listened as a guidance counselor told the four refugees about the attendance policy—that was important—and explained that fighting would get them a one-way ticket home. She said that teachers were impressed with the dedication of the southern Sudanese refugees who already were enrolled. The counselor also reminded the refugees that school buses did not go to Open Campus. Students were responsible for getting there themselves, either by taking public transportation or by driving or riding with a friend. If you're driving, the counselor said, remember that traffic is awful around the school.

The volunteers could vouch for that.

"That light on LaVista can stop you for ten minutes," Bill said.

"And coming up North Druid Hills is tough," Linda said.

The guidance counselor nodded. "North Druid Hills Road—it can take a long time," she said.

On the way out, Susan stopped to chat with the counselor. "Thank you so much for having them at the school," she said. "It's an answer to a lot of prayers."

The next day, the young men from southern Sudan, accompanied by American volunteers who had befriended them, were back at Open Campus, in the gymnasium this time, to register for classes. Rows of blue plastic chairs with aluminum legs rested in the middle of the gym floor, arranged in blocks and cordoned off by yellow ropes. Prospective students sat in the chairs clutching paperwork, waiting to be called to the first of about a dozen tables arrayed in front of the gym walls. Administrators sat behind the tables, telling young men and women to read this form and sign that one and then move on to the next station to read and sign more forms. Tiffany Byers and Bill Morgan guided refugees through the process. Tiffany sat with a young man named Wal Deng Wal and waited as he read every line of the attendance policy. He lifted a page and peered at a yellow sheet underneath.

"It's just a copy," she said.

He signed and dated the form.

"Make that look like a 9," Tiffany said.

He did.

"Is that a T?" she asked.

He corrected the letter.

"Better, better," said a school administrator sitting across the table. "Even I can read it upside down."

The refugees in apartment 40-G knew about Open Campus, but none seemed too interested. Jacob had dedicated himself to receiving his GED diploma on his own, and Peter was waiting to see what happened with a handful of Sudanese who had applied to Georgia Perimeter College. Daniel sent off for information on the seminary in Iowa that the Catholic priest had told him about when he was in Sioux Falls. Marko had heard about other Lost Boys in Atlanta getting into high school after receiving "birth certificates" that showed they were under eighteen. Volunteers would go to court to become their legal guardians and then use the birth certificates to enroll them in high school. He would find out more later about how that happened. John and William were working at the meatpacking plant without a clear idea of whether they would get into school, though they were hearing more about a path to school that led from Atlanta to Washington, D.C.

In the spring of 2002, a few months before the first Sudanese refugees enrolled at Open Campus, a Lost Boy named Abraham Chan had moved from Seattle to Atlanta. He met Neal Kelley, the network engineer who was going to Clarkston after work so often that his coworkers would kid him about coming to work in the same clothes he had worn the day before. Neal spent huge chunks of his weekends and most of his weeknights in Clarkston, a forty-five-minute drive from his home in the suburbs north of Atlanta. If he found himself in an apartment of Lost Boys late at night, as he often did, Neal would sleep on the couch and go straight to work the next morning. As his involvement deepened, Neal won the respect of many of the men from southern Sudan by learning to speak Dinka, which he did with the help of tapes and workbooks from Kenya. Some Lost Boys started calling Neal "Agutthon," a Dinka term that, roughly translated, means "the man who killed the bull," an unlikely nickname for a man who grew up as the neighborhood geek in a rough section of Queens, New York.

As a boy, Neal had a reputation as "the little scientist," the kid who spent hours in his own little world, flying model airplanes while others played stickball. It wasn't the worst of neighborhoods, he would say, but he had seen people shot and killed, had seen firsthand the violence that drinking can unleash. Neal never touched alcohol. He liked to point out that the word *toxic* was part of the word *intoxication*. Neal did not touch coffee, either. He had a broad smile and an easy laugh. A computer nut, Neal and some buddies got the idea, in the high-tech mania of the 1990s, to create a new kind of magazine that would cover the booming hip-hop world. Instead of text and photos on the printed page, the magazine would come on a CD that consumers would buy and plug into their computer. They would see articles, photos, and ads, just like in a traditional magazine, but could also watch video clips of live performances and hear interviews with the stars. While promoting his idea for an "enhanced CD," Neal made connections that led to Lisa "Left Eye" Lopes of the hip-hop group TLC, the most successful female trio in recording history. She was a sexy singer from Atlanta who was famous for her abilities on stage, for her habit of wearing eyeglasses with a condom in place of the left lens, and for burning down the mansion of her boyfriend, an Atlanta Falcons football star, after a quarrel one evening in 1994. After Neal showed Lisa a prototype of one of his CDs, she got him an audience with one of the titan producers in the hip-hop world. When it became obvious that, despite their interest and kind words, the producers were not biting, Lisa gave Neal ten thousand dollars to promote his hip-hop CD magazine. It went nowhere, but Neal and Lisa remained friends.

After he read a newspaper story about the Lost Boys and began spending so much time in Clarkston, he took several of the refugees to the star's house in suburban Atlanta. One refugee who met Lisa, Abraham Diing Akoi, told her a friend in Nairobi had a poster of her on his wall. They called the friend from Lisa's house and, once he realized it really was Left Eye calling from Atlanta, the man broke into one of her songs. She sang into the phone right along with him.

Abraham said he told Lisa, "Soldiers killed our parents when we were very young," and said she "was wondering how people who were very, very small were able to survive." She seemed as taken as Neal with the refugees and even invited six Lost Boys into her studio. They recorded songs she planned to use as backup vocals on a CD she was producing for another female hip-hop group. Talking with the refugees, she said, made her wonder how she would have reacted to the trauma that visited them in childhood: "Once I start seeing the picture in my mind of what they describe happened, I can't help but imagine myself in that situation." A few months after meeting some Lost Boys in Atlanta, Lisa was killed in a car wreck while on vacation in Honduras. Her death upset Neal, but he did not wallow or brood. Just hours after hearing that his friend was dead, Neal was at work, sad but not distraught. He was optimistic by nature, and his usual cheerful guffaws were on display weeks later as he answered his cell phone one weekday afternoon.

"Hey man!" Neal said and then laughed, even before the caller had said much of anything. He smiled and nodded. "Yea, Abraham Diing got laid off, but *hakuna matata*," he said, throwing in some of the Kiswahli he'd been learning. "No problem, man!"

Yet it was a problem. People were being laid off. And those who were able to keep their jobs wondered whether they would ever go to school. So Neal was possessed with inspiration after he got to talking one night with Abraham Chan, the man who had moved to Atlanta from Seattle. They were thumbing through a book that listed opportunities for vocational training when Abraham pointed to an entry about a program called Job Corps. He told Neal he had applied to enter the program while in Seattle.

Run by the U.S. Department of Labor, Job Corps receives more than $1 billion a year in public money to offer academic and vocational training to poor students ages sixteen to twenty-four at 118 campuses around the United States. Students studied for the GED exam and learned a trade, such as carpentry, data entry, or plumbing. For up to two years, the federal government would pay a student's room and board and provide an amount of spending money that increased the longer they stayed. The rationale was that investing tax money for an "at-risk" population would save public money in the long run in the form of decreased welfare payments, higher taxes paid by people who could earn more with a diploma and a trade, and cost savings for people who might otherwise be incarcerated. Nearly 2 million people have been through the Job Corps program since its founding in 1964. The government said fifty-five thousand of the seventy thousand participants in any given year leave having passed the GED or having completed a course of vocational training.

To Neal, it sounded like a perfect solution. He spoke with a woman who worked for an Atlanta company that interviewed and processed Job Corps applicants. She had not heard of the Lost Boys of Sudan, so he faxed her some information. A few weeks later, she gave a presentation about Job Corps at one of those Saturday morning meetings at the Lost Boys Foundation. As curiosity grew, Neal asked the contractor to make sure that any of the Lost Boys in Atlanta who joined the program were sent to the same Job Corps campus. They had functioned as a group for so long and would do better in an unfamiliar place, Neal said, if they could compare notes with friends. Most refugees were reluctant to go at first, preferring the comfort of a large community of Lost Boys to the unknown of this federal program that seemed too good to be true, but a few people applied. The first two Lost Boys left Atlanta for the Job Corps campus in Washington around March 2002 and called back with positive reports. Neal encouraged others to apply and soon morphed into a walking advertisement. Two converts visited apartment 40-G one day in May 2002 to tell the six roommates that a friend had called from Job Corps to endorse it without reservation. "He said they were welcomed," one visitor said. "The only thing he talked about is the noise in the compound."

Two weeks later, Neal knocked on the door of apartment 40-G. Peter and Daniel rose to greet him. They made small talk, Neal all smiles and laughs, and then the conversation turned to Neal's passion. He asked whether they had thought about going to Washington.

"We don't know the advantages of Job Corps and we don't know the disadvantages," one of them said. "So inform us."

Neal started with the testimony of Lost Boys who already had left Atlanta for Washington. They could focus on studying without having to worry about work. Every day, it seemed, Neal heard from Lost Boys in Atlanta who had spoken with friends in Washington. They all received glowing reports about Job Corps. "I don't want to send you someplace that's not working," he said.

He faced a tough crowd in apartment 40-G. Peter sat on the edge of a couch to the left of Neal, looking at the floor. He leaned forward and rested his forehead in the palm of his left hand and did not say anything. Daniel lay on another sofa against the opposite wall, his eyes closed, right hand over his head.

"What I'm trying to do is find an option, another path," Neal said. "The most important thing is that you learn to make decisions on your own." He waited for questions that did not come. "This option will work," he said. "I would not send you someplace that I would not go myself." Neal was a motivational speaker now, a preacher at revival. "You are not acquiring an education by yourselves," he said. "You will teach the multitudes of people who are left behind. The foundation of a New Sudan will come from you guys." His voice rose. "What defines you?" he demanded. "What makes you? If this is the only path that is available, and I hope to God it is not, then it's the path you must take."

When he stopped for a breath, the only sounds were from the black-and-white television perched atop a dresser in the living room. It was just after 7:30 p.m. and *Wheel of Fortune* had merged into *Jeopardy!* Alex Trebek was talking with a contestant. "Odd hair growth on your chin," Trebek said.

"What is a beard?"

"Right!"

Peter and Daniel seemed relieved when Neal ended his pitch and stood up to say good-bye. They appreciated Neal's time and energy. Many refugees were following his advice on how to receive the education they craved, but most of the men of apartment 40-G had other ideas. Peter and Daniel harbored visions of other paths to education, Jacob had committed himself to studying on his own for the GED exams, and Marko was thinking more and more about trying to find some way to go to high school in Georgia.

William, however, was foundering. He wanted an education as much as anyone but had no real prospects, so he listened when his roommates told him later what Neal said about Job Corps, how instructors spent time on academics and also taught trades that could lead to better-paying jobs in the future. He was intrigued.

DRIVING

Peter was working long hours at the meatpacking plant. He had received a promotion that came with a raise. Now the company paid him $9.55 an hour to run a machine that wrapped meat in plastic for shipment to grocery stores. He told Susan Gordon and Linda Amick that he planned to quit his job and go to college if he could pass the Test of English as a Foreign Language (TOEFL), required of many foreign-born students applying to colleges and universities in the United States. Susan and Linda promised to help him apply for financial aid and register for classes at Georgia Perimeter College. In the meantime, Peter wanted to buy a car.

Most southern Sudanese refugees in Georgia rode public buses and trains to work in low-wage jobs in warehouses, hotels, department stores, and factories. After work, they were stuck in Clarkston for lack of a car, restricted to their apartments and places within walking distance. A trip to the grocery store could take a few hours, including the walk there and back. They walked to church at the community center on Sunday unless an American volunteer took them there. They walked everywhere. Of course, they had always walked everywhere, but they were not in

Kakuma anymore. It did not take long for many of the refugees to see the automobile as a ticket to unrestricted mobility and freedom. Before they could hit the roads, though, they had to learn to drive.

Peter spent hours studying the Georgia driver's license manual. On the first Monday in May 2002, he passed a written test and then identified road signs and passed an eye test to receive a learner's permit. Five days later, Cheryl Grover pulled into the parking lot of Olde Plantation Apartments to pick him up for his first driving lesson. Peter wore his USRP sweatshirt and pants with a plaid pattern of pastel yellow, green, and white, as if he were bound for a retirement-community golf course. He climbed into Cheryl's white Infiniti I30 and rode with her to an empty parking lot at Georgia Perimeter College. "You could be going to this college next year, huh?" Cheryl said.

"Yeah."

"Maybe driving to the college."

"Yeah."

Peter sat in the passenger seat, watching Cheryl press pedals with her feet. She stopped in the middle of a parking lot, turned off the engine, and told Peter to step out. Before she started the lesson, Cheryl wanted to point out a few things. The tires, for example. She squatted by the front left tire and fingered the tread. "You can see the ridges," she said. "These are brand new tires."

He touched where she had touched.

Police can pull you over for having a broken taillight, Cheryl told him, so make sure they work. She told Peter to stay behind the car while she got into the driver's seat, put the key into the ignition, and started the engine. The first thing Peter noticed was an antenna on the right side of the trunk sliding up quietly. Then the red brake lights came on. Cheryl demonstrated one turn signal and then the other. He nodded. She stepped out again to show him the spare tire and windshield wipers. "Let's see," she said. "What am I forgetting?"

When Cheryl and Peter got back into the car, Peter settled into the driver's seat. "It's important that you have confidence that you have driving skills for any driving conditions," Cheryl said. "It's important that new drivers feel confident, especially here in Atlanta, where the traffic is so heavy all the time." She showed Peter how to put the windows up and down, turn on the headlights, and adjust the side and rear-view mirrors. Then she pointed to space underneath the steering wheel. "The one on the right is the gas pedal. The bigger one in the middle—"

"Brake," Peter said.

"—is the brake pedal. It's important to leave a distance of two car lengths between you and the car in front of you." To help him visualize what two car lengths might look like, she got out and walked in front of the car. Peter watched through the windshield without saying anything. Cheryl got back into the car, thought for a minute, and told Peter to turn the key. The engine hummed to life.

Peter pointed to a lever by the steering wheel: "What of this one?"

"This one has two functions. It's your turn signal, okay? This also controls the lights of the car," Cheryl said. "You and all your passengers should be wearing the seat belt and you don't move your car until they are wearing the seat belt."

"Yeah," he said.

"What I want you to do is—is make sure I have my seat belt on," she said.

Peter laughed. She reached down to buckle her lap belt.

When you drive, you don't want any distractions, Cheryl said. No radio. No conversation. No turning to face other passengers. Keep your eyes on the road. The car tends to move in whatever direction the driver looks. That's just human nature, she said.

Then, finally, the driving. "Put your foot on the brake pedal," Cheryl said. Peter pressed the accelerator. The engine revved. "No. The brake pedal." Cheryl explained the typical gears on an automatic car and what the letters stood for on the gearshift: P for park, R for reverse, N for neutral, D for drive. As Peter pressed the brake pedal, she moved the gearshift to D. Then she told him to ease his foot off the brake pedal. The car moved forward. Peter smiled. After the car had rolled about twenty feet, he pressed hard on the brake pedal and a force pushed Peter forward in the driver's seat and then back again.

"I understand now," he said. "Use the brake without a big push."

"Yes. Press gently."

He took his foot off the brake pedal again and let the car move without using the accelerator. As the car rolled forward, Cheryl suggested he turn the steering wheel. The car drifted left and then back to the right. Peter turned the wheel left, and the car drifted past the center line and headed for the curb.

"Steer to your right," Cheryl said. "No! No! Brake!" Peter hit the brake hard. The car stopped a few inches from the curb. "Okay!" Cheryl said. "That's okay!"

Peter said nothing.

"The hard part about turning is seeing where the curbs are. I think you sense that," she said. "Do you see how sometimes you turn it too much one way or the other? The car tends to want to go straight by itself." For the next twenty-three minutes, he practiced lifting his foot from the brake pedal and steering right and left without accelerating. "Go ahead and use the accelerator gently," Cheryl said. "Very, very gently."

"I am to press down on the accelerator?"

"Yeah."

"Now?"

"Yes."

Peter pressed down, and an invisible power pushed the car forward. He laughed.

"There you go," Cheryl said. "Good. Very good. Very nice, Peter!"

A few minutes later, after drifting again, Peter jammed the brakes down and screeched to a halt about a foot from a concrete island. Cheryl didn't miss a beat. "Okay. Good," she said. "Let's practice putting it in reverse." After backing up and moving forward and backing up again, Cheryl showed him how to pull into a parking space. It was tricky, but Peter did it several times.

"You did very good, Peter," Cheryl said. "I'm very proud of you."

One of Peter's roommates, John, got his turn a month later. Two of his friends were getting lessons from a friend named Jeremy Paden, a doctoral candidate studying Spanish literature at Emory University. He and his wife attended Dee Clement's church and volunteered with the Lost Boys after hearing a presentation Dee made at a church dinner. They got to know six refugees in the same apartment. For much of June and July 2002, Jeremy had been giving driving lessons to two of the six. He took it slowly at first, going to parking lots and doing about the same things Cheryl had done with Peter. Finally, on a Friday morning in August, Jeremy decided it was time for a lesson in real traffic. When he went to their apartment to pick them up, John came bounding down the stairs.

"I just got my learner's permit. Can I go?" he asked.

Jeremy said he could ride along. John got into the backseat and rode with Jeremy and his two students to a neighborhood in Avondale Estates, a quiet, residential community just east of Atlanta. Jeremy yielded the driver's seat to one of his students, who did well. Jeremy was impressed, but when John, in the backseat, asked whether he could drive, too, Jeremy said no.

"He just looked crestfallen," Jeremy recalled. "I shouldn't have given in, but the street was empty, no traffic."

In the passenger seat, Jeremy explained the brake and gas pedals and reminded John to check his side and rear-view mirrors before moving. John pressed the accelerator. Jeremy's light-blue four-door 1990 Pontiac Grand Prix glided forward under John's command, but turning in one direction or another was not as easy as it looked. The car swerved right and then left. It surged forward. Both men in the backseat shouted "Brake! Brake!" as the car banked hard left, heading straight for the curb. John tried to brake, but his foot smashed the gas pedal instead. Jeremy tried to yank the wheel to the right but John clasped it in a death grip. The Grand Prix jumped the curb and smashed into a dogwood tree about five inches thick. Jeremy looked around after the car finally stopped moving; no one was hurt. He stepped outside and saw the tree embedded about ten inches into the engine compartment. Jeremy said John looked "absolutely sick, just physically sick with himself. He just said over and over again that he was sorry. He felt horrible that I had trusted him with something of mine. He said, 'I was hoping we could be friends, but I understand if you don't want to be my friend.'"

Jeremy reassured him. "Don't worry about it," he said. "This happens. I wrecked a few cars when I was learning to drive."

The car was totaled, but it could have been much worse. Jeremy had paid only five hundred dollars for it in the first place (he had bought it from his in-laws).

Owning a car gave Lost Boys a certain prestige and a sense of independence. A refugee with his own car no longer had to depend on others for a ride. He was the one offering rides. Jon D. Holtzman, an anthropologist who worked in Minnesota studying southern Sudanese refugees from the Nuer ethnic group, reported that "the automobile has come to have a special significance for Nuer in Minnesota. . . . Nuer joke that 'In Africa, we have cows; here we have cars.' Although spoken in jest, this statement shows a conscious engagement of Nuer with American culture, which, as they have correctly assessed, is deeply focused on the automobile."

Holtzman found that Nuer refugees "were already thinking about and talking about cars" when they lived "in refugee camps half a world away." Yet when they were in Minnesota, working long hours at low-wage jobs, they came to realize that "a car constantly gives you problems" because "few Nuer can afford a car that is in good condition. They frequently purchase cars from unscrupulous dealers who take advantage of the Nuer's lack of experience and inability to assess the condition and value of a car." In addition, many refugees drove without a license or insurance and frequently got into wrecks, experiences mirrored by the Lost Boys in Atlanta. "In just over three years that the average Nuer had been driving, 84 percent had had an accident, had a car repossessed or impounded, or been forced to abandon a car because of irreparable mechanical problems," Holtzman wrote. Despite the problems, owning a car allowed "Nuer to shop more easily and visit friends. In fact, Nuer who do not themselves have cars generally have to ask friends for rides, and this has real or potential social costs. Nuer speak of 'annoying people,' of putting a burden upon them with too frequent requests." Owning a car let refugees "attain at least the symbols of a class position that most of them could not have hoped to have held in Africa."

So it was in Atlanta. Volunteers such as Neal Kelley started making trips to used-car lots, where Lost Boys would plunk down one thousand to six thousand dollars for cars of varying quality. Many viewed buying a car the same as buying groceries or clothes. They were impatient when told that some Americans spend weeks going from dealership to dealership, researching prices, hunting for the car they wanted at a price they were willing to pay. If they had the money, the refugees figured, why wait? They would leave home in the morning and return with a car in the afternoon.

John had a typical experience. At the first dealership, a salesman young enough to have acne on his cheeks materialized just as John cupped his hands to peer through the driver's-side window of a 1996 Toyota Camry with 186,000 miles. The salesman wore a beige sports coat and dark hair slicked back from his forehead. The sticker said thirty-five hundred dollars, but the salesman told John he might be able to talk his manager down to thirty-two hundred. At another dealership, John shook hands with a salesman who chomped gum and swung his arms wildly as he walked. He wore sunglasses and lowered his head when he spoke to look at you over the top of his shades. He said things like, "This way, my man, I'll set you up," and, "This baby has forty-nine thousand miles—and they're original." As John described what he wanted—a reliable car that cost about three thousand dollars—the salesman looked at him over the tops of his sunglasses, put his hand on John's shoulder, chomped his gum, and nodded while repeating, "Of course. Of course." John followed the man past row after row of shiny new Ford Expedition SUVs. They stepped through an open gate at the back of the lot and entered a small square patch of land covered with gravel and enclosed by a tall chain-link fence. There were seven or eight used cars here, and the salesman told John that one of them was just what he was looking for: A silver 1989 Mercury Marquis with burgundy seats. The salesman said an elderly man had owned it and kept it in his garage most of the time (it was the one with forty-nine thousand original miles). John stared at the big boxy car. He raised his right hand and pointed.

"This one is the motherfucker," he said.

Several months earlier, John had overheard neighbors tossing around that word, apparently near a full-sized sedan like the Mercury Marquis he would later see at the dealership. He had interpreted the word to refer to the car and not, perhaps as it had been intended, to the person driving it.

John joked about it after he left the Ford dealership to ride a half-mile north to a Saturn dealership, where he found a forest-green 1995 SL2. The "service engine" light came on, but a salesman pledged to correct whatever problem triggered the warning. A few days later, John returned to take the car to a mechanic for inspection. He waited there with a friend, Nathaniel, talking about the time he totaled a car the first time he got behind the wheel. Nathaniel was telling John about his wreck when his cell phone rang. Nathaniel's friend, Santino, was calling to say he had just smashed up his car. Santino had been driving when he saw a group of people walking on the sidewalk. He looked at them, lost control, and ran off the road. A few weeks later, Peter Anyang steered his Nissan Maxima into another car while merging onto I-285. No one in Peter's car was hurt, but Lost Boys had been killed in car wrecks in Arizona and Pennsylvania since the resettlement had begun. Nevertheless, the prospect of a wreck did not deter John or any other Lost Boys in Atlanta any more than it did their Nuer counterparts in Minnesota.

While most refugees endorse the American emphasis on the automobile, many struggle with other elements of the culture. They perform a delicate balancing act in deciding which aspects of their old culture will suit them in the United States and which will be a liability. Women from countries with traditional gender roles, such as Iran and Pakistan, find themselves in a country where women can work and, if the mood strikes, wear short skirts and tight blouses. They and their daughters must decide which custom to follow, a decision that is particularly difficult for school-aged refugees surrounded by Americans their age. Refugees from Asian countries that frown on divorce discover that nearly half of all marriages dissolve in the United States without the stigma that divorce would carry in their native countries. At home, refugees must decide whether to speak English or their native language. They also face decisions about what to cook—hamburgers and fried chicken, or more traditional fare?

Before wrestling with these larger questions, though, many Lost Boys in Atlanta spent time trying to decipher the unwritten rules that govern everyday life. One rainy Sunday, William walked to an automated teller machine with Peter and Marko. It was his first time using an ATM card. He entered his personal identification number and followed the on-screen instructions, but the machine did not spit out any money. Peter discovered the problem—William was trying to withdraw $148, but the machine only dispensed amounts in multiples of $20. Another time, Jacob and some friends decided to drive to Kentucky to visit friends in Louisville. They rode for three hours on I-75 before noticing they had not crossed into Tennessee, which was to have happened about an hour and a half into the trip. They had gone south instead of north.

The unknown stirred fear. When Cheryl Grover took the young men in Apartment 40-G to Lake Lanier, about thirty miles north of Atlanta, they asked if crocodiles or hippopotamuses lurked in the lake. Another time, on a hike in a state park north of Atlanta, Peter asked whether lions stalked the forest.

One night, as Peter sat in the living room of Apartment 40-G reading a GED study guide, someone pounded on the front door. William had just stepped out of the shower, but the others were asleep. Peter heard voices on the other side, shouting, but he could not understand what they were saying.

"That must be people attacking us," William said.

He raced to his room.

The noise stirred Jacob from bed. He ventured into the hallway and asked Peter who was at the door. Peter said he had looked through the peephole but saw no one in the dark. Peter dialed 911 and told the operator, "Someone is knocking at my door very hard but I can't see who it is." The operator sent an officer. As he waited, Peter turned off the lights, walked to the door, and looked through the peephole again. This time he saw a man in a police uniform with a piece of paper in his hand. Cautiously, Peter said, he opened the door to see two police officers. They had come to Apartment 40-G in search of a man who used to live there. Peter recognized the man's name—mail addressed to him arrived occasionally. Realizing their mistake, the officers turned to walk down the staircase just as another officer pulled up in the parking lot, sent to investigate after Peter's call for help.

There were other miscues. Some of the first Sudanese refugees to leave Atlanta for the Job Corps campus in Washington did not bother to tell their landlord or employer they were leaving. They finished their shifts as hotel janitors one day and just never came back, causing headaches for the resettlement agency that had found them jobs. The agency had a hard enough time finding jobs for refugees, especially as the economy slowed. The hotel threatened to stop hiring refugees if more quit without giving notice. And it was not just the hotel managers who were put out. When the young men went to Washington, they left pots, pans, plates, and bowls in the kitchen of their apartment, trash in the garbage can. Dee Clement spent hours cleaning their apartments.

Many refugees said they had no difficulty understanding southern drawls, but for the life of them they could not understand much of what their African American neighbors were saying. Several Lost Boys said they had come to the United States expecting warm relations with African Americans and were surprised to sense indifference, if not hostility. For one thing, African Americans at Olde Plantation asked Lost Boys if they were gay. They were suspicious to see Sudanese men holding hands, a customary practice for Dinka and Nuer that carries no sexual connotations. Most Lost Boys picked up quickly on the American taboo against grown men holding hands.

John got to talking about race relations with a manager at the meat plant where he worked. The manager told him about slavery and segregation.

"I fail to understand, actually, what is the problem between these groups, the whites and the blacks," John said. "I don't know who is wrong and who is not wrong."

In trying to sort out the complexities of American culture, refugees relied on caseworkers, volunteers, neighbors, and, inevitably, on images dancing on their television screens. William bought a pair of baggy denim jeans with a Georgetown Hoya stitched on the back pocket "to look like everyone else." One of the young men studying at Open Campus High School braided his hair into cornrows to look like the hip-hop artists he saw on television. Other Lost Boys still wore the mishmash look that came from donated, secondhand clothes, but some came to the church at the community center in shiny athletic jerseys, baggy pants, and pricey, stylish sneakers. Television conveyed hundreds of messages, not the least of which was that Americans celebrated sex. That message oozed out of music videos starring curvaceous young women spilling out of skin-tight bikini tops, fingers on full, rounded lips or on long, sensuous legs.

"You know," Peter said one afternoon, "a lot of the ladies on the TV are very beautiful, but one cannot know what is on the inside."

Like men their age around the world, many Lost Boys of Sudan in Atlanta were thinking about women. Had war not forced them from home, many would have by this stage in their lives taken part in Dinka courtship rituals that lead to marriage. As a traditional Dinka song says: "For a woman, a man spears an animal. For a woman, a man keeps his cattle." Courtship in Dinkaland, Francis Deng writes, historically involved a dance at which young men would "stand singing, roaring unnecessarily with laughter," or singing verses that could be insulting "to give girls the impression that a man is witty and hot-tongued." After men and women danced, some couples made plans to see each other again. Typically, they would set a date on which a man would set off to visit the woman and travel "whatever the distance in spite of the weather. The harder the trip, the more convincing his intentions and the better the result." The couple would sit talking outside her home for the first of several sessions. Later, the man's friends or relatives might visit the woman's family to speak on his behalf. It was an elaborate ritual that frowned on premarital sex only in the sense that it might lead to pregnancy and "harm the marital interests of the girl."

The Dinka traditionally emphasize marriage and producing children as overriding goals of life. Ongoing war in Sudan has not changed that focus, but it has disrupted the patterns of courtship. Dinka men in refugee camps lack the cattle to pay a dowry, so many get married with a dowry of whatever money they can scrape together or the promise of future payment. For the young men resettled in the United States, the rules were even less clear. About one hundred of the thirty-eight hundred refugees in the group known as the Lost Boys of Sudan actually were girls. Many were identified by brothers who also were being resettled. Aid workers estimate that while boys made up the overwhelming majority of unaccompanied minors in Kakuma, their numbers included up to two thousand girls who missed out on the chance for resettlement. One reason the girls were not recommended for resettlement was that many of them had been placed with foster families in Kakuma who would have opposed resettlement for fear of missing out on a dowry when the girl got married. In addition, since older Sudanese men played a big part in reviewing lists to determine which refugees were in Kakuma before 1995—and which, therefore, qualified for resettlement—some aid workers suspect the elders overlooked girls in favor of boys who may or may not have been in Kakuma in time to qualify. Nevertheless, some Lost Boys in the United States remembered the women. Occasionally they would ask when the girls were coming.

Finding an American woman seemed impossible, though there were attempts. One afternoon, Dee Clement was helping a young man move from one apartment to another when a magazine fell out of a sofa they were carrying. When it landed on the ground, a sexy blonde woman smiled up from a page on the pavement. The man Dee was helping asked whether she could help him find someone like the woman in the magazine. Dee did not know if he was joking, but she suddenly felt very self-aware. A Somali man sat on his deck, watching, perhaps listening, and Dee did not want him to think that she was "in the business," that "the lady in the white truck" was someone you could turn to "for a good time." In a voice loud enough for the Somali man to hear, she told the young Sudanese man that she couldn't do anything for him.

She was not the only woman picking up on impulses felt by men who had a hard time envisioning when and how they might meet a woman. Cheryl Grover answered the phone in her house one day to hear a young southern Sudanese man she knew well announce, apropos of nothing: "I wish to be circumcised." It was not an overture aimed at Cheryl. She recalled it as a poignant remark from a young man beginning to think that he would one day like to find a wife, a man whose culture required that he be circumcised before having an intimate relationship with a woman. Cheryl called a doctor, who said the operation would cost twelve hundred dollars, more than the young man could afford. Adrian Jelks, the International Rescue Committee teacher, said that most men were deferential and polite to her but that one or two got fresh. She recalled walking down a staircase with a refugee who pulled her head toward him and tried to kiss her. She turned in time for him to kiss her cheek. He asked whether she would like to share the wealth he was accumulating at seven or eight dollars an hour. Adrian recalled a few hugs that lingered too long, and a man who called twelve times one night. "I had a talk with him," she said.

The young men were not alone among refugees in the obstacles they faced in trying to find a mate. The psychologist and author Mary Pipher notes that "dating, sexual relationships and courtship are complex even for native-born Americans. These activities require judgment and the ability to send and receive subtle signals. They involve understanding the nuances of flirting and knowing how to set limits and negotiate consensual sex." Many Lost Boys had a tough time interpreting unspoken gestures, a challenge compounded by their fluency with a literal, archaic brand of the English language, though they refined their language skills over time. Once, while two young men in Louisville, Kentucky, were talking with an American woman there, one wondered why she and her husband did not have children. "How long have you been married?" he asked.

"Seven years," she said.

"What is wrong with you that you do not have a child? Is it your problem or is it your husband's problem?"

His companion admonished his indelicacy. "You're not supposed to say, 'What is wrong that you don't have children?'" he said. "You're supposed to say, 'Do you plan to have children?'"

Police charged one of the young men in Atlanta with loitering for the purpose of soliciting a prostitute, a misdemeanor. His defenders said he was walking from an Ethiopian restaurant toward a motel that, unbeknownst to him, was frequented by prostitutes and their customers. They said police arrested him after mistaking him for a john. Abraham Yel heard about the arrest and went to the DeKalb County Jail to visit the man, but jailers told him for four straight days that they had no record of the man he was asking about. Abraham was adamant. The man wasn't home, and Abraham was sure police had taken him to jail. On the fifth day, a clerk tilted a computer screen toward Abraham and showed him a dozen mug shots. Did he recognize anyone? He did. The jailers had booked the man as "John Doe," a name Abraham had never before heard.

Volunteers in other parts of the United States reported Lost Boys having similar scrapes with the law. Most were fairly minor, but police in Boston charged a nineteen-year-old Lost Boy with rape after saying he burned a woman with a cigarette, threw her to the ground, and assaulted her. Refugees were also victims of crime. Attackers in Nashville tied up one of the Lost Boys and shot him to death in an apparent robbery. A young man in Jacksonville, Florida, was shot in the leg while another in Los Angeles said he was beaten up at a bus stop. Four or five young men who had been resettled in Atlanta were attacked in their apartment complexes. One said some neighbors beat him up because they mistakenly believed he had insulted one of their girlfriends. Another time, police charged a Lost Boy in Atlanta with loitering at 3 a.m. The man said officers stopped him and asked why he was walking at night. He told them he had just gotten off work and had taken the bus to Clarkston. Now he was walking home. Nevertheless, the police gave him a ticket. It seemed odd to Linda Amick, who was emerging as the person to call when refugees had to go to court. Linda had escorted several of the refugees to court, mainly to answer to traffic charges, and she went with the young man charged with loitering. As the judge read the police report, Linda got the sense that he didn't think it was too serious. Some guy walking down the sidewalk in the middle of the night. Big deal. The judge looked up and asked Linda whether she knew about the woman. Linda froze. She turned to the man beside her.

"What woman?" she said.

"No woman," he said.

Before much else could happen, the judge dismissed the charges and sent the young man home with a warning. On their way out, Linda said, she asked the man what the judge was talking about. "No woman," he repeated.

A police report is scant on details but provides a few clues. It says the man was walking down the street with a woman when a police car drove by. He bolted. Suspicious, the officer stopped his patrol car and found the Sudanese man "buttoning his pants as he walked out of the bushes." He said "he had fallen down in the woods and had passed out and just woke up and walked out of the woods."

Some volunteers heard rumors that prostitutes propositioned some

Lost Boys. Asked about this, one refugee said, "Yes, some prostitutes have come to these apartments, but I have no interest in them. Why would you? You lose your money and you lose your energy. And you expose yourself to HIV. What benefit is there?"

The more Lost Boys watched television and thought about women, though, the more they wanted to fit in. This was especially true when it came to their teeth. Most Lost Boys in Atlanta, like so many other Dinka, had many years earlier undergone a ritual that removed their lower teeth. Elders had been pulling out the six lower front teeth of Dinka children for as long as anyone could remember. "As with circumcision," Deng writes, "the Dinka do not give any explanation for the custom other than that it is esthetically pleasant and helps shape the mouth to be handsome. They say that unextracted lower teeth push the lower lip outward and make the lower jaw repulsive. Teeth are removed at about the age of ten in an operation more painful than circumcision. It is done by an expert with a fishing spear. The tip of the spear is placed between the teeth and is pressed back and forth to loosen the roots of the teeth and tear them from the gum. The tip of the spear is then forced to the roots and the whole tooth is plucked."

Like many Lost Boys in Atlanta, Peter was missing his lower front teeth. It did not affect his ability to speak Dinka, but sometimes, when he spoke English, Peter had trouble pronouncing certain words because of the movement of air over the space of his missing teeth. Another man from southern Sudan in Atlanta, the high-school student with cornrows, admitted to feeling self-conscious about his lack of teeth. "I want to look like other people," he said. "I feel that I'm missing something in my body which is very important." Another Lost Boy in Atlanta said, "Some Americans think I have a disease in my mouth." Many of the Lost Boys had noticed that only the poor and unintelligent lacked lower front teeth in the United States.

They found a champion in Dr. Gail McLaurin, a periodontist who read a newspaper story about the Sudanese refugees in 2001 and volunteered her services. She screened seventy-five refugees one morning at the Lost Boys Foundation and soon was extracting infected front teeth and performing other services. Dr. Gail, as the refugees called her, donated tens of thousands of dollars' worth of her services. She wanted to implant false lower front teeth in refugees who were missing them, but it was expensive. First, Dr. Gail would have to install costly implants that would anchor the replacements. A dental company donated some implants, but it was only a start. Dr. Gail still had to come up with fees to pay a lab to make specific teeth for specific recipients. In 2002, she provided new bottom teeth to a handful of refugees. Meanwhile, a clinic that provided low-cost dental care to low-income patients provided dentures in place of missing teeth to about a dozen young men. "I've never seen a group that values their teeth like they do," Dr. Gail said. "They want to sound intelligent."

That was obvious as the one-year anniversary approached of the day an airplane delivered Jacob, Peter, Daniel, and Marko to Atlanta. They had been supporting themselves for months as they chased their dream of education.

Jacob learned in the summer of 2002 that he had passed two of the three GED exams he had taken—science and social studies. He had failed literature interpretation but could take it again. In the meantime, he took GED tests in two more subjects, math and writing. He felt confident about math but worried about writing. An essay question required him to write about a movie he had seen, but Jacob had only seen one movie, with Dee, and he had had a hard time following it. Instead of writing about a film, he focused on *Things Fall Apart*, a 1958 Nigerian novel set in that country's colonial era in the 1800s. Jacob left uncertain about his results and was stunned two weeks later when he got the results. Not only had he passed both sections, he had received a higher score on the writing section than on any other tests he had taken. Now Jacob had passed four of the five GED sections. Literature interpretation was all that was left. Once he conquered that, it was off to college.

Peter had his eyes on college, too. He had been saving money and planned to enroll if he passed the Test of English as a Foreign Language. Marko talked vaguely about going to high school but he had no concrete plans to get there. Daniel had pinned his hopes on the Catholic seminary in Epworth, Iowa. In June, around the one-year anniversary of his arrival in the United States, Daniel wrote an essay in support of his application.

"My parents they do encourage me indeed to become a priest when I was in Sudan," he wrote. "They have strong faith in Jesus Christ. They were all Christian of Roman Catholic Church. They were farmers and their lifestyle was going well even if there was great persecution in Sudan because of the religion division."

Daniel said he liked to read the Bible and play soccer.

"About the ladies, I don't have any connection with the ladies at all. Even I don't talk with the girls when I was in Africa and right now," he wrote. "I do controlled myself not to talk and involving too much activities with the females because I have this dream of mine that I want to be a priest.

"My main objectives as to why I want to become a priest is that just to preach the good new of Jesus Christ to the people who don't know the words of God all over world round, like in our country Sudan, most people they don't know about God at all that is why majority of the people from Sudan were Muslim. Ninety-five percent in Sudan were Muslim.

"I do believe that, God is with us in any situations that we had faced for the last few years because if I recalled back many difficulties we had facing during for the past nineteen years of civil war in Sudan. In those years, nobody was taking care of us at all but God was the one who taking care of all us. He do protects us from all in any disaster, destruction, and genocide for example, we had cross the desert from Sudan to Ethiopia in 1987. We had facing some obstacles like, thirsty, hunger, wild animals and many other things, and indeed God manages to protect us from all these thing. During in our exile, God put his protection on so much, and in this case, I have decided to serve God and his people here on earth."

DON'T GET OBSESSED

Along with his application to Divine Word College, Daniel needed a physical and some shots. Jacob suggested he call Carolyn Geddes, a volunteer who was taking a lot of refugees to the doctor. She was a semiretired travel agent who lived in the suburbs north of Atlanta with her husband, Jim, a retired engineer. She had done volunteer work throughout her life, at a hospital in New York City and with the Salvation Army. She had traveled extensively because of her job and said she sympathized with immigrants and refugees. She said she knew how overwhelming it was to be in a foreign country and not know the language or many of the customs. Life in the United States is so fast paced, she said, so frantic. Sometimes she wondered how immigrants and refugees could succeed without American guides. Like Dee Clement, Carolyn had worked with Bosnian refugees for several years. She explained her commitment to volunteering by saying she enjoyed it and, simply, "It's work that needs to be done."

Since Carolyn and Jim had moved to Georgia in 1985, their daughter had grown up and moved to Australia. In the fall of 2001, they were talking about moving to Charleston, South Carolina, to be near a niece, but Carolyn had doubts she did not fully understand. "Something was holding me back," she said later, "but I didn't know what it was." Then she read a news story about the Lost Boys. "The minute I saw the story I knew that was what was to be done," she said.

It had been a year since she had stopped working closely with the Bosnians. Now Carolyn turned to her husband. "This is my next calling," she said.

"Carolyn," he said, "don't get obsessed."

Yet Carolyn was soon spending nine, ten, sometimes eleven hours a day taking refugees to and from doctor's appointments, calling employers on their behalf, and troubleshooting a thousand problems that would seem minor to someone who has lived in the United States for any length of time. A refugee with no experience receiving and paying bills would receive a health-insurance statement that said "This Is Not an Invoice" and mistake it for a bill. The needs were overwhelming. Carolyn spent thousands of dollars of her own money to pay for clothes, eyeglasses, and prescriptions. Her home-based travel business suffered. "A lot of things have been pushed to the side," she said. "They had so many things that needed attending to."

Other volunteers were spending just as much time and money. Linda Amick spent three thousand dollars in three months to buy eighteen sets of tires. The treads were worn thin on many of their cars, she said. No wonder Lost Boys were having so many wrecks. Susan Gordon and her husband, Kevin, paid $1,350 a year for Jacob's younger brother and sister to go to boarding school in Uganda. She also was spending hundreds of dollars here and there, buying clothes, prescriptions, whatever. Who could keep track of how much money they were spending? Volunteers like Neal Kelley and Dee Clement were spending money and time, too, so much that it might as well have been a full-time job. One weeknight at 10:30 a refugee called Carolyn to say he had a terrible headache. She rose, dressed, and drove thirty miles to take him Tylenol, apple juice, a banana, and yogurt. The amount of time volunteers invested strained some marriages and contributed to at least one divorce. In that case, there were other problems, the wife said, but her husband seemed jealous because she spent so much time away from home.

As the months passed, the connection deepened between volunteers and refugees. Many Lost Boys started calling the volunteers Mom or Mother, as in "Mom Carolyn," which would roll off the tongues of Daniel and Marko more and more in the months to come. Other refugees occasionally called caseworkers and volunteers Mother. This is partly because they want to express gratitude and partly because, in some cultures, the word *mother* applies not just to one's biological parent but to many women of childbearing age. Yet the word was not far off the mark, at least not in a legal sense, for volunteers like Linda Amick.

Linda volunteered in January 2002 and got to know three young men especially well. One had eye problems. A doctor had diagnosed him with trachoma, a disease that comes with cloudy pupils and causes one's eyelashes to scrape painfully against the cornea. Linda called his resettlement agency to ask whether a caseworker planned to take him to a doctor. The caseworker said yes, but Linda felt that the agency was not acting quickly enough. After two or three calls, she started calling doctors herself and eventually got him into an operating room for a surgery paid for by Medicaid. Linda took him into her house while he recuperated. He never left.

Linda soon realized that what he and two roommates really wanted was to go to school, so she took them to Lakeside High School. Administrators referred her to the county school system's International Center, which evaluated foreign-born students. The International Center asked to see the men's birth certificates. That was a problem. They did not have birth certificates. None of the Lost Boys did. Years ago, United Nations workers had eyeballed them and guessed their ages, assigning each one a "birthday" of January 1 and a year that seemed to fit his age. In lieu of a birth certificate, the school system asked to see their I-94s, the arrival record that immigration authorities give noncitizens entering the United States. But the I-94s said the three men were nineteen or twenty, too old to go to high school in Georgia, so Linda came up with a plan: She would have them "aged" at seventeen, become their legal guardian, and enroll them in school. So she took them to a friendly dentist and cardiologist for X-rays of their wisdom teeth and wrist bones. Though an inexact and controversial science, examining dental and wrist-bone X-rays can give doctors a fairly reasonable estimate of someone's age. The results were letters that said they were about seventeen. Next Linda applied to become their legal guardian so they could enroll in high school (anyone under eighteen must have a parent or guardian to go to high school in Georgia). When the probate court awarded a temporary guardianship, it was enough for Linda to get three Lost Boys into high school. Attending school meant that they could not work full-time, so Linda invited two of the young men to live with her along with the man suffering from eye problems.

Divorced, Linda had two children of her own, a son in college and a daughter who lived in the Atlanta suburbs. What she did was controversial. By changing their age to make them young enough to need a guardian and then using that guardianship to enroll them in high school, Linda alarmed the young men's resettlement agency. The agency worried that immigration authorities would become suspicious when the men applied for legal residency and, ultimately, citizenship. Authorities might question why the men claimed one age when they entered the United States and another after they arrived. The agency director and a representative of the federal Office of Refugee Resettlement in Washington visited Linda and the three young men living with her. Linda said they pointed out that the three Lost Boys were brought to the United States as adults and, like other adult refugees, were expected to find jobs and support themselves, not go to high school. After a half-hour or so, Linda said, she asked them to leave.

"It's time to go," she snapped. "This meeting is over."

After the resettlement agency wrote a letter to the probate court opposing Linda's request for guardianship, a judge declined to approve it. Linda's temporary guardianship expired after a few months, but it made no practical difference. Administrators at the high school did not notice. The young men kept going to class. Two did fairly well in tenth and eleventh grades, earning B averages, but the third failed every subject except English as a Second Language. There were problems at home, too. Linda eventually asked him to leave. Just like that, he was back on his own, with no job and no school. He moved in with some friends and returned to his resettlement agency to ask for help finding a job. His experience deepened convictions at the resettlement agency that Linda had acted rashly.

The two who remained thrived in Linda's house. They had spent months in a typical apartment in Clarkston, hearing the typical loud music pulsing through the typical thin walls, trying in vain to kill the typical roach that darted across the typical kitchen floor past the typical leaky toilet. Now they lived in a split-level house with a well-manicured lawn. Linda kept it clean. The refrigerator was full. Even so, Linda worried. The resettlement agency had blocked her attempt to become their guardian. If the school caught on, there could be problems. Eager for permanent guardianship, Linda called a probate court clerk who told her there would be no problem if only the men had birth certificates. Later, Linda talked with the young men in her house.

"Can't you get a birth certificate?" she asked. "That would resolve all our problems if you could get one of those. Other boys have gotten one."

The young men bought a phone card, called Africa, and—voilà!—birth certificates showed up in the mail a few weeks later. They said the two were sixteen, the perfect age for them to continue studying at Lakeside High.

Linda's story encouraged other volunteers. Dee Clement followed her lead and became the guardian of two men who had obtained birth certificates listing them as minors. At least two other Lost Boys lived with Americans who had befriended them in Georgia, including one who lived with one of the three women who constituted the controversial Lost Boys Foundation. It was an arrangement that let a refugee desperate for education go to high school.

Marko noticed. He talked with contacts in Africa and sent them money to obtain a birth certificate, too. It looked as official as anything you'd find in the county courthouse. It listed his father's name—Ayii Aguer—and his place of birth—Madhol. It said "Republic of Sudan" and "Certified by the Ministry of Foreign Affairs" and listed his birth date as October 8, 1986. That meant Marko was sixteen when the birth certificate arrived in the summer of 2002. He clearly was younger and less mature than his roommates, so the age seemed to fit. It also was consistent with accounts Marko gave of leaving home in the late 1980s. Marko said he remembered few details about the trip around southern Sudan in 1987 or 1988, and if he had been too young to remember, he would have been around sixteen when he arrived in Atlanta. Now, armed with a birth certificate, Marko was looking for someone to become his guardian, to help him the way Daniel was getting help.

After Daniel had asked for her help in getting a physical exam and shots, Carolyn had taken him to an internist from India who had seen dozens of Lost Boys for free. She had been impressed that Daniel had applied to go to seminary. Weeks later, Carolyn was thrilled when he called her with big news. He had received a letter from Divine Word College: the admissions office had accepted him.

Daniel Khoch was going to college.

Carolyn had attended Catholic elementary school, high school, and college and had clear ideas about how he should dress. Carolyn said she "didn't want him looking like some poor refugee kid," so she drove him to Macy's.

"Let's start with the trousers," Carolyn said.

Daniel tried on navy pants.

"Oh boy do you ever look great!" Carolyn said.

She bought Daniel pants, underwear, socks, and brown and black Rockport shoes. She spent several hundred dollars to outfit Daniel "because it had to be done." Daniel thanked her. He had just sent his mother seven hundred dollars to travel from Khartoum to her village in southern Sudan. He also had just finished repaying his loan to the International Organization for Migration (refugees are required to repay the cost of their airfare to the United States).

"I'm helping you now because that was the opportunity I had," Carolyn said. "And you will have the opportunity to help someone else one day and you'll help them. That's what God would want."

She explained later: "Here's a guy trying to do the best thing for himself and finding his vocation. You figure these opportunities come up, you're supposed to take them."

Later, Carolyn gave Daniel shirts from the Gap and J. Crew. Susan Gordon gave him one of her husband's sports coats, four pairs of her brother's Dockers pants, a blue dress shirt, several ties, and some Gucci loafers.

As the time drew closer for Daniel to leave, Marko said he would miss his friend, but their time apart, when Daniel was in South Dakota, had prepared him for a more prolonged separation. Besides, this was different. Daniel was going to school. Marko understood that. They all wanted to go to school.

On a Saturday morning, after the others had gone to work, Daniel dressed smartly in a short-sleeved blue plaid shirt with blue cotton pants. He picked up his Northwest Airlines ticket and a black suitcase and rode with Carolyn to the airport. There, he took a train to concourse D, rode the escalator up, and turned right. He strode past a yogurt shop and newsstand and past posters advertising flights to a city with skyscrapers at night, aglow in neon ("Electrifying Asia") and to someplace where an athletic man windsurfed on a brilliant blue sea ("Shoot the Breeze"). He handed his ticket and Georgia ID card to a woman behind the counter at gate D-15.

"Okay," she said. "You're all set."

Daniel moved to his right and then turned to disappear down a tunnel leading to the plane. The next day, he called Mom Carolyn to say he was "very, very far from any place" but happy to be in school. Divine Word College in tiny Epworth, Iowa, has about one hundred students, many from countries such as Jamaica, Canada, Vietnam, Indonesia, Norway, and China. The school caters to men who plan to serve as Catholic missionaries around the globe. Instructors teach English as a Second Language and GED-prep classes as a prelude to undergraduate work. Over the next several months, word of the school's existence traveled through communities of Lost Boys in Atlanta, Dallas, and other cities. Soon, eighteen students were from southern Sudan.

Like Daniel, Abraham Yel planned to go to seminary. He pinned his hopes on a seminary in South Carolina, but an American friend found out that the school lacked accreditation. So he settled on classes at Atlanta Christian College. Susan Gordon took him to tour the campus and meet with an admissions counselor.

"Have you finished high school?" the counselor asked.

"No," Abraham said.

When the counselor said Abraham needed a GED diploma, Susan asked whether the counselor had ever heard of the Lost Boys of Sudan. The counselor had not. Susan told the story and gave the counselor a tape of the *60 Minutes II* segment that included interviews with Abraham. The counselor left and returned in a few minutes to say that Abraham could take five credit hours a semester until he received his GED diploma or until he completed twenty-eight credit hours. Then he could enroll full-time. Within weeks, Abraham was rising most weekdays at 5 a.m. in his apartment near Clarkston to walk to a MARTA station, ride a train to downtown Atlanta, change trains, ride south, and pick up a bus that stopped at the college in time for classes that began at 7:30.

Abraham started classes about the time of the one-year anniversary of the arrival of the men of Apartment 40-G. When their lease was up at Olde Plantation Apartments, the roommates moved into different apartments. Peter, Marko, William, and Kuan would rent a second-floor unit at a complex across the street from Olde Plantation. All of them except William were from the same part of southern Sudan, a place called Modhol in the Bahr El-Ghazal region. Jacob moved into an apartment with other men from Bor, his region of southern Sudan. John, who was also from Bor, moved in, too, only by now he had changed his name to *Daniel*, paying a lawyer $500 for what he could have done on his own at probate court for about $105. He said he had the wrong name all along, that he had inherited a ration card with the name John on it in Kakuma and that the United Nations used those ration cards to draw up the list of refugees eligible for resettlement. A smattering of Lost Boys around the United States also changed their names after being resettled, often explaining that in the refugee camps they had been given names that were not their own. Others who were at Kakuma said the United Nations had relied on a years-old list of unaccompanied minors in the camp to come up with the names of refugees to recommend for resettlement. They said some young men whose names were on that list had left Kakuma by the time the United States started to resettle the Lost Boys. That created some openings that were filled, the theory went, by young men who assumed identities to travel to the United States.

As they settled into their new apartments, the former roommates of apartment 40-G began trying to craft plans to emulate the success Daniel Khoch and Abraham Yel enjoyed in getting into school.

Peter had studied for the Test of English as a Foreign Language but after taking it he worried about his performance. His concerns were misplaced—he scored higher than many other refugees who had taken it. Peter talked about studying computers for two years, finding a job that paid better than the meatpacking plant, and working for a while. Maybe after he saved more, he would return to school.

William had talked about going to the seminary, too, but his heart was not in it. He applied to go to the Job Corps campus in Washington and settled in to wait. Months later, news: he was in. On the morning he left Atlanta, William walked into his living room in those baggy jeans with the Georgetown Hoya on the back pocket. He stood by his suitcase and wondered aloud about how he was dressed. Maybe the blue jeans were too casual, he said. William disappeared into his bedroom and came back out in a beige suit with white stripes. Carolyn Geddes arrived a few minutes later. He followed her downstairs, climbed into her minivan, and rode away.

Jacob was still working the overnight shift at Target and studying on his own for the GED exam. He had passed four of the five sections and was as close as any Lost Boy in Atlanta to receiving his high-school equivalency diploma. Only the dreaded literature-interpretation section stood in the way, the part of the test with figurative language that confuses so many nonnative speakers. Four months after taking it for the first time, Jacob signed up to take it again.

"I will not give up," he said. "I will take it until I pass."

The results came two weeks later. His score was 390, up from 350 the first time but below the 410 minimum. Jacob had not recognized some of the words in the reading section, and if he did not recognize some words, how was he ever going to pass?

"I had the belief that I can do it myself, but I realize I cannot make it by myself. I need help," he said.

Susan arranged tutoring sessions with Linda Austin, a retired teacher who had volunteered to teach some of the Lost Boys of Sudan. Jacob and Linda met on the Saturday and Sunday before he was to take the literature-interpretation section for a third time. A little rattled but determined, Jacob again walked through the main doors at the Fulton County Schools Staff Development Center. On the wall to his left was a framed photograph of a bald eagle at twilight, mist enveloping a stand of fir trees below. "Dare to Soar," it said. "Your attitude almost always determines your altitude in life."

Jacob turned left and started down that long hallway of cream-colored cinderblocks. A few more steps and he saw another framed picture on the wall. Waves smashed into a rocky coast at dawn or dusk. "Courage does not always roar," the poster announced. "Sometimes it is the quiet voice at the end of the day saying 'I will try again tomorrow.'"

Twenty seconds later, on that inexorable march toward the test that had defeated him twice, Jacob passed another image on the wall, a boat on calm waters. "Success is a journey," this one said. "Not a destination."

Finally, Jacob walked back into room 103 and settled into a chair at a table by himself. He did not take off his heavy black winter coat. The red-and-blue-plaid scarf stayed around his neck. With a pencil, Jacob darkened the bubbles corresponding to his name.

Suddenly, there was some excitement in the room. The instructor chided a young man in the room for opening his test booklet before the appointed hour. She reminded him the test was timed. A minute later, the student did it again. Another warning. After he opened it a third time, the instructor confiscated the booklet. The man leaped up. "I paid for this fucking test!" he said. The instructor told him to leave. In a huff, he did. During a break, Jacob saw the man arguing with a security guard in the hallway.

After the test started, Jacob was surprised to actually understand the poetry. Something about a man courting a woman at night. He stands outside her window and signals for her to join him. Jacob answered questions with a confidence that increased as time passed. He cruised through an essay about two French women in 1940. One woman lends her friend a diamond necklace. The friend loses the jewelry and tries to pass off a replacement as the original. Seven questions remained unanswered when the instructor told the students to hurry up and finish, time was running out. Jacob guessed. Even so, he felt that the tutoring had helped. Things seemed to be clicking this time. He seemed closer to college than at any time since he had come to the United States.

And so he was stunned when the results came two weeks later.

He scored 380.

Jacob had failed literature interpretation a third time.

PEACE?

The old pressure to receive an education had never felt stronger to Jacob than it did in the first few months of 2003, after he took the literature-interpretation portion of the GED test for the third time. If he did not pass that section, he would not receive his high-school equivalency diploma. If he did not receive the diploma, how would he go to college? And if he did not go to college, what contribution would he make in the future? Would the southern Sudanese in Kakuma see him as someone who squandered a chance in the vaunted land of opportunity? Jacob thought back to his first night in the United States, when he had sat up in bed in a dark hotel room in New York City and had written three questions in a blue day book.

What have you plan for me?

What are going to be my achievements here in US?

What is my future and what am I going to be in NS [New Sudan]?

Jacob and other southern Sudanese youth around the United States were wrestling with that last question. What role would they play in New

Sudan? If they attended high school and college in the United States, and if they did well, many hoped to return to rebuild the southern Sudan, to anchor an educated class as architects of an ambitious reconstruction. They and other educated southerners would teach children, treat the sick, run businesses, and plant crops. They would be among those who would judge the guilty, repair the plumbing, police the streets, and pave the roads. Many Lost Boys in the United States arrived with plans to return when peace stopped the war that had flushed them from home in the first place. As time passed, some changed their view. They had a more difficult time imagining themselves leaving a country that offered such security and opportunities to make money and, eventually, go to school. Others wanted to return home one day to find a bride and contribute to rebuilding southern Sudan. Many refugees thought about it in the abstract, but a growing number began to wonder whether they would be confronted with a decision sooner rather than later. For a variety of reasons, the calculus of war was changing in Sudan. Suddenly peace seemed within reach.

Oil was one reason. Crews discovered oil in southern Sudan in 1978, but exploitation did not begin until 1998. International companies were harvesting about four hundred thousand barrels of oil a day by 2000, making Sudan a medium-scale oil exporter. Eager to clear the way for drilling, the Sudanese military often attacked villagers who happened to live on land above oil reserves. Oil money doubled the government's defense spending and strengthened its battlefield position, though neither side was poised to achieve complete military victory. Despite an infusion of cash that paid for deadly new weapons, including attack helicopters, the Sudanese military still had to contend with a rebel army that had the lethal ability to conduct guerrilla war. The SPLA continued combat operations and occasionally attacked oil pipelines to disrupt productions. The rebels' military position strengthened in 2002 when Riek Machar, the Nuer rebel leader who had split from the movement in 1991, reunited with John Garang, the Dinka leader of the SPLA. Nevertheless, analysts said the government's increasing military strength provided an incentive for the rebels to negotiate before oil money tilted the balance of power too sharply in favor of Khartoum.

The government suddenly had a reason to negotiate, too. Its interest came amid a general war weariness and a belief that acceding to American pressure to negotiate would increase the chances that the United States would remove Sudan from its list of countries that sponsor terrorism. The government's interest in negotiation would increase after the terrorist attacks in New York and Washington in September of that year and a change in presidential administrations in Washington in 2001.

Whatever else it may have meant, the election of President George W. Bush after one of the most contested elections in U.S. history led to major changes in the American approach to Sudan. The administration of President Bill Clinton had viewed Sudan as a threat to the national interest, mainly because of Sudan's support for militant Islamic groups the United States considered terrorist organizations. The main goal of the Clinton administration was to isolate and contain Sudan. The administration also wanted to end the war, but that was a distant, secondary objective. American officials pursued isolation and containment by supporting economic sanctions, meeting opposition groups, and sending representatives into southern Sudan. In 1995, the U.S. ambassador to Sudan, Donald Petterson, delivered a secret note to General Bashir, the Sudanese leader, and Hassan al-Turabi, the Islamic cleric widely regarded as the power behind the throne. The message said the United States was "aware of Sudan's involvement in terrorist plots against us" and that, if such plots were carried out, it would result in "the international isolation of Sudan, in the destruction of your economy and in military measures that would make you pay a high price."

Despite its efforts, the United States failed in the 1990s to reform or change the regime or relieve the humanitarian crisis. A perception that the United States was out to overthrow the government deepened after the American military bombed the El Shifa pharmaceutical factory in Khartoum in August 1998. Clinton said he had ordered the strike in retaliation for the bombings of U.S. embassies in Kenya and Tanzania by the al-Qaida terror network of Osama bin Laden. He said that the plant manufactured the deadly VX nerve agent and that bin Laden helped finance the plant, but Sudan's leaders denied any such production. Amid the controversy, former president Jimmy Carter called for an investigation to determine exactly what the plant produced (he would later say the plant "was completely committed to producing human and veterinary medicines").

Carter had credentials when it came to Sudan. The former president visited the Horn of Africa several times after leaving office. He met with representatives of the Sudanese government and SPLA to encourage them to negotiate an end to the killing, mediating talks between the government and rebels in 1989. A few years later, Carter hosted rival leaders of the rebel movement in Atlanta at the Carter Center, his nonprofit organization that fights disease and promotes peace, human rights, and democracy, mainly in parts of the world that rarely make the evening news. Carter encouraged a negotiated settlement between rival factions of southern Sudanese rebels, who were then embroiled in a war that had started as a struggle for leadership of the opposition but had promptly devolved into a bloodbath pitting one ethnic group against another. The mediation effort was unsuccessful, but Carter persisted. In 1995, he negotiated a cease-fire that allowed medical workers to visit more than two thousand villages in southern Sudan as part of Carter's campaign to rid the world of Guinea worm disease.

People contract the disease by drinking water infected with tiny fleas carrying the Guinea worm larvae. Inside the human body, larvae grow into worms that break through the skin in painful blisters. Victims rarely die, but most can't work or go to school for at least two months. Infections can disrupt everyday life, particularly in the rural settings. Farmers who contract the disease around the harvest, for example, can't get crops out of the ground. That diminishes a community's food supply and increases the odds of hunger. When Carter started his drive to fight the disease, in 1986, it seemed like an impossible task. The disease affected 3.2 million people, mainly in Africa and Asia. To reduce the number, the Carter Center taught hundreds of thousands of people in remote areas to safeguard local drinking-water supplies by staying out of ponds or lakes if they were infected (the worm releases larvae in water; people who drink that water unknowingly ingest the larvae). Since the center began its campaign, the disease has been stamped out in Cameroon, Chad, India, Kenya, Pakistan, Senegal, and Yemen, and there were only about thirty-five thousand remaining cases worldwide in 2004. Nearly 80 percent of these cases are in southern Sudan. The Carter Center also has been active in sub-Saharan Africa in efforts to combat trachoma—the eye disease affecting one of the Atlanta Lost Boys—which is caused by a microorganism, and river blindness, transmitted by the bite of a certain black fly.

Carter said the civil war in Sudan "has been the most long-lasting and devastating war in the world," and he maintained contact in the 1990s and beyond with key figures in the war. In addition, in 1999 Carter almost single-handedly negotiated an end to a dispute between Sudan and Uganda—officials in each country had accused the other of supporting rebel groups fighting their respective governments. Carter shuttled between the two leaders during a meeting in Kenya much as he had shuttled between President Anwar el-Sadat of Egypt and Prime Minister Menachem Begin of Israel to broker the Camp David Accords in 1978. In March 2002, Carter traveled to Sudan to promote his center's health projects. He also met with top government and rebel officials to encourage them to negotiate. By then, Carter also had discussed the war with a new U.S. president.

The former president and his wife, Rosalynn, traveled to Washington in the winter of 2001 for the inauguration of President George W. Bush. Carter joked that he was one of the few Democrats at the inauguration who did not have to be there. Disappointed as a Democrat, Carter said the election gave him fresh hope nonetheless for a new U.S. policy toward Sudan. He had long since become disillusioned with what he saw as the Clinton administration's "misplaced policy of trying to overthrow the government in Khartoum. . . . Every time we tried to have a balanced mediation between the north and the south, the U.S. government would intercede and subvert the effort with the intention of overthrowing the northern government, which they were not able to do." Carter chalked up Clinton's stance to a "very ill-advised woman" in the administration who "had an obsession against the Sudanese government." He said the policy caused "one of the main disharmonies between me and the Clinton administration."

So Carter was prepared when President Bush chatted with him on inauguration day there on the reviewing stand, telling Carter as a courtesy just to say the word if he needed anything.

"Mr. President," Carter said, "there's only one thing I want you to do for me and that is to initiate peace talks in Sudan in a balanced way."

Later, in a reception room at the capitol, the nation's thirty-ninth president spoke again with the forty-third chief executive. Carter repeated his request that Bush push for a negotiated settlement. The new president said he wouldn't forget Carter's request. He said he would look into it. About a month later, Carter returned to Washington to meet with Secretary of State Colin Powell and National Security Adviser Condoleezza Rice to urge again that the United States use its influence to try to jump-start peace talks.

Carter was not the only one urging the new president to pay attention to the war in Sudan. Evangelical Christians, a group Bush was much more likely to pay attention to, also were urging the Republican administration to get involved. They had worried for years about the persecution of Christians in southern Sudan. They were alarmed by reports of Arab tribal militias enslaving southern Sudanese Christians. Experts would say evangelical groups viewed the civil war imprecisely through a narrow prism, as a conflict pitting Muslims against Christians, and that they failed to grasp the complexities of a war that is more a competition for power and resources than a religious battle. The experts point out that southern fears of northern domination predate Christianity in southern Sudan. They also point out that the rival Dinka and Nuer rebel groups who slaughtered each other in the early 1990s were, in some cases, Christians killing Christians, ostensibly at least, and that large swaths of southern Sudan are not home to Christians at all but to people who follow animist religions, which deify natural objects, such as rocks or trees. Nevertheless, evangelical Christians increasingly were successful in the late 1990s at calling attention to widespread suffering in southern Sudan. Partly as a result, Bush made Sudan a priority. In September 2001, four days before the terrorist attacks on New York and Washington, Bush appointed former senator John Danforth of Missouri, an Episcopal minister, as his special envoy to Sudan. Danforth's involvement in the next year would prompt the Sudanese government and rebels to agree to a six-month cease-fire in a mountainous area southwest of the capital, but the most powerful impetus for peace was a force that most of America did not see coming.

In a televised address twelve hours after the terrorist attacks of September 11, 2001, Bush warned that the United States would "make no distinction between the terrorists who committed these acts and those who harbor them." He said, "America has stood down enemies before, and we will do so this time." The next month, the United States led an attack on the Taliban regime of Afghanistan, which sheltered bin Laden and his al-Qaida colleagues. The assault swiftly destroyed the Taliban leadership and replaced it with an interim government, all the while continuing military operations to find and kill members of al-Qaida. Events in Afghanistan were keenly noted in Sudan, which feared becoming a target of American wrath in the war on terrorism.

Eager to be removed from the U.S. list of states that sponsor terrorism, leaders in Khartoum had offered even before the terrorist attacks to share intelligence information on bin Laden and al-Qaida with FBI counterterrorism investigators. Carter said Bashir, the Sudanese president, had told him in the late 1990s that Sudan wanted to distance itself from groups listed as terrorist organizations by the U.S. government. "Every time I would go to Sudan, which was pretty often," Carter said, "they would tell me that any member of the CIA, any member of the U.S. Congress, any representatives of the U.S. government could come to Sudan and they would be given unimpeded access" to the government's information on groups like al-Qaida in Sudan.

U.S. authorities had rebuffed the overtures amid questions about their legitimacy. They had kept Sudan on the list of countries that sponsor terrorism. The terrorist attacks of September 11, 2001, intensified the Sudanese government's desire to distance itself from terrorist groups, especially after the U.S. waged war on a country that it said sheltered terrorists. Leaders in Khartoum stepped up their efforts to cooperate. Not only did Sudan open its intelligence files on bin Laden's al-Qaida network to the CIA and FBI, it reacted to U.S. pressure to negotiate with the SPLA. Khartoum also negotiated in the hopes of receiving more foreign investment to increase oil production.

Garang, leader of the rebel Sudan People's Liberation Army, told an audience in Atlanta that included dozens of Lost Boys in the spring of 2002 that a coalescence of several factors, notably the government's desire to distance itself from international terrorism, seemed to be setting the stage for peace. "As a result of the horrific events of September 11, this factor of international pressure" on the government of Sudan "has increased," he said. "So has the prospect for a negotiated settlement. . . . The international community is focusing on the Sudan as a result of terrorism and the concern for terrorism after September 11."

In July 2002, the Sudanese government and rebels reached a remarkable agreement that paved the way for formal peace talks. According to the agreement, Islamic law would only apply in northern Sudan. Six years after a formal peace agreement, people in southern Sudan would vote on whether to secede from the country to form an independent nation. Both were major concessions from the government. The U.S. ambassador to Sudan from 1995 to 1997, Timothy Carney, said the agreement "open[ed] a massive opportunity for reaching a just and durable peace." Negotiators from the government and rebel SPLA made substantial progress in subsequent peace talks and seemed close in the fall of 2004 to a final peace deal, though a separate conflict in the Darfur region of western Sudan, where government-backed Arab militias waged a campaign of killing and rape that the U.S. Congress condemned as genocide, overshadowed the peace talks for most of 2004.

Expectations for peace in southern Sudan also were high among aid organizations such as CARE, the international humanitarian organization that has its U.S. headquarters in Atlanta. Its president, Peter Bell, traveled to Sudan in November 2002 and sensed a distinct change from previous visits. He met government officials who seemed genuinely interested in peace. "This is truly a historic moment within Sudan," he said. "This is the most serious peace process over the decades of the civil war." He recalled meeting about 40 Dinka farmers in Bor, near Jacob Magot's hometown. He told them several Dinka from Bor lived in Atlanta. They seemed surprised. The farmers asked what Bell thought about the prospects for peace. When he said he thought the chances were fairly good, "farmers who had been very somber suddenly broke out into fervent applause and cheering."

Political attention to Sudan in the United States led to passage of the Sudan Peace Act, signed by President Bush on October 21, 2002. It set aside $100 million for three years for "assistance to areas outside government control to prepare the population for peace and democratic governance, including support for civil administration, communications infrastructure, education, health and agriculture," the State Department said. More significantly, the law required the president to review the progress of peace talks. He was to determine every six months whether the government and rebels were negotiating in good faith. If he concluded that the Sudanese government was not acting in good faith, the president was to seek a resolution in the United Nations Security Council for an arms embargo. He also was to instruct American financial institutions to oppose loans, credits, and guarantees by international financial institutions and to "take all necessary and appropriate steps to deny Sudan's government access to oil revenues in order to ensure that the funds are not used for military purposes."

Lost Boys in Atlanta followed the news.

Abraham Yel organized a special church service in September 2002 to discuss the peace talks and the recent SPLA capture of two key towns in southern Sudan. Fifty-eight worshippers stood and sang in the old classroom at the community center, wearing short-sleeved plaid madras shirts, khaki slacks, golf shifts, and baggy blue jeans. A young man in a black T-shirt that said "Chevrolet Racing" passed around the collection plate.

Abraham stood in front of his flock in his priest's collar under a white robe with a green sash. "We came to United States, whereby you have something to eat, you have your doctor, but we need to think about our brothers and sisters back at home," he said. "I still feel that I'm part of southern Sudan and those who are facing the government. We need to help our brothers by all means, financially and, even if you want to go back and fight, it will be okay. But going to school here is one part of fighting in southern Sudan."

The congregation interrupted him with applause. Light streamed in through blinds on windows facing the street. A fan hummed.

"September 11 is everyday life in Sudan. Our property, our houses, everything is burned down and we are killed. Some of us are captured," Abraham said.

An elderly Sudanese preacher who followed Abraham led the young men in a shout of support for the SPLA, using a term that translates very roughly into "Yea!" or "Hurray!" The old man shook his fist in the air and shouted, "SPLA oyee! SPLA oyee! SPLA oyee!" Electrified, the congregation chanted with him and pumped their fists in the air.

Abraham said that the people who had attacked the United States on September 11 were the same ones attacking southern Sudan. "Wake up, Africa!" the preacher screamed. "We shall never, never come to an agreement with the north!"

Heavy applause filled the room.

"I don't understand the Arab," he screamed over the din. "It is only the Jews and the Israelis and the southern Sudanese who understand the Arab. You are now called upon to wake up! Wake up and contribute what you are supposed to contribute!"

A few minutes later, one young man in the congregation stood up and wrote "His Mercy Endures Forever" in black ink on a dry-erase board. Another man urged everyone to behave well so as not to jeopardize their role in New Sudan. "Let's watch out for moral and social decay," he said. "Each and every person here among us is important to our country."

It went without saying that each and every person in the congregation was important because he had the chance to receive an education that would prepare him for a role in rebuilding Sudan. No one needed to be reminded of the old pressure to study and learn. Whether or not negotiations would end the war, many Lost Boys were as eager as ever to find their way into a classroom.

GENTLEMEN OF THE FUTURE

Marko knew that several young men from southern Sudan were in high school. More than two dozen were studying at Open Campus High School, the alternative school for older students, by the winter of 2003. A handful of others attended traditional high schools. Most had received birth certificates from Africa that showed them to be under eighteen. Others were taken by American friends and volunteers to sympathetic dentists and doctors for X-rays of their wisdom teeth, which tend to come in after late adolescence, and of their wrist bones, which fuse at about the same time. Volunteers used birth certificates or letters from dentists or doctors to establish that a particular refugee was a minor. Then they applied to become that refugee's legal guardian. At least five Lost Boys in Atlanta traveled that route to high school in 2002. Stuck in a grueling job at the meatpacking plant, Marko sensed that finding a guardian would be the only way he could go to school. The eleventh- and twelfth-grade classes at Open Campus were above his level. Even the pre-GED classes at Job Corps intimidated him. More so than many of the southern Sudanese refugees, Marko needed an education on the ninth- or tenth-grade level. The only place he was going to get that was in high school. Carolyn Geddes knew it. She had taken a liking to Marko—there was something warm and inviting to her about the way he laughed so easily. So she talked with her husband and decided to become Marko's guardian, inviting him to live with her and her husband in the suburbs north of Atlanta. He quit his job at the ever-cold meatpacking plant and moved into a spare bedroom with two twin beds and a National Geographic map of Africa on the wall.

In August 2003, Marko started classes at Kell High, a new school with thirteen hundred students that was in such an affluent suburb that chairs in the library had ports for laptop computers. For the first week, he couldn't find his way through the maze of lockers, from one class to the next, but teachers and a kind guidance counselor looked out for him. They made sure a student accompanied him to his next class until he got down the routine. It took Marko little time to figure how to get from his locker to Ms. Wilkins's first-period English as a Second Language class. He strode in on a typical Wednesday morning in New Balance tennis shoes, khaki pants, and a neatly pressed button-down shirt with thin stripes of red, white, green, and blue. Marko sat in the front row and read a message on the dry-erase board: a quiz Friday would cover chapters seventeen through twenty.

"Congratulations to the girl's tennis team for beating the team from East Cobb," a voice said on the morning announcements. "Congratulations to Kell High School's first Model United Nations meeting. All students did a great job. Go Longhorns!"

Ms. Wilkins passed around copies of *USA Today* and told students to turn to page 3A to read a story with the headline "Soldiers Killed in Army Helicopter Crash." Marko turned to the back of the front section but saw only a weather map. Nothing about a helicopter crash. He looked through the Sports and Life sections. Ms. Wilkins was patient. Marko turned to another student and finally, after turning each page, arrived at page 3A. He and three other students in the class took turns reading aloud, stopping for definitions of words and terms that were unfamiliar, such as "Sgt." Ms. Wilkins asked how many people survived the crash, where the survivors were being treated, and in which state the helicopter crashed.

"How many people were on the helicopter?"

"Thirteen," Marko said.

"Do we know what time it crashed?"

"Yeah."

"What time?"

"About 2 p.m.," Marko said, and then it was his turn to read aloud: "The ground at the crash site was covered in snow, Bohr said. Rescue crews reached the scene at 3:30 p.m."

The next student to read paused before an unknown word.

"'Evacuation,'" Ms. Wilkins said. "What is the root word?"

"*Evacuate*," Marko said.

"What does that mean?"

"To move from one place to another place."

The student who was reading continued: "An incident in which Black Hawk helicopters were shot down in Sol-am—"

"Somalia," Marko said.

"—in 1993 was the subject of the 2001 movie *Black Hawk Down*."

Next, on to the Sports page, where a story ran with a picture of a woman kissing a horse. Under the headline, "Flying Out of the Gate," was a smaller one that read: "Jockey Shannon Uske, 17, a winner in her debut, studies under old pro in chase of lifelong dream." The story said she went to a barn owned by a "73-year-old Hall of Famer, H. Allen Jerkens, who became her mentor and friend."

Ms. Wilkins looked around the room. "What's a Hall of Famer?" she asked. Silence. "What's a Hall of Fame?" Nothing. "What's fame?"

Marko never had heard of a "thoroughbred" or a "peppermint-loving mare." No one in Kakuma spoke of "jockeys," but Marko was a quick study. He did not hesitate when Ms. Wilkins asked about the function of adjectives.

"They tell us about nouns," he said.

"What part of speech is *learns*?"

"A verb," he said.

After the bell rang, Marko slung a backpack over his right shoulder and walked to PE for a game of basketball. Later, he went to a computer-repair class. Most students were tinkering with circuit boards and hard drives, but Marko had little experience with computers. To ease him into the subject, his teacher asked Marko to define *CD-ROM* and *desktop* and have him practice creating and saving documents in Microsoft Word.

At lunch, Marko sat in the cafeteria with a pretty preacher's daughter who kept a picture of Vin Diesel, muscle-bound heartthrob and action-movie star, tucked in the inside flap of a notebook. Marko asked whether she wanted to go to an upcoming celebration for southern Sudanese. She laughed. She said she was only fifteen and didn't know if her father would let her go on dates. She did ask Marko for details, though. That was something.

In English, Marko read with an eye toward spotting topic sentences along with students from Guatemala, Ecuador, Mexico, and Iraq. The students and teachers had been intrigued with Marko ever since he read an autobiography to the class.

"My name is Marko Ayii and I am seventeen years old. I was part of a group of 3,800 boys resettled in United States by your government," he wrote. "I want to get a good education in America so that I can return to Sudan when war is over. Then I can help to develop my country when we live in peace again.

"I do not know anything of my parents, sister and brother even though I have tried to find them. No one can travel to locate refugees because of war or fighting." The memory of his family had not faded. "My father was a brave Dinka man with many cows, symbol of my culture," Marko wrote. "My parents know nothing of me now."

That was about to change.

In the spring of 2003, a Sudanese refugee in Nashville returned to southern Sudan with a video camera. He was from the same village as Marko and Daniel. He told them before he left that if he made it back to Modhol, he would ask around and try to find out what had become of their families. After he returned, he sent word to Atlanta that Daniel and Marko should come to Nashville. There, in an apartment, with Carolyn Geddes at his side, Marko watched a television screen flicker to life. Images appeared of their old home, the vast, flat landscape of southern Sudan. Marko and Peter and Daniel stared at the screen, transfixed. Peter recognized a river from his childhood, and grass huts like the ones he used to call home. Now they were looking at a woman standing under a tree. She looked so old, but Daniel recognized her. His mother. She spoke with the same voice he had heard that night on the phone, when he had sat alone in his room in Clarkston and called Khartoum. She had used money Daniel had sent to travel with two daughters to their village in the Bahr El-Ghazal region of southern Sudan.

Then another woman stared out at them from the television screen, also old and tired and gaunt. The man from Nashville who had traveled with a video camera to Modhol turned to Marko. "That is your mother," he said.

The man from Nashville had told Marko only moments earlier that his mother was alive, but no one had told him he would see her on the video. Yet there she was, peering out at Marko from across a universe of time and space, looking incredulous when told that her son was alive somewhere far off, across the ocean, in the United States. If he is alive, she said, why doesn't he come here to help me?

Marko doubled over on the sofa and wailed through unabashed tears. Carolyn put her hand on his back. She would say later she had never heard such visceral emotion, tears that would not stop. In a span of less than fifteen minutes, Marko had learned that his father and a brother were missing, presumably dead, but that his mother was alive. He had left home at such an early age that he could not remember what his mother looked like, but Marko did not doubt it was her on the videotape. The first thing he did after regaining his composure was ask what he could do to support her. Since his father and brother were gone, the responsibility to help her fell to him, but he was a high-school student with no job. Even if he had money, the place his mother lived was so remote that he could not send her anything. The reality sunk in that all he could do was receive an education as quickly as possible. The sooner he finished his studies, the sooner he could "become somebody," as he put it, and maybe return to southern Sudan to meet his mother.

Daniel came back to Georgia for a break in the summer of 2003. He had taken English classes in his first year at Divine Word College and was frustrated that instructors had not yet let him take a crack at the GED exam. He planned to start academic classes in the fall and did not waver in his dream of becoming a priest. He talked often that summer to Peter, the oldest of the six young men who had spent their first year in Apartment 40-G of Olde Plantation Apartments. Having scored well on the Test of English as a Foreign Language, Peter had applied for admission to Georgia Perimeter College with help from Linda Amick, the volunteer who had two Lost Boys living with her. He knew that the Lost Boys Foundation had paid about five hundred dollars to each of about a dozen Lost Boys at Georgia Perimeter, so he and another refugee bound for college went to the foundation's office one day in mid-2003. The foundation had raised at least $181,000 in their name, ostensibly to help the Lost Boys pursue their education, so Peter and his friend asked whether they could apply for one of the five-hundred-dollar stipends they kept hearing about. Peter's friend did the talking, but the foundation's executive director, Barbara Obrentz, told them they should not have come in unannounced: "She said she didn't want to listen to what he was saying unless he called and made an appointment," Peter said later. Since Peter was there for the same reason, he did not say anything. Back in his apartment, he called the foundation and left his name, phone number, and the reason he had called. "Nobody called me back," he said. The next day, he called again. "There was no answer back," he said. Peter paid his own way to Georgia Perimeter College, using money he had saved from working at the meatpacking plant. He hoped to take the computer and commerce classes he craved. He had quit his job at the meatpacking plant and found work at a printing business that demanded twelve-hour shifts. It was not unusual for Peter to work from 6 p.m. to 6 a.m. and spend much of the morning and afternoon in class.

For Jacob, the approaching second anniversary of his arrival in Atlanta was cause to worry. Other refugees were in high school or college or studying at Job Corps. He was struggling to pass the GED exam that would open the door to college. Jacob had done well on the math, science, writing, and social studies portions of the test. He needed only to pass the fifth part—Interpreting Literature and the Arts—to receive a diploma. After failing the test for the third time, Jacob returned to the home of Linda Austin, the retired English teacher.

He settled into a wicker chair at a table in her dining room and said little as she spoke, watching her with wide eyes, rarely pausing to touch the plate of grapes Linda had set to his right. She opened a practice test and began giving advice. There was so much to cover. When they practiced reading excerpts from a play, Linda realized that Jacob did not grasp that some lines conveyed stage directions ("Corie's mother, Mrs. Banks, staggers in the door, bouncing off it and coming to rest paralyzed against the railing"). How was he supposed to know that? Jacob spoke fluent English, in addition to Dinka, Arabic, and Kiswahli, but he had never read plays. How was he supposed to know they were printed as dialogue between characters (in this case, "Mother" and "Corie") or that the phrases in brackets or parentheses ("moves up toward windows," for example, or "trips over platform") were directions for actors on a stage?

On another page, Jacob read a review from *Time* magazine of a movie about a high-school basketball team. "Norman and his charges are such stuff as Rocky Balboa and the Karate Kid are made of," it said, "not to mention old Frank Capra movies." How was Jacob supposed to know about Rocky Balboa or the Karate Kid? He had only seen one movie in his life. Linda knew that only in time would Jacob understand such cultural references. She tried to give him no-nonsense advice. Read the questions first, she said. Then read the passage trying to find the answers. Skip a passage if you find that you just can't understand what it's about, she said. Otherwise you'll waste valuable time trying to decipher it. Better to guess at the answers and move on. She told him to skip over slang he did not understand, such as "there was nothing better to chew on than last week's game," and try to discern the main point, meaning, and tone of a passage from the parts he could understand.

At the end of their last tutoring session before Jacob's fourth attempt at literature interpretation, Linda walked Jacob to the door. "I know you'll pass," she said, "but if you don't, I'll see you right back at this table."

Jacob took the test and went about the next few days trying in vain not to think too much about it. After a week of waiting, Jacob walked down the street to the community college where he had taken the test. He found a woman who gave him his score. He walked back in high spirits and composed an E-mail to six American friends. "Literature stood in my way for a long time," he wrote, "but I made it possible last Saturday because of you."

Jacob had passed. He was on his way to college.

"My best regard and thank to all of you for the help you have all rendered to pass my literature and the entire GED exams," he continued. Jacob singled out Cheryl Grover and other friends for giving him GED-preparation books, encouragement, and writing tips. "Thanks to Susan Gordon and her husband, Kevin," he wrote. "These are great characters in my life. First of all, Susan helped me a lot on my GED. . . . Susan Gordon and Kevin are taking care of my younger brother in one of the best schools in Uganda and my sister, too, sending money for their school and their living expenses. This helps me a lot on my school because I am not thinking too much about them for they are in good condition. Linda Austin," he continued, "thank you very much for you hit the hammer right to the nail. I passed literature simply because of your advice. You are my best teacher and I will not forget all you told me until I will achieve the best of my education.

"I have no word in English to express the depth of what I feel about you all, but let me say thank you again. God will bless you all and your families."

The next month, Jacob started classes at Georgia Perimeter College. He and Peter studied English in the same class. When Daniel came home from Iowa for the summer, Jacob walked from his apartment to one where Daniel was staying. They talked about school and a little of everything. Most weekends, Carolyn or her husband would bring Marko to Clarkston. Sometimes he saw Jacob at church in the community center, but on the last Sunday in June, near the end of his second full year in the United States, Jacob wasn't there.

He was at a cathedral instead, dressed in a blue cap and gown for his high-school graduation. About a dozen fellow refugees sat in the back of a cavernous sanctuary for a ceremony to honor Jacob and three others from southern Sudan who were among 150 people to receive diplomas for passing the GED exam. They sat in red-cushioned wooden pews and smiled as parents shushed babies and cameras flashed. The graduates sat front and center and listened to a brief address from the general manager at a distribution plant of the Gates Rubber Company.

"It was not easy, but you persevered," he began, in the tradition of commencement speakers. "The GED is just a first step." Thirty-six years ago, he said, he had received a GED diploma. When he raised it in his right hand, as proof, the audience applauded. He had used it, he said, as a stepping-stone to an associate's degree, then a bachelor's degree, and then a master's degree. He had gone from sweeping floors and packing boxes to running the distribution plant. After another word or two of encouragement, the speaker wished the graduates well and concluded his remarks, a short speech very much out of character for commencement speakers.

Next at the podium came a figure who told the graduates to get ready. The first row of men and women in caps and gowns rose. Soon a speaker started reading names, and then a second row of young men and women rose to hear their names called, and then there were the graduates, gliding into the light on a stage with a huge U.S. flag in the background, to shake hands with one person and receive a diploma from another. Some of the graduates thrust up their arms in victory as they walked toward the future. Others beamed at people in the audience. When this name or that was called, a wave of friends or relatives popped up among the sea of seated guests to scream "All right, Kristy!" or "Way to go, Towanda!"

Ten minutes into this ritual, the speaker called the name that the audience members from southern Sudan had been waiting to hear: "Jacob Magot."

Jacob strode more quickly than the others, arriving only a few steps behind the woman in front of him. He looked somber as he shook hands, picked up his diploma, and paused for a photo at the bottom of some stairs. Later, after he moved the yellow tassel on his cap from left to right, Jacob marched out with the graduates. He passed through sanctuary doors to enter a vestibule packed with souls in blue caps and gowns, parents and siblings and boyfriends and girlfriends. From there, propelled by the same force that had pushed him for years, Jacob opened an outer door and stepped into the sunlight of another summer afternoon alive with promise. Several friends waited in the shade of some trees on one side of the church. They shook his hand and posed for pictures with him and the three other graduates from southern Sudan. Jacob tried to savor the moment, but he could not linger. He worked most Sunday afternoons, and his supervisor had given him just enough time off for graduation. Jacob would go to work two hours after the ceremony and clock out around midnight, then return to Clarkston for a few hours' sleep. He was a gentleman of the future, like the old Dinka song said. Even if he tired, he would endure. He would find its sweetness later on. Jacob would rise not long after the sun. He would leave his apartment and walk toward the campus of Georgia Perimeter College. He had class in the morning.

EPILOGUE: NOVEMBER 2004

Three years after an airplane delivered Jacob Magot, Peter Anyang, Daniel Khoch, and Marko Ayii to new lives in the United States, violence in their native country is attracting increasing international attention. To crush a fledgling rebellion in the western region of Darfur, the Sudanese government has armed and cooperated with nomadic Arab militias in a campaign of looting, rape, and murder that has killed tens of thousands of black African farmers and forced at least 1 million others from their homes. Humanitarian organizations draw parallels to mass killings in Bosnia, Cambodia, and Rwanda. The U.S. Congress calls it genocide, and the news media is suddenly paying more attention to bloodshed in Sudan. The violence threatens to undo remarkable progress both sides have made toward ending an unrelated north-south civil war that has killed 2 million people since 1983, mainly civilians in southern Sudan.

Meanwhile, the U.S. Refugee Program is stabilizing after changes that followed the terrorist attacks of September 11, 2001. The United States admitted about fifty-two thousand refugees in 2004, compared with seventy thousand the year before the attacks and twenty-seven thousand the year after. Half of the refugees the United States welcomed in 2004 were from Africa, a dramatic increase from years past and, by all accounts, a sign of things to come. With the Cold War over and a shrinking pool of refugees in Indochina and the former Soviet Union, the refugee flows produced by repression in countries such as Sudan, Ethiopia, Liberia, and Somalia have emerged as major sources for those few of the world's refugees whom the United States resettles.

In Atlanta, about 150 young men known as Lost Boys continue to work and study. A small group of American volunteers still shuttle the young men to medical appointments and help them study. Dee Clement became the guardian for one young man so he could go to school. He lives in her house. Carolyn Geddes became the guardian for Marko Ayii. She opened her home to him so he could attend high school. Carolyn is still a presence in the lives of other refugees, too, helping them find doctors and letting young Sudanese men stay in her house while they recover from surgery. Neal Kelley spends so much free time with the Lost Boys that he can carry on decent conversations in Dinka. Cheryl Grover, the real-estate consultant whom the International Rescue Committee had matched with the young men in apartment 40-G of Olde Plantation Apartments, occasionally trades e-mails or phone calls with Jacob, Peter, Daniel, or Marko, but she has gradually reduced her involvement, a withdrawl that resettlement agencies encourage as refugees become self-sufficient. Susan Gordon continues to take refugees to doctor's appointments and offer advice when they get a traffic citation. She spends countless hours helping them get into school. She is particularly close to Jacob Magot, taking him to services at the Decatur First United Methodist Church most Sunday mornings. The Lost Boys Foundation, which three years earlier had raised high hopes in Atlanta, has little relevance in the everyday lives of most of the refugees, though it is providing generous college scholarships to about a dozen young men. Its founder has focused on publicity, writing a children's book and working with an author and with filmmakers who are planning a feature film. She has virtually no day-to-day contact with most Lost Boys in Atlanta. The corps of volunteers who have maintained contact with the refugees have after three years divided them into two groups: those who are in college or are likely to attend and those who will probably settle for jobs that require little advanced education. Roughly two in three Lost Boys in Atlanta have received or are on track to receive high-school equivalency degrees, but some seem destined to push a broom or work on an assembly line.

The community was shaken in July 2004 by the death of a twenty-one-year-old refugee. Separated from his parents in childhood, he had walked across southern Sudan in the late 1980s with the group that came to be known as the Lost Boys, but he was not in the group of thirty-eight hundred Lost Boys the United States resettled in 2000 and 2001. The man had been reunited with relatives in Africa and had moved to Egypt before the United States offered shelter to him and his family as refugees. He died in Atlanta of head injuries sustained in a drunken dispute over ten dollars, and police charged one of the Lost Boys with involuntary manslaughter. A month later, a twenty-four-year-old refugee among the Lost Boys of Sudan was shot and killed in an apparent robbery in Louisville. The deaths in Atlanta and Louisville followed the killing in May 2003 of one of the Lost Boys in Nashville. The Atlanta case generated strong feelings. Some young men say the death was an accident; others were angry when the authorities dropped charges for lack of evidence that a crime had been committed.

Daniel Khoch was far from the controversy that followed the death. He was in Kenya that summer for a reunion with the mother he had last seen in 1986. A newspaper story that described Daniel reconnecting by phone with his mother inspired Mona Edwards, a medical office manager in suburban Atlanta, to pay to fly Daniel to Kenya, where his mother was staying. He first caught sight of her as a taxi delivered him to an apartment building about 7 a.m. one day. Daniel said that his mother looked "so old" but that he recognized her at once. "She came running and gave me a hug," he said. "It was my first time to see my mother and be happy again." Daniel learned that his father was missing and two sisters were dead, but other siblings were alive and well, including a thirteen-year-old brother that he had not known he had. To his mother he described the United States as "full of freedom." When she asked who took care of him, he mentioned Edwards, whom he calls "Mom Mona." Daniel spent about five weeks with his mother. "I told her good-bye and maybe

I will meet you again sometime," he said. After his mother returned to southern Sudan, Daniel flew back to the United States and spent a week in Georgia before returning to Divine Word College in Epworth, Iowa. He has spent two years there, earning mostly Bs and Cs but also one D, in ancient philosophy, where he found the writings of Socrates impenetrable. He still hopes to become a priest.

Marko Ayii also had trouble understanding some school assignments. His tenth-grade classmates at Kell High School intuitively knew when they read *To Kill a Mockingbird* that blacks in Alabama in the 1930s were relegated to second-class status, but Marko had no frame of reference to grasp that without being told.

The students at Kell got to know Marko during an assembly in his sophomore year. After administrators showed the *60 Minutes II* segment about the Lost Boys, Marko marched to the podium and told his life story. The students gave him a standing ovation. Months later, after a fund-raising drive coordinated by the National Honor Society, Marko received more applause during a pep rally when he accepted the two thousand dollars that had been raised to help several Lost Boys pay for tuition and textbooks. At the end of a typical school day, Marko takes a nap and then tackles homework. Carolyn's husband, Jim, an engineer, helps Marko with science and math. Jim also gave him driving lessons in the weeks before Marko started the eleventh grade.

A grueling schedule defines Jacob Magot's routine. Several days a week, he attends class at Georgia Perimeter College from 8 a.m. to nearly one o'clock, rests for two hours, and then works until almost midnight. Jacob often studies as late as 3 a.m. and sleeps for five or six hours before getting up to do it all over again. More than once, while driving home from work late at night, Jacob has wrecked his 1996 Toyota Camry but escaped injury. On one occasion, he fell asleep on I-285, the perimeter highway that encircles Atlanta, and crashed his car into the median wall. Another time, also drowsy, he rear-ended a car that was stopped at a traffic light, totaling the Camry. The most frightening wreck came a few weeks later, after Jacob climbed into a roommate's car with plans to drive to a store to buy a calling card. He said he put the car in reverse and tried to turn, but the steering wheel seemed locked. The car surged backward and hit a parked car. Jacob tried to move the car back to a parking space, but the car zoomed forward. He is not sure exactly how it happened, but the car hopped a curb, smashed through a wrought-iron fence, sped three or four feet down a gently sloping dirt hill, and plunged over a concrete retaining wall. It fell seven feet straight down and smashed into a sidewalk in an accident that could have been fatal had the driver's side airbag not deployed. Shattered glass littered the sidewalk for weeks, but Jacob did not receive a scratch. A few months later, he quit his job as a shopping-center security guard to work food service in the DeKalb County Jail, less than a mile from his apartment. The new job makes his schedule a little less hectic because Jacob no longer has to drive forty-five minutes to and from work.

Peter Anyang has changed jobs, too. He worked for months at the meat-packing plant south of Atlanta, trading one position that paid $8.45 an hour for another that paid $9.55. Then he worked twelve-hour overnight shifts at a printing company. The problem with that job, aside from the fact that it ended around dawn and that Peter spent the next several hours in college, was that it came with an irregular schedule. Some days, the company needed Peter; other days, it did not. Peter eventually joined a southern Sudanese friend at a job that offered a more regular schedule. The *Atlanta Journal-Constitution* pays Peter $12.00 an hour to stuff inserts into the newspaper at one of its suburban offices. He usually works from 3 p.m. to 11 p.m. three or four days a week. Like Jacob, he often studies as late as 3 a.m. and sleeps for a few hours before rising at dawn to go to Georgia Perimeter College, where he takes classes that he hopes will lead to a career in business or computers. After a few semesters, Peter had earned an A, two Bs, a C, and a D. Although his frequent fatigue makes studying hard, he never wishes he was back in the refugee camps or in southern Sudan, where people can only dream of attending a college like the one where he studies.

Peter's attitude about the future has changed after three years in the United States. He had arrived planning to obtain an education and return to southern Sudan, where he would use newly acquired skills to rebuild his country. Now he talks about becoming a U.S. citizen and spending the rest of his life in the United States. He wants to go back to southern Sudan, but only to visit. There are many ways to rebuild a war-torn country, he says, mentioning as possibilities working for a company or nonprofit organization that operates in southern Sudan. Peter had once dreamed of marrying a Dinka woman and having eight or nine children. He asked shortly after coming to Georgia why so many couples in the United States limited themselves to one or two children. Now he sees that it would be difficult to pay for clothes, medicine, and education for eight or nine children. He has no idea how he will find a wife, but after he does, he figures, they will have no more than two or three children.

Sometimes Peter thinks back to those first weeks in apartment 40-G, when he had marveled at the Americans who always seemed so pressed for time. Now he is as busy as everyone else. He had not used a phone before coming to the United States but now he occasionally calls friends in Africa. There is no question but that Peter has changed. As strange as it would have seemed when his flight landed in Atlanta on July 18, 2001, Peter is home. He acknowledged as much in the kind of eloquence he is prone to in casual speech. Peter sat on the edge of his couch one Sunday afternoon. The world outside his apartment had once seemed so foreign. Now he belongs. "When you walk into a dark room, your eyes squint and you can hardly see anything," Peter said, "but you stay for a while and your eyes adjust." He paused. "Then you can see for some distance."

NOTES

Preface

p. xi   "Lost Boys": Some individuals in the group of refugees known collectively as the Lost Boys of Sudan point out the imprecision of that title. They are not lost in the most literal sense of the word, nor are they boys. The name is used here and throughout the text because it has become such a well-known identifier for a group that has much in common but is not, as few groups are, a homogenous whole. The text similarly refers to refugees resettled "in Atlanta" for the sake of simplicity. As noted in the text, most were actually resettled in and around the city of Clarkston, a part of metropolitan Atlanta that is about twelve miles northeast of downtown Atlanta.

p. xii   "best obtainable version of the truth": Bernstein often is quoted in lectures and articles as saying that the news media has abandoned its traditional purpose—pursuing the "best obtainable version of the truth"—in favor of a focus on topics of trivial and fleeting importance. One of many such references can be found in the Winter 2003 issue of *Richmond Alumni Magazine*, produced for alumni of the University of Richmond.

p. xiv   "multiple and recurring civil wars": Johnson, *The Root Causes of Sudan's Civil Wars*, xiii.

p. xiv   "the most long-lasting and devastating war in the world": Former president Jimmy Carter made this comment in an interview with the author on October 27, 2003. Carter noted that the death toll in fighting in the Democratic Republic of the Congo recently exceeded that of the war in Sudan but that for many years, the Sudanese war was the "most . . . devastating" in terms of human suffering.

Landing

p. 4   "In the United States, education is accessible to everyone . . .": Center for Applied Linguistics, *Welcome to the United States*, 53.

p. 5   "they first saw a moving staircase": This account is based on interviews with several refugees who were at the Brussels airport that day.

p. 5   "teenagers and young men": Refugees who came to be called the Lost Boys of Sudan were assigned ages by relief workers. They traveled without birth certificates and cannot be certain of their ages.

p. 6   "with 56 ethnic groups split into more than 570 tribes that speak at least 100 languages": Peterson, *Me against My Brother*, 178.

p. 6   "Atlanta, Boston, Chicago, Cleveland . . .": This list of resettlement sites was supplied by the U.S. State Department's Bureau of Population, Refugees, and Migration.

p. 6   "dying young boys" and "walking skeletons": The march of thousands of "dying young boys" across southern Sudan, toward Ethiopia, was described in *Sydney Morning Herald*, "New Ethiopia Famine Takes Toll Of Young," as it appeared in the *Washington Post*, April 18, 1988. An account by the Associated Press, appearing under the headline "Civil War Refugees: Sudanese Swamping Ethiopian Camps," appeared in the *San Francisco Chronicle* on April 29, 1988. It quoted the head of the Ethiopian desk in the U.N. High Commissioner for Refugees office in Geneva as referring to the boys as "walking skeletons."

p. 6   "walking hundreds of miles . . .": Boys walked various distances, depending on their starting points. Those who walked the farthest typically came from villages in the Bahr El-Ghazal region of southern Sudan. As noted elsewhere in the text, many walked roughly 450 miles, about the distance from New York to Cleveland.

p. 6   "all had the dull concentration camp stare . . .": Quoted in Roger Rosenblatt, "The Last Place on Earth," *Vanity Fair*, July 1993, 116.

p. 6   "some estimated that three in five boys . . . died": Precise and reliable counts of the death toll are impossible to come by. This estimate is drawn from Victor Malarek, "Eyes of Dinka Boys Reflect Journey to Hell and Back," the *Globe and Mail*, March 31, 1990. That articles identifies Kingsley Amaning as head of the sub-office for the United Nations High Commissioner for Refugees in Gambella, Ethiopia, and quotes his estimate that three of every five boys who left southern Sudan died along the way to the camp at Panyido, Ethiopia. Other sources estimated that 20 percent of the boys who left homes around southern Sudan died en route to Ethiopia.

p. 7   "Jacob said he was five or six . . .": This account is based on several interviews with Jacob Magot conducted in 2001 and 2002. The goal here is to present his account without embellishment. It should go without saying, for obvious reasons, that corroborating his account is impossible, but there is no doubt that southern Sudanese boys like him experienced horrors in 1987 and 1988 almost identical to what he describes.

p. 10 "nearly 250,000 . . . fled": The exact number of southern Sudanese refugees who fled Ethiopia in May 1991 is impossible to verify. This estimate comes from Peterson, *Me against My Brother*, 239.

p. 11 The article appeared in the June 1992 issue of *Life* magazine, under the headline "Lost Boys of the Sudan." It was written by Edward Barnes.

p. 12 "74 percent of the boys were survivors of close shelling or aerial bombardment . . .": Peterson, *Me against My Brother*, 242.

p. 13 "more than three of four refugees admitted since 1980 came from the Soviet Union, Indochina, or Bosnia": The link between U.S. foreign policy and refugee-resettlement priorities is well documented. The figures cited here come from an analysis, conducted by the author, of refugee-resettlement figures furnished by the U.S. Committee for Refugees.

p. 14 "The federal government would pay their rent and power bill for up to four months . . .": As described elsewhere in the text, various federal programs provide assistance to refugees for various periods of time. The amount and duration of assistance that any given refugee receives depends on which program he or she participates in.

p. 14 "One lesson you will learn quickly . . .": Center for Applied Linguistics, *Welcome to the United States*, 5.

p. 15 "resettle 156 . . .": The State Department says it resettled 156 Lost Boys in metro Atlanta in 2001.

Bread in the Dishwasher

p. 19 "if you believe that life begins at conception . . .": Daniel and his roommates happened upon an episode of *Inside Politics* that aired on CNN on July 19, 2001.

p. 22 "In Boston, a Sudanese man . . .": Sara Corbett, "The Long, Long, Long Road to Fargo," the *New York Times Magazine*, April 1, 2001.

p. 22 "In a grocery store in Fargo, North Dakota . . .": Corbett, "The Long, Long, Long Road to Fargo."

p. 24 Population estimates are from the U.S. Census Bureau.

p. 26 "highest concentration of African and European . . .": Based on the author's analysis of figures from the U.S. Census Bureau.

p. 34 "When you are an educated person . . .": This account is based on a tape recording of what was said at the Kakuma Refugee Camp the day before Peter Anyang left. Anyang provided the tape and translated from Dinka into English.

The Spoiling of the World

p. 37   "The Dinka historically have viewed . . .": Much of the description in this chapter, particularly of Dinka history, culture, and tradition, is drawn from the published works of Francis Mading Deng as well as interviews with him.

p. 37   "the evil forces of illness and death": Francis Mading Deng, *The Dinka of the Sudan*, 2.

p. 37   "a source of dignity and pride . . . highlighted by the institution of *toc* . . .": Deng, *The Dinka of the Sudan*, 85.

p. 37   "are thought to be attractive . . .": Deng, *The Dinka of the Sudan*, 86.

p. 38   "the dream of every Dinka": Deng, *The Dinka of the Sudan*, 93.

p. 38   "important for the welfare of the Dinka . . .": Deng, *The Dinka of the Sudan*, 3.

p. 38   "Traditionally most southern peoples live in spread-out settlements . . .": Deng, *War of Visions*, 186–87.

p. 38   "the blazing sun . . .": Deng, *The Dinka of the Sudan*, 3.

p. 38   "to a Dinka, his country, with all its deprivations . . ." Deng, *The Dinka of the Sudan*, 6.

p. 39   "too poor to warrant its conquest": Quoted in Peterson, *Me against My Brother*, 177.

p. 39   "Arab Muslims with superior weapons . . .": Deng, *War of Visions*, 39.

p. 40   "You are aware that the end of all our effort . . .": Quoted in Deng, *War of Visions*, 47. Also see Scroggins, *Emma's War*, 43.

p. 41   "the British navy seized fifteen hundred slave ships . . .": Scroggins, *Emma's War*, 45.

p. 41   "one man in command of a small flotilla . . .": This and other quotations in this passage are drawn from Scroggins, *Emma's War*, 48.

p. 43   This account of Gordon's death is drawn from Scroggins, *Emma's War*, 59.

p. 44   "Those were terrible . . .": Quoted in Deng, *War of Visions*, 51.

p. 44   "would come with camels and donkeys and mules . . .": Quoted in Deng, *War of Visions*, 73.

p. 44   "The Dinka would beat the drums of war . . .": Quoted in Deng, *War of Visions*, 74.

p. 45   "would go . . . and would kill any people he found . . .": Quoted in Deng, *War of Visions*, 74.

p. 45   "It is impossible . . .": Quoted in Deng, *War of Visions*, 71.

p. 45   "slavery has indeed remained . . .": Deng, *War of Visions*, 74.

p. 46   "a museum of nature": Deng, *The Dinka of the Sudan*, 138.

p. 46   "brought the longest period of peace and security . . .": Deng, *War of Visions*, 82.

p. 46   "a race of long-legged, well built people . . .": Quoted in Deng, *The Dinka of the Sudan*, 1.

p. 47   "idea of progress was quite foreign . . .": Quoted in Deng, *War of Visions*, 206.

p. 47   "The Dinka became increasingly aware . . .": Quoted in Deng, *War of Visions*, 207.

p. 47   "The most popular game in our house . . .": Deng, *The Dinka of the Sudan*, 153.

p. 48   "Learning is good / We have found it so . . .": Quoted in Deng, *The Dinka and Their Songs*. Deng quotes a similar song from that era in *The Dinka of the Sudan*, 153: "I am a small boy / But I am a gentleman of the future / I am the goodness of my land / And I will do my best / Teach me that my mind / May accept the word of learning / Learning is power / Learning is best."

p. 50   "For a people . . .": Deng, *The Dinka of the Sudan*, 139.

p. 51   "The feud of the Southerners with the Northerners . . .": Quoted in Deng, *The Dinka of the Sudan*, 139.

p. 51   "a clash of identities . . .": Deng, *War of Visions*, 26.

p. 52   "deny the strongly African elements . . .": Deng, *War of Visions*, 3.

p. 52   "Until recently . . .": Deng, *War of Visions*, 5.

p. 52   "intent on liquidating . . .": Deng, *War of Visions*, 142.

p. 52   "it became the policy . . .": Deng, *War of Visions*, 144.

p. 52   "Chiles were put . . .": Quoted in Deng, *War of Visions*, 144.

p. 53   "Instead of the liberal president . . .": Deng, *War of Visions*, 170.

A Bitter Wind

p. 57   The account of what happened at Ed Da'ein is drawn from Scroggins, *Emma's War*, 94.

p. 57 "only naked bodies . . .": Quoted in Human Rights Watch / Africa, *Civilian Devastation*. See the section entitled "Unaccompanied Minors and Recruitment of Child Soldiers" and the subheading "Conditions in the Ethiopian Refugee Camps."

p. 57 "When they come in the camp, they're not able to stand": Quoted in "Civil War Refugees," Associated Press, April 29, 1988.

p. 57 It is impossible to estimate precisely the number of people who died while walking from southern Sudan toward the refugee camps in Ethiopia. The estimate of eight thousand deaths comes from "New Ethiopia Famine Takes Toll of Young," *Washington Post*, April 18, 1988.

p. 57 "plane they use to bomb the people": This and other material in quotes comes from a brief autobiography that Daniel Khoch wrote in Atlanta while teaching himself to type.

p. 60 "a friendly Ethiopian government . . .": For a concise description of relations between the Ethiopian government and southern Sudanese rebels in the 1980s and early '90s, see Peterson, *Me against My Brother*, 202.

p. 61 The report of Human Rights Watch / Africa mentioned here is *Civilian Devastation*.

p. 61 "boys interviewed by social and relief workers . . .": Human Rights Watch / Africa, *Civilian Devastation*. Quotes from the report in this section come from a part of the report entitled "Unaccompanied Minors and Recruitment of Child Soldiers."

p. 62 This description of the tradition of "boy soldiers" in East Africa is drawn from Human Rights Watch / Africa, *Civilian Devastation*. See the section entitled "Unaccompanied Minors and Recruitment of Child Soldiers" and the subheading "Historical Background for Boy Soldiers in Southern Sudan."

p. 63 This description of the refugee camps at Dimma, Itang, and Panyido is drawn from a videotape entitled *Wandering Children: A Report on Sudanese Refugee Children*, produced by Harold Linde for the U.S. Committee for Refugees in September 1990.

p. 63 "among the most chauvinistic . . .": Deng, *War of Visions*, 401.

p. 63 The population estimates for the camps at Dimma, Itang, and Panyido come from Human Rights / Africa, *Civilian Devastation*.

p. 64 "In the first few years, the Red Army fought . . .": Quoted in Human Rights Watch / Africa, *Civilian Devastation*. See the section entitled "Unaccompanied Minors and Recruitment of Child Soldiers" and the sub-heading "Military Training for the 'Red Army.'"

p. 66　"the acrid camp smell of constantly burning cooking fires . . .": Peterson, *Me against My Brother*, 239–40.

p. 66　For an in-depth and richly detailed account of the split within the SPLA in 1991, see Scroggins, *Emma's War*.

p. 66　Description of conditions at Palataka comes from Johannes Zutt, *Children of War*.

p. 67　"some relief workers suspected . . ." Human Rights Watch / Africa, *Civilian Devastation*. See the section entitled "Unaccompanied Minors and Recruitment of Child Soldiers" and the subheading "Those Passing through Pochalla and Their Flight from Pochalla to Avoid Government Attack."

p. 68　"12,241 unaccompanied minors and 6,600 'teachers and dependents . . .'": Human Rights Watch / Africa, *Civilian Devastation*. See the section entitled "Unaccompanied Minors and Recruitment of Child Soldiers" and the subheading "Those Passing through Pochalla and Their Flight from Pochalla to Avoid Government Attack."

p. 68　The estimate of 10,500 unaccompanied minors in Kakuma comes from Human Rights Watch / Africa, *Civilian Devastation*. See the section entitled "Unaccompanied Minors and Recruitment of Child Soldiers" and the subheading "The Flight from Sudan to Refuge in Kenya."

p. 69　"a fat cow, a radio . . .": Quoted in Jennifer Parmelee, "'We Think God Has Been Punishing Us: War in Sudan Sets Boys on Trail of Terror," *Washington Post*, February 1, 1994.

p. 69　"If I am not dead" and "If I am alive . . .": Quoted in Zutt, *Children of War*, 30.

p. 70　"We were uneducated . . ." and details of the clash in June 1996 that killed six boys and injured one hundred others are drawn from Karin Davies, "Refugee Camp in Kenya Offers Skills Training for Sudanese Fleeing War Education: Programs in Kakuma, Where About 47,000 Dwell, Teach Residents Carpentry and Bookkeeping, Among Other Things, to Help Them Rebuild Homeland," Associated Press, September 8, 1996.

p. 70　"one of the most traumatized groups of children I have ever met . . .": Magne Raundalon, a specialist in treating children for the effects of war, quoted in Parmelee, "'We Think God Has Been Punishing Us': War in Sudan Sets Boys on Trail of Terror," *Washington Post*, February 1, 1994.

p. 70   "People were shot . . .": Quoted in Zutt, *Children of War*, 37.

p. 70   "I saw their bones . . .": Quoted in Zutt, *Children of War*, 38.

p. 70   "It all comes back as a film . . .": Quoted in Zutt, *Children of War*, 38.

p. 71   The sixty-six thousand population estimate at Kakuma in 1999 comes from Ann M. Simmons, "Lost Boys of Sudan Look West," *Los Angeles Times*, February 3, 1999.

Selective Compassion

p. 77   "would displace more people . . .": Reliable estimates of displaced populations often are hard to determine. The U.S. Committee for Refugees estimated in 2004 that more than 5 million Sudanese were displaced from their homes, more people than in any other country. The committee estimated that 4.8 million were displaced within Sudan and another six hundred thousand were refugees outside of the country.

p. 77   The figures on the nationality of refugees resettled in the United States from 1982 to 2002 come from the author's analysis of figures supplied by the United States Committee for Refugees.

p. 80   "eleventh on a list of nations . . .": These figures come from the U.S. Committee for Refugees, *World Refugee Survey 2004*, 15.

The Level of Responsible People

p. 81   The description of O'Keefe's background and his impressions of Kakuma are based on interviews with him conducted in 2003.

p. 84   "59 percent of all slots go to Europeans . . .": Quoted in John Daniszewski, "Black Caucus Seeking More African Refugees / Few Still Have a Chance to Come to America," *Los Angeles Times*, May 10, 1998.

p. 85   The Refugees International report was written by Mary Anne Fitzgerald.

p. 85   "beasts are sacrificed . . ." and "for excitement is high . . .": Deng, *The Dinka of the Sudan*, 69–70.

p. 88   The dialogue between O'Keefe and Kreczko has been reconstructed based on interviews with both participants.

p. 88   The account of Deng's conversation with a State Department official about the possible resettlement is based on an interview with Deng.

p. 89   The conclusion that word got back to refugee-resettlement officials in Washington is based on interviews with Terry Rusch, director of refugee admissions, and two other officials in the U.S. State Department's Bureau of Population, Refugees, and Migration.

p. 89 "just be honest . . ." and "very uncomfortable": This account of a reluctance to discuss events in the Ethiopian refugee camps is drawn from an interview with Terry Rusch, director of refugee admissions in the U.S. State Department's Bureau of Population, Refugees and Migration, conducted in Washington on May 16, 2003.

p. 90 "equate wealth with money": This quote is taken from a news story about the resettlement that aired on the CBS program *60 Minutes II* on May 15, 2001.

p. 91 "The United States is a large, diverse country . . .": Center for Applied Linguistics, *Welcome to the United States*, 5.

p. 91 "When you first arrive . . .": Center for Applied Linguistics, *Welcome to the United States*, 27.

p. 91 "One of your first goals . . .": Center for Applied Linguistics, *Welcome to the United States*, 37.

p. 91 "all communities have fire departments . . ." and "the telephone number to dial . . .": Center for Applied Linguistics, *Welcome to the United States*, 24.

p. 92 "Once you are settled into the community . . .": Center for Applied Linguistics, *Welcome to the United States*, 58.

p. 92 "I don't know much about America . . .": These quotes are taken from the *60 Minutes II* segment.

p. 93 "So when you are there in the United States . . .": This and other quotes from Kakuma are taken from a tape recording of what was said at the Kakuma Refugee Camp the day before Peter Anyang left. Anyang provided the tape and translated from Dinka into English.

p. 94 "There is a reason for the existence of everything . . .": Based on interviews with Jacob Magot in 2001 and 2002. The questions quoted at the end of this chapter are based on the author's review of notes in a pocket-size calendar Jacob Magot brought with him from Kenya to the United States.

Are Y'all Resettling Any of These Guys?

p. 96 "If you don't know how to swim . . .": This and other quotes on this and subsequent pages, as indicated in the text, are drawn from a story about the resettlement that aired on the CBS program "*60 Minutes II*" on May 15, 2001.

p. 97 "This is snow . . .": Corbett, "The Long, Long, Long Road to Fargo."

p. 101 "Hunted by lions and hyenas . . .": Edward Barnes, "The Lost Boys of the Sudan," *Life*, June 1992.

p. 104 Details of the initial assistance available to refugees resettled by the United States government are based on a review of a standard "Reception and Placement" contract from the U.S. State Department.

Body Language in the Workplace

p. 114 "What we want to tell you . . .": This quotation comes from a tape recording of what was said at the Kakuma Refugee Camp the day before Peter Anyang left. Anyang provided the tape and translated from Dinka into English.

p. 115 "[E]ntry-level jobs . . . are those which require . . .": Center for Applied Linguistics, *Welcome to the United States,* 42.

September 11, 2001

p. 123 "harassment of civilians . . ." and "shooting of civilians . . .": Douglas H. Johnson, *The Root Causes of Sudan's Civil Wars*, 61.

p. 124 "Zionists . . .": Peterson, *Me against My Brother*, 181–82.

p. 124 "Even the director . . ." Peterson, *Me against My Brother*, 181.

p. 125 "carried hope to Muslims . . ." and "Khartoum hosted . . .": Peterson, *Me against My Brother*, 184.

p. 126 "established a construction company . . .": Donald Petterson: *Inside Sudan*, 96.

p. 128 "[O]n 21 June 1995 . . .": The quotes on this and following pages come from Gaspar Biro, *Situation of human rights in the Sudan: Interim report on the Situation of Human Rights in the Sudan Prepared by Mr. Gaspar Biro, Special Rapperteur of the Commission on Human Rights, as of 8 March 1995* (New York: United Nations, 1995).

p. 129 "the problems are exaggerated": This and other quotes from Turabi are taken from Doug Struck, "Sudan: An Unseen Tragedy," *Baltimore Sun*, April 21, 1993.

p. 129 "was part of an unstoppable . . . .": Peterson, *Me against My Brother*, 185–86.

p. 129 "there has been enmity between the two peoples . . .": The British ethnologist referred to here is E. E. Evans-Pritchard, as quoted in Peterson, *Me against My Brother*, 218.

p. 129 "Nuer warriors marched on the Dinka heartland . . .": Peterson, *Me against My Brother*, 218.

p. 131 The exact number of noncitizens detained in the months after September 11, 2001, is in dispute. The federal government was reluctant to divulge many details of the detentions. It put the number of immigrants detained at eight hundred; immigrant advocates quoted a figure of around twelve hundred.

p. 131 Figures on the nationality of noncitizens deported in the year after September 11, 2001, are drawn from data from the former Immigration and Naturalization Service, obtained and analyzed by the author in his capacity as a staff writer at the *Atlanta Journal-Constitution*.

Chasing the Wind

p. 134 Jacob Magot and his roommates received limited benefits as part of the federal Matching Grant program. The federal government provided two hundred dollars in spending money for up to four months. Then refugees were expected to support themselves.

p. 138 "As with other refugees . . .": The quotations attributed to Julianne Duncan in this section are drawn from a report entitled "Sudanese 'Lost Boys' in the United States: Adjustment After Six Months," presented to the United States Catholic Conference on May 30, 2001. Other information about Duncan's impressions comes from an interview with her conducted in 2002.

p. 144 The accounts of Mary Williams's visit to the church in Clarkston and to Abraham Yel's apartment are drawn from interviews with her and Abraham Yel.

p. 145 Information about Mary Williams's background comes from interviews with her, a biography produced by her foundation, and published reports.

p. 147 The speaker who said the Lost Boys Foundation "wanted me to talk about my miserable life as a Lost Boy" is Emmanuel Solomon Gai.

p. 148 The description of Angelina Jolie's visit to Atlanta is based on interviews with several refugees who met with her on that visit.

p. 148 The refugee who said Williams told him she could see he did not trust her is Abraham Nyok. He recounted the meeting in an interview. His account was corroborated by other refugees and volunteers who were present.

p. 150 "I thought he was going to ask me for a check . . .": This episode of the *Oprah Winfrey Show*, entitled "People Helping Children of the World," aired on May 9, 2002.

p. 152 Financial information about the Lost Boys Foundation quoted here is based on the organization's Form 990 of the Internal Revenue Service for 2002.

p. 152 "The Lost Boys Foundation promises . . .": About eighty Lost Boys in Atlanta approved a letter to the editor about the foundation that was published in the *Atlanta Journal-Constitution* on September 24, 2003. Coming in response to a news account of the controversy, it said "the foundation exists only to meet its interests and not ours as Lost Boys, in whose name its officials solicit the hard-earned money of Americans." It said volunteers acting apart from the foundation helped access education and that "we have decided not to be used" by the foundation. The letter was signed by Jacob Magot, Stephen Bayok, and Daniel Alier. It ran with a letter in support of the foundation, penned by a refugee who lived with one of three foundation employees. He said the foundation "provided hope for all the Lost Boys" and "helped us by seeking out the opportunities we need so that we can become successful members of the global community."

p. 153 The amount of money John sent to relatives and friends in Africa was reconstructed by reviewing his receipts of the transactions.

Can You Name Your Sisters?

p. 157 The dialogue on these pages was reconstructed based on separate interviews with Marko Ayii, Dee Clement, and Daniel Khoch.

p. 159 The account of Daniel Khoch's time in Sioux Falls, South Dakota, is based on several interviews with him as well as with Tami Trussell.

p. 160 The dialogue on these pages was reconstructed based on separate interviews with Marko Ayii and Daniel Khoch.

p. 162 "Kwol, son of Arob . . ." and "there is no precise moment . . .": Deng, *The Dinka of the Sudan*, 40.

p. 164 The dialogue was reconstructed based on an interview with Dee Clement.

p. 165   "the bloodiest . . .": Deng, *The Dinka of the Sudan*, 70.

p. 165   The dialogue was reconstructed based on interviews with Daniel Khoch.

This Is Your Future

p. 173   The dialogue here is reconstructed based on an interview with Adrian Jelks and others to whom she relayed accounts of the conversation.

p. 174   The presentation by Barbara Obrentz of the Lost Boys Foundation at the church in Clarkston caused a very public controversy. This account of that visit is based on interviews with her, Neal Kelley, Susan Gordon, Abraham Yel, and several other people who were there that day.

Driving

p. 186   The dialogue on these pages and the account of the wreck are drawn from separate interviews with Jeremy Paden and John.

p. 188   "the automobile has come to have a special significance . . .": Jon D. Holtzman, *Nuer Journeys, Nuer Lives*, 64.

p. 188   "were already thinking about . . ." and "in refugee camps . . .": Holtzman, *Nuer Journeys, Nuer Lives*, 69–70.

p. 188   "a car constantly gives you problems" and "few Nuer can afford . . .": Holtzman, *Nuer Journeys, Nuer Lives*, 64.

p. 188   "In just over three . . .": Holtzman, *Nuer Journeys, Nuer Lives*, 67.

p. 188   "Nuer to shop . . .": Holtzman, *Nuer Journeys, Nuer Lives*, 69.

p. 191   The account of someone knocking on the door of Apartment 40-G is based on interviews with Peter Anyang, Jacob Magot, and their roommate, William.

p. 193   "For a woman . . .": Deng, *The Dinka of the Sudan*, 87.

p. 193   The quotations on this page relating to traditional Dinka courtship rituals are taken from Deng, *The Dinka of the Sudan*, 86–92.

p. 195   "dating, sexual relationships and courtship . . .": Mary Pipher, *The Middle of Everywhere*, 202.

p. 195   Dialogue reconstructed based on an interview with Beverly Bartlett.

p. 196   The dialogue here, as well as the overall account of what transpired in court, is based on interviews with Linda Amick.

p. 197   "As with circumcision . . .": Deng, *The Dinka of the Sudan*, 66.

Don't Get Obsessed

p. 201 The dialogue between Carolyn Geddes and her husband, Jim, is reconstructed based on an interview with Carolyn Geddes.

p. 204 The quotation from Linda Amick and the account of how refugees living with her received birth certificates are based on interviews with her.

p. 205 The dialogue here is based on interviews with Carolyn Geddes.

p. 206 The account of Abraham Yel's visit to Atlanta Christian College is based on an interview with Susan Gordon, who accompanied him to the college.

p. 209 The account of an unruly student was supplied by Jacob Magot.

Peace?

p. 212 Oil production estimates are taken from "U.S. Policy to End Sudan's War," prepared in February 2001 by a task force of the Center for Strategic and International Studies. Francis Deng and J. Stephen Morrison were co-chairs.

p. 213 Donald Petterson, former U.S. ambassador to Sudan, described in his book and in an interview presenting a "very harsh message to President Bashir" that threatened to "essentially destroy the Sudanese economy" in the event of Sudanese-sponsored terrorism against the United States. See Petterson, *Inside Sudan: Political Islam, Conflict and Catastrophe*, 74–75. Quotations from the message itself are drawn from David Rose, "The Osama Files," *Vanity Fair*, January 2002.

p. 214 "was completely committed . . .": Former president Jimmy Carter made these remarks in an interview with the author on October 27, 2003.

p. 215 "has been the most long-lasting and devastating war in the world . . ." Former president Jimmy Carter made this comment in an interview with the author on October 27, 2003. Carter noted that the death toll in fighting in the Democratic Republic of the Congo recently exceeded that of the war in Sudan but that, for many years, the Sudanese war was the "most . . . devastating" in terms of human suffering. Other quotations attributed to him in this chapter are taken from that interview.

p. 216 "Mr. President . . ." The dialogue here is reconstructed based on an interview with former president Carter.

p. 217 For an account of possible efforts by the Sudanese government to cooperate with U.S. intelligence agencies before September 11, 2001, see Rose, "The Osama Files."

p. 218   "open[ed] a massive opportunity . . .": This quotation is taken from an interview with Timothy Carney, former U.S. ambassador to Sudan. Portions were reprinted in the *Atlanta Journal-Constitution* on July 31, 2002.

p. 218   "This is truly a historic moment . . .": Peter Bell made these comments in an interview in November 2002 with Moni Basu of the *Atlanta Journal-Constitution,* who kindly allowed the author to attend and participate in the discussion.

Gentlemen of the Future

p. 223   "The ground at the crash site . . ." and "An incident in which Black Hawk helicopters . . ." and "Jockey Shannon Uske . . ." and "73-year-old Hall-of-Famer . . .": The articles quoted here ran in *USA Today* on March 12, 2003.

p. 224   The dialogue and description from the trip to Nashville is based on interviews with Marko Ayii, Carolyn Geddes, and Daniel Khoch.

p. 226   The description of Jacob studying at Linda Austin's house is based on separate interviews with Linda Austin and Jacob Magot.

BIBLIOGRAPHY

American Council on Education. *Tests of General Education Development: Official GED Practice Tests*. Austin, Tex.: Steck-Vaughn, 1998.

Center for Applied Linguistics. *Welcome to the United States: A Guidebook for Refugees*. Washington, D.C.: Refugee Service Center, 1997.

Deng, Francis Mading. *The Dinka and Their Songs*. Oxford: Clarendon, 1973.

——. *The Dinka of the Sudan*. Prospect Heights, Ill.: Waveland, 1972.

——. *War of Visions: Conflict of Identities in the Sudan*. Washington: Brookings Institution, 1995.

Holtzman, Jon D. *Nuer Journeys, Nuer Lives*. Needham Heights, Mass.: Allyn and Bacon, 2000.

Human Rights Watch / Africa. *Civilian Devastation: Abuses by All Parties in the War in Southern Sudan*. New York: Human Rights Watch, July 1994.

Johnson, Douglas H. *The Root Causes of Sudan's Civil Wars*. Bloomington: Indiana University Press, 2003.

Peterson, Scott. *Me against My Brother: At War in Somalia, Sudan, and Rwanda*. New York: Routledge, 2000.

Petterson, Donald. *Inside Sudan: Political Islam, Conflict, and Catastrophe*. Boulder, Colo.: Westview, 1999.

Pipher, Mary. *The Middle of Everywhere: The World's Refugees Come to Our Town*. New York: Harcourt, 2002.

Scroggins, Deborah. *Emma's War: An Aid Worker, a Warlord, Radical Islam, and the Politics of Oil: A True Story of Love and Death in Sudan*. New York: Pantheon, 2002.

United Nations. *Situation of Human Rights in the Sudan: Interim Report on the Situation of Human Rights in the Sudan Prepared by Mr. Gaspar Biro, Special Rapporteur of the Commission on Human Rights, as of 8 March 1995*. New York: United Nations, 1995.

U.S. Committee for Refugees. *World Refugee Survey 2004*. Washington, D.C.: Immigration and Refugee Services of America, 2004.

Werner, Roland, William Anderson, and Andrew Wheeler. *Day of Devastation,*

Day of Contentment: The History of the Sudanese Church across 2000 Years. Nairobi: Paulines, 2000.

Zucker, Naomi Flink, and Norman L. Zucker. The Guarded Gate: The Reality of American Refugee Policy. New York: Harcourt Brace Jovanovich, 1987.

Zutt, Johannes. Children of War: Wandering Alone in Sudan. New York: UNICEF, 1994.

ACKNOWLEDGMENTS

This book would not exist had it not been for the assistance of innumerable people offering their time, information, and insight. Foremost among them are Peter Anyang, Marko Ayii, Daniel Khoch, and Jacob Magot. They allowed a writer to enter their lives and ask question after question, maintaining a good-natured patience even when an author's presence must have been trying. To them I owe a debt of gratitude that can never fully be repaid. Others who provided invaluable help include Daniel Deng, William Dut, and Abraham Yel Nhial as well as Linda Amick, Dee Clement, Carolyn Geddes, Susan Gordon, Cheryl Grover, Cyndie Heiskell, Neal Kelley, and Janis Sundquist.

Many people at the Atlanta office of the International Rescue Committee were particularly helpful, including Robin Harp, Adrian Jelks, Mathew Kon, and Clare Richie. I also am grateful to Kay Trendell at Lutheran Services of Georgia and the Reverend Sandra Mullins at Refugee Resettlement and Immigration Services of Atlanta.

Experts who informed sections on Sudanese culture and history and U.S. policy toward Sudan include Timothy Carney, former president Jimmy Carter, John Danforth, Francis Mading Deng, Abdullahi An-Na'im, Donald Petterson, John Prendergrast, and Jemera Rone. At the U.S. State Department, Mike O'Keefe kindly shared information about the resettlement of southern Sudanese youth in the United States, as did Terry Rusch, Jessica Yutacom, and others. Hiram Ruiz at the U.S. Committee for Refugees helped me locate hard-to-find publications and one videotape relating to southern Sudanese refugees in the late 1980s and 1990s.

For helpful comments on the manuscript, I am indebted to Susan Abramson, Tom Crick, Deborah Scroggins, David Mozersky, Barbara Thompson, Joel Wurl, and Norman Zucker. Editors at the *Atlanta Journal-Constitution* encouraged the pursuit of this story and allowed me to conduct reporting for the newspaper that also proved of value to this work. They include Keith Graham, Hank Klibanoff, Sylvester Monroe, Raman Narayanan, Barbara Senftleber, Cheryl Segal, Bill Steiden, Susan Stevenson, and Julia Wallace. Nancy Grayson at the University of Georgia Press conceived of this book and shepherded it from the idea stage to publication with able assistance from Andrew Berzanskis and Jennifer Reichlin. Molly Thompson offered a sharp editor's eye that strengthened the book.

Finally, I am grateful to my wife, Lynn, for her patience, understanding, and support as I researched, reported, and wrote. My hope is that she understands, while perusing these pages, the reasons her husband invested so many hours conducting interviews away from home or typing in the living room late at night.

INDEX

Juba, 52
Jubilee Partners, xv, 140–41

Kakuma, refugee camp in: agency
    delegations visit, 84–85; conditions
    at, 69–70, 86; cultural orientation
    sessions at, 18, 90; refugees arrive
    at, 12–13, 68–69, 82–83; resettled
    refugees send money to, 113–14
Kapoeta, 11, 67
Kell High School, 222, 234
Kelly, Neal, 174, 177–79, 180–81, 188,
    201, 232
Khoch, Daniel: desires to become a
    priest, 71, 169, 198–99, 205–6, 225,
    234; family of, 160–63, 165–66,
    233–34; memories of, from Africa,
    57–59, 65–66, 67–68; moves to
    South Dakota, 155–56, 157–60;
    returns from South Dakota, 164
Kon, Mathew, 15, 16, 17–21, 23, 27,
    110
Kreczko, Alan, 86–88
Kuol, Gordon Kong, 66

League of Nations, 75
Life magazine, 11–12, 101
Lopes, Lisa "Left Eye," 178–79
Lord's Resistance Army, 72
Lost Boys Foundation: controversy
    over, 146–47, 148–49, 151–52,
    168, 226; creation of, 144–46,
    147–48; current focus of, 232; and
    fundraising, 150–51; and Open
    Campus High School, 172, 174
Lost Boys of Sudan: background of, xi,
    xiii, 2; and courtship and marriage,
    193–95; journeys of, to and from

Ethiopia, 6–7, 57, 59–60, 64–69;
    media coverage of, 95–98, 101,
    103–4; mental health of, 12, 70–71,
    138–40; U.S. resettlement of, xi, xii,
    5–6, 88–89, 92, 95–98
Lutheran Immigration and Refugee
    Service, 84, 85
Lutheran Ministries of Georgia (later
    Lutheran Services of Georgia),
    99–100, 103, 109

Machar, Riek, 66, 67, 129
Machar, Simon, 123
Magot, Jacob: current life of, 234–35;
    and employment, 115–16, 119–21,
    136–37; family of, 72; and GED
    exam, 154, 167–68, 169–71, 198,
    208–10, 226–27; graduates from
    high school, 228–30; memories of,
    from Africa, 7–8, 10, 63, 71
Mahdi, Sadiq al-, 124, 141
Mariam, Mengistu Haile, 10, 53, 59
Matching Grant program, 106
McLaurin, Gail, 197–98
Morgan, Bill, 176
Mosley, Don, 140–41
Mou Mou, Lueth, 22
Mubarak, Hosni, 127

Narus, 10, 68
New York Times, 11
New York Times Magazine, 97–98
Nhial, Abraham Yel. *See* Yel, Abraham
Nimeiri, Jaafar Muhammad, 52, 53
Nuer, 63, 69, 70, 129–30, 188

Obrentz, Barbara, 174, 226
oil, in Sudan, 212